Women Writing On Family

Tips
on
Writing
Teaching
and
Publishing

Also by the Editors

Carol Smallwood

Women and Poetry: Tips on Writing, Teaching and Publishing by Successful Women Poets (co-ed.), McFarland, forthcoming.

Library Management Tips That Work (ed.), American Library Association, 2012.

Pre-and Post-Retirement Tips for Librarians (ed.), American Library Association, 2012.

Compartments: Poems on Nature, Femininity, and Other Realms, Anaphora Literary Press, 2011. Nominated for the Pushcart Prize.

The Frugal Librarian: Thriving in Tough Economic Times, American Library Association (ed.), 2011.

Writing and Publishing: The Librarian's Handbook (ed.), American Library Association, 2010.

Librarians as Community Partners: An Outreach Handbook (ed.), American Library Association, 2010.

Lily's Odyssey, All Things That Matter Press, 2010.

Contemporary American Women: Our Defining Passages (co-ed.), All Things That Matter Press, 2009.

Suzann Holland

Library Management Tips That Work (contributor), American Library Association, 2012.

Currently working with the permission of the Laura Ingalls Wilder estate to complete a monograph tentatively entitled *The Little House Literary Companion*.

"No Easy Targets: Six Libraries in the Economy's Dark Days," *Public Libraries*, July/August 2009. Reprinted in The PLA *Reader for Public Library Directors & Managers*, edited by Kathleen Hughes: Neal-Schuman, 2009.

2010 *Public Libraries* Feature Article Award Winner Monograph chapter "Municipal, County, and Regional Governmental Archives" in *Local and Regional Government Information (How to Find It, How to Use It)*, edited by Mary Martin: Greenwood Press, 2005.

"Censorship in Young Adult Fiction: What's Out There and What Should Be", *Voice of Youth Advocates*, August 2002.

Endorsements

"Family is what creates us, sustains us, bedevils us, confuses us, loves us, destroys us, and defines us. For writers--particularly women writers--family is also a rich vein of subject matter that can be both nourishing and overwhelming, often at the same time. This volume examines a wide variety of family-related issues from points of view that range from the practical to the philosophical, but all focused on how they impact women who write."

—Eleanor Lerman, author of *The Sensual World Re-Emerges* (Sarabande Books, 2010) and *Janet Planet* (Mayapple, 2011), among other volumes

"*Women Writing On Family: Tips on Writing, Teaching and Publishing* is like a good conversation with writer-friends who share their experiences and help you think about your own approach to writing and publishing. If you want to preserve your family history for future generations, write a memoir, or just explore your own family's stories, this book is full of accessible and useful suggestions."

—Ellen Bass, poet and faculty in the Pacific University MFA program; *The Human Line* (Copper Canyon Press, 2007)

"From how to deal with relatives who feel betrayed to finding bits of time to write while raising children to blogging and writing for the internet, *Women Writing On Family: Tips on Writing, Teaching and Publishing* is a major resource for women who write about family in nonfiction, fiction, and poetry. Lela Davidson's essay about using research and creative imagination to bring your ancestors to life on the page, Rosemary Moeller's on writing with respect about devoutly religious families and communities when you are a freethinker, and Kezia Willingham's on taking the risk to write your own truth are just a sampling of the gems of advice, technique, professional tips, and encouragement that make up this valuable book."

—Linda Rodriguez, *Heart's Migration* (Tia Chucha Press), 2010 Thorpe Menn Award for Literary Excellence

"This is a comprehensive work that belongs on any nonfiction writer's bookshelf. Not only does it address the legal and emotional costs that come with the challenge of writing about family, it offers insights into how one can nurture a rewarding writing career in conjunction with a demanding day job and family obligations."

—Jennifer Tang, New York City librarian and freelance writer for *Newsweek, L.A. Times,* and *Fitness* magazine

"This extraordinary collection of insightful, well-written essays will serve splendidly as both guidebook and motivator for any woman who is writing seriously and living her life fully. Matters as diverse as family dynamics, realistic time-management, marketing strategies---even ways of writing more effectively—are covered here with great sensitivity and common sense."

—Marilyn L. Taylor, Ph.D., Wisconsin Poet Laureate, 2009-2010; *Going Wrong* (Parallel Press, 2009)

"Writing about family carries out the writing instructor's dictum of writing about what you know, but brings along the very family issues that draw writers to the subject in the first place. Besides a range of thoughtful pieces that capitalize on family strengths yet confront any issues head on, *Women Writing On Family* offers new writers sage advice on finding the time to write, using the Internet to advantage, and successfully publishing their work--on any topic."

—Phyllis Holman Weisbard, University of Wisconsin System Women's Studies Librarian, and Publisher, *Feminist Collections: A Quarterly of Women's Studies Resources*

"With all the rhetoric today about family, it is nice to see a volume that actually deals with family in way that is creative, honest, and tasteful. *Women Writing On Family: Tips on Writing, Teaching and Publishing* provides sensible guidelines to use and savor. Not to be missed by those studying family history. The stories and ideas contained within are jewels of wisdom that women will find useful. Oh and men can get something out of this book too!!!!"

—Robert G. Weiner, associate humanities librarian, Texas Tech University; contributor, *History of the Holocaust* (Routledge, 2011); Editor, *Captain America and the Struggle of the Superhero* (McFarland, 2009)

"The essays in *Women Writing On Family: Tips on Writing, Teaching and Publishing* are written by experts in the field who balance keen intellect and practical tips with a sensitivity for personal histories. This is an a must have work for anyone interested delving into the complex and rich world of family histories."
—Sarah Passonneau, Iowa State University, assistant professor

"It is only natural for women, traditional keepers of language and storytellers, to share their experience on writing memoirs and recording a family history. From conception to delivery, this anthology covers a wide variety of aspects that a woman writer may encounter on her journey."
—Vera Gubnitskaia, Youth Services Manager, Orange County Library System; contributor: *Librarians As Community Partners: An Outreach Handbook* (ALA editions, 2010)

"As women, we have unique perspectives on life experiences. These experiences deserve an audience. This book will be invaluable to women needing guidance with the emotional, ethical, and professional avenues of getting their stories in print."
—Colleen Driscoll, Breitung Township Schools, Michigan, Media Specialist

"If you're interested in learning how to craft and market stories about family, *Women Writing On Family* features a wealth of experienced writers and editors to help you through every phase of the process. This comprehensive book deals honestly with the emotional, legal and practical aspects of writing close to the heart."
—Kerol Harrod, Writer/Co-Producer of Library Larry's Big Day, Denton Public Library, Denton, Texas; First-Place Winner of 2010 TATOA Programming Awards

"This is a book of practical advice on writing about a sometimes messy subject, the family. Read the whole thing through, or dip in a topic you are interested in, and you'll come away with a clear view on how to start and finish writing."
—Wayne Jones, Queen's University, Kingston, Ontario

"People interested in writing, teaching, and publishing family-focused stories, narratives, poetry, or books will appreciate the practical and helpful contributions in *Women Writing On Family: Tips on Writing, Teaching, and Publishing.* Including tips on writing fiction and nonfiction as well as publishing, marketing, and promotion, this excellent anthology is timely, important, and especially relevant for writers interested in the family."

—Donald G. Frank, Professor Emeritus, Portland State University

"Just as every place has a story, so does every family. *Women Writing On Family* gives you the essentials on writing, teaching and publishing about family. Real, detailed advice from women who know. If you want to share your family stories, this book is not to be missed."

—Chris Helvey, author of *Purple Adobe* and Editor-in-Chief of Trajectory

"From finding inspiration to practical advice about marketing and legal issues, these experienced authors' essays serve as a roadmap for anyone putting pen to paper to capture their family's story."

—Jason Kuhl, Library Operations Director, Arlington Heights Memorial Library, Arlington Heights, Illinois

"The contributors, all published authors, to *Women Writing On Family: Tips on Writing, Teaching and Publishing* provide invaluable help to women authors on the more difficult than expected task of turning their family experiences into quality, marketable literary works. This rich treasure trove of advice ranges from finding time to write to crafting family history through a personal style to publishing and promoting the resulting publications in the Internet age."

—Dr. Robert P. Holley, Wayne State University, Detroit, Michigan, contributor, *Writing and Publishing: the Librarian's Handbook* (ALA Editions, 2010), author of over one hundred publications

Women Writing On Family

Tips on Writing, Teaching and Publishing

Editors

Carol Smallwood & Suzann Holland

KPH

First Edition 2012
The Key Publishing House Inc.
Toronto, Canada
Website: www.thekeypublish.com
E-mail: info@thekeypublish.com
ISBN 978-1-926780-13-9

Copyediting & proof reading Jane Albert
Cover design David Stevenson
Typesetting Andrew Miller

Library and Archives Canada Cataloguing in Publication is available. Printed and bound in USA.

Published by a grant and in association with The Key Research Center (www.thekeyresearch.org). The Key promotes freedom of thought and expression and peaceful coexistence among human societies.

KPH

The Key Publishing House Inc.
www.thekeypublish.com
www.thekeyresearch.org

Dedication

Audrey Gouine; Betty and Marion Drust,
for sharing family history

Carol Smallwood

For the supportive staff and board of the
Monroe Public Library

Suzann Holland

The truth is rarely pure, and never simple.

Oscar Wilde

Table of Contents

Part VIII Building Your Confidence **295**

Foreword

I so wish I had a book like this while I was working on my collection of personal essays, my memoir. This was the first thought that came to my mind when I was asked by Carol Smallwood to write the foreword for this very useful collection of essays. Writing about family is easier said than done. What we have to remember is that thinking about something is not the same as putting those very thoughts down on paper, especially when we have to deal with facts, emotions, and feelings. We are taught that sincerity in writing makes the most impact. Yet, when it comes to writing about family, do we truly reveal everything indiscriminately? And if we want to, then how do we go about it in the best and fairest possible way?

Reading Martha Engber's essay would have taught me how to write about my difficult aunt without offending the other members of her family. Lela Davidson would have taught me how to write about grandmothers with more relevant details. That would have truly enhanced my own essay on my dear grandmother. Yelizaveta Renfro, whose work I admired while we were in MFA workshops together, would have taught me a thing or two about incorporating family in nonfiction. Granted that the memoir is about myself, but then what relevance does the "I" have without family? The title of Kezia Willingham's essay was exactly what I was doing whilst writing my book. Maybe my family would have had an easier time if I had read this essay first!

We are all familiar with the adage that "writing cannot be taught." But we do need guidance. All of us have our own distinct voices when writing the personal essay, but a general overview of the "how to" or "when" or "why" is a must before and during the writing process. This anthology strives to do just that and succeeds admirably. It covers all aspects involved with writing about family-from the craft of writing to legal issues involved and essays that serve as a guide to finding time to write and using the Internet as a research tool amongst others. There are also valuable writing exercises for you before you start on your own account of your family. And last but not least, there are essays on marketing strategies for your work. It is an "all-in-one" anthology, a must for any writer of creative nonfiction, and especially one who is thinking of writing about family.

During the publication process of my own book, I remember chickening out and removing offending material as late as when I was reading proofs from the publisher. Maybe I would have left them in or at least reworded them had I read the essays in this collection. Now I will always be left with the thought, "what if?"

Supriya Bhatnagar

Director of Publications, Association of Writers & Writing Programs (AWP), editor of *The Writer's Chronicle,* author of the memoir *and then there were three ...* (Serving House Books, 2010).

Introduction

In our experience, we've found that women have a special interest and talent in writing about family. No matter if we are poets, essayists, short story writers, journalists, novelists, non-fiction writers, or one of the growing numbers of memoir writers, we often turn to family for inspiration or subjects.

In the often quoted Proust passage from, *The Remembrance of Things Past*: "When nothing else subsists from the past, after the people are dead, after the things are broken and scattered, the smell and taste of things remain poised a long time, like souls bearing resiliently, on tiny and almost impalpable drops of their essence, the immense edifice of memory." I believe many women substitute family for "smell and taste," their memory essentially through family; "We think back through our mothers if we are women," Virginia Woolf noted.

As girls, we often grew up playing with dolls, played house trying to master our mother's high heels, carefully observing our families. Jane Austen used her family circle extensively in writing her unforgettable characters--and made her narrow domestic world timeless, and universal.

Women know all too well the struggle to get published. An invaluable website co-founded by Cate Marvin, associate professor in creative writing in the College of Staten Island, City University of New York, and Erin Belieu, director of the creative writing program at Florida State University addresses the need for female writers to engage in conversations regarding the critical reception of women's creative writing today. The statistics regarding the publishing disparities regarding women are well documented at the Vida: Women in Literary Arts Website.

Supriya Bhatnagar, Director of Publications, AWP, Editor of *The Writer's Chronicle*, notes in the Foreword: "We are all familiar with the adage that 'writing cannot be taught.' But we do need guidance." It is hoped this anthology with thirty-nine contributors fills this goal.

Contributors were asked to each write and given Gustave Flaubert's solid advice: "Whenever you can shorten a sentence, do. And one always can. The best sentence? The shortest."

The anthology's fifty-five chapters were arranged under: Part I Personal and Legal Issues about Family Topics; Part II Finding Time to Write with Career and Family; Part III Making the Most of Your Family Experience; Part IV Writing Exercises and Strategies; Part V Exploring Family in a Variety of Genres; Part VI Finding Your Writing Style; Part VII Publishing, Marketing & Promotion; and Part VIII Building Your Confidence.

No matter how long you've been writing or whatever your goals are: becoming published, critiquing/editing your work or that of others, developing your teaching skills, enhancing your knowledge as a student, writing for yourself or saving your work for posterity, this collection is for you.

Carol Smallwood, Suzann Holland, co-editors

Part I

Personal and Legal Issues about Family Topics

1. Family Secrets: How to Reveal What Matters Without Getting Sued, or Shunned

Martha Engber

How could we not want to divulge family secrets? Such revelations can often explain who we are and how we got that way. Yet revealing private information, even if done so to lift ourselves from beneath hidden burdens, often means exposing others. Stepping on their rights can result in lawsuits, and even more devastating for women, the permanent destruction of relationships.

That's why you, as a female writer, should understand three things before deciding to write about family ghosts: your motivation; the legal and emotional consequences; and how to mitigate both.

Your Rights

The U.S. Constitution under the First Amendment gives you the right to free speech. How you express yourself will determine how people react to what you've written.

If you're bent on revenge, you'll probably choose an inflammatory approach that incites anger and ignores others' privacy. In turn, they may sue you, shun you, or both. While you may think, too bad, a negative tactic means you might lose an opportunity to heal, something you may not appreciate until it's gone. That and you could jeopardize your chance of getting published. With the rise in popularity of memoirs and creative nonfiction, publishers are increasingly wary of stories that could leave the publishing house open to scorn or lawsuits. Consider Random House, which was put on the defensive when certain events in James Frey's memoir, *A Million Little Pieces*, were found to be untrue.

If you're motivated to write an honest account in the name of self-discovery or a wish to help others, however, you're more likely to choose a safer legal and emotional course that respects others' rights.

Others' Rights

The living people you mention in your story have two basic rights. The first is a right to privacy, which means people should not have to suffer from the revelation of private information that embarrasses or portrays them in a false or offensive way. If they feel you've made them look bad, they can sue you for libel, which is a written statement that gives an unjustly favorable impression without just cause and with the intention to incite public contempt.

Say you write that your aunt is an alcoholic. She could sue, saying this portrayal casts her in a negative light that exposes her to public ridicule. If she proves you meant to embarrass her, have no proof of her alcoholism, and that the information isn't integral to your story, she'll have won three major points against you.

If you try to get around her objections by implying she's a drunk, rather than saying so, she could still sue. The same is true if you hint she's connected to criminal activity without providing any proof, such as police records.

But what if she's a celebrity? That depends, given the definition of famous and well known is purposely vague so each case can be considered individually. If you divulge her secrets just to sell books, she has grounds to sue. But if you show the connection between her story and yours, you're in a much stronger legal position.

Now let's say your aunt is deceased. Could her descendants sue you? No, because the dead have no right to privacy.

The second right people enjoy is the right to publicity, or the chance to profit from the commercial use of their names, likenesses or personas. If you make money on your story through the sale of books, related articles, screenplays and advertisements that promote the work, the people you feature can sue, saying your profit proves their identities have commercial value and they deserve a piece of the financial pie.

No federal laws protects a person's right of publicity and of all 50 states, only 19 currently have laws regarding the matter. Of those laws, some only cover the rights of celebrities while others address individuals, including minors. In most cases, the right of publicity extends for decades after a person's death, meaning the right can be passed to descendants for a specified number of years.

If you're still not sure how to handle the rights of those you're writing about, consult an attorney who specializes in entertainment or intellectual property law or check accurate libel information like that in the *MLA Style Manual* and *Guide to Scholarly Publishing* by Joseph Gibaldi. The investment could save you a lot of time, money, worry and emotional trauma.

Emotional Consequences

Working through painful memories can help you find peace and closure. But revealing hidden aspects of your family can also harm good relationships or sever fragile ones. To curtail emotional trauma, write down the names of everyone you mention in your book, both alive and dead. Then attempt to determine:

- how your story depicts them
- how they'll react
- how your depiction will affect others in your family, including those not mentioned

Realize that what might seem harmless to you might be embarrassing or controversial to someone else. That same difference in perspective can mean your perception of an honest portrayal may strike someone as erroneous.

Lastly, be mindful that how you paint one person could jeopardize your relationship with another. For example, if you write that your now-deceased grandfather was a suspected murderer, a reputation your family worked hard to suppress, you might wound your mother who had to live with the social stigma. Is inclusion of the fact worth damaging your relationship with her?

Strategies

Once you determine who might be affected by the airing of private information, there are at least five ways to further reduce your risk of legal and emotional upheaval:

Include your family in the writing process.

Have them read your work and offer their opinion. This may seem stupid, because why would they help uncover what they worked hard to hush up? But this tactic can open an avenue for discussion that may lead to healing. If not, at least you've given them a chance to offer their perspective.

If they object to particular material, negotiate with them. Agree to cut smaller facts they find embarrassing in exchange for the inclusion of what you find most important to your personal journey.

If they agree to your portrayal and the information you've included, get their consent in writing. But what if you've tried talking and negotiating and your relatives still threaten to sue?

Stick to verifiable facts from credible sources.

You can't be sued for stating facts that are a matter of public record. Such information can be found in police records, school transcripts, medical documentation, court transcriptions, the sworn testimony of witnesses and other concrete evidence.

If you write that your uncle punched you in the stomach, for example, yet no one witnessed the event or the aftermath—neither the bruise nor your distress—he could sue and possibly win because there's no way to check your allegations. Whereas he would have no recourse if you stuck to the facts listed on the police record documenting the incident.

The key to this defense is that the source of the facts is credible. If you repeat libelous material—say by referencing a newspaper article that includes incorrect information—you can be sued for libel.

Be clear this story is from your point of view.

Rather than state your opinion as fact, such as, "I looked at him and knew he was a criminal," use phrases such as "I thought" and "he seemed" that communicate your subjectivity. For example, "I never felt comfortable around him and always suspected he was a criminal at heart, though he was never arrested for anything."

You can use the same method to show your perspective might be different than someone else's: "I knew, or thought I knew, that he hated me from then on. Later I asked him about that night and he said he didn't hate me, but rather, was hurt I would think so poorly of him."

Fictionalize certain people or details to make them unrecognizable.

This is an excellent strategy if you: don't want to hurt family members' feelings or violate their right to privacy; can't reach them to gain their consent; or have been refused their consent.

If you choose this tactic, make people unrecognizable to themselves, or if they know they're the basis of your fictional character, to the public. You can make them into another person by using a different name, physical appearance, gender, etc. Or you can combine the features of many people to represent the particular challenge they posed.

For instance, rather than write about one person, "This six-foot balding guy who wore a Rutgers, NY, bowling shirt and came to me about a shoddy penile implant job…" you could write, "I used to get a string of middle class businessmen who wanted me to solve their sexual dysfunctions, which were probably due more to boredom than to actual physical problems."

Wait to tell your story until key characters have died.

This is an excellent strategy if you know what you plan to write will destroy someone you care about. This path is also appropriate if you're afraid the person, or group of people you're writing about, might exact revenge, whether physical, monetary or emotional.

Given the complexity of family dynamics, you'll most likely need to use a combination of these strategies to deal with each person who will be affected by the publication of private family information. As you work through these issues, keep track of your attempts to contact people, their reactions and what strategies you used to maintain their right to privacy or publicity. Such records will prove your ethical and professional reasoning to publishers, the media and readers. More importantly, you'll have the satisfaction of knowing you did everything in your power to be fair to others and honest and sincere in the telling of your story.

Resources

If you still feel uneasy about revealing family secrets, do further research until you feel certain you've taken every precaution necessary to protect yourself and your work. Here are two great resources to get started:

Couser, G. Thomas. *Vulnerable Subjects: Ethics and Life Writing.* Ithaca: Cornell University Press, 2003.

FindLaw. Copyright 2011, Thomson Reuters. findlaw.com

Are You Emotionally Ready?

Now that you've decided on the most ethical and professional way to reveal family secrets, the question remains: are you emotionally ready?

To find out, ask yourself the following:

Do you know why you're writing the story?

If you can tell someone, in one sentence, why you're writing this story, you probably know your motivation. If you fumble for an answer, however, you may not have unearthed the reason. Keep digging until you do, since the answer will tell you if you're ready to reveal those secrets to the world.

There are a number of good reasons for unearthing sensitive family information: a desire to help and inspire others; a need to heal; an attempt to process what happened. If you're out for revenge, however, consider setting the story aside until your anger abates. After all, readers love witnessing the personal growth of an author over the course of his or her story, whereas there is no growth in revenge.

Can you let someone read your material?

If you can't pry your fingers from the manuscript you've asked your friend to read, don't. Your distress, whether due to embarrassment or fear, signals that the story is still too personal for you to relinquish.

How honest have you been in recounting your story?

Self-censorship is a natural way for people to protect themselves against painful feelings and thoughts. If you feel compelled to make your life appear rosier than reality by ignoring, cutting or changing key details, you've probably run into areas you're not ready to address.

Have you thought about how readers might react?

What would you do if someone read your story then sent an email stating you're a liar, whore or traitor? What if your friends distanced themselves based on what they learned about you? What if strangers revealed their own dark secrets and asked you for advice?

These are scenarios you should contemplate before seeking publication. Keep in mind that the more poignant your story, the more comments—both positive and negative—your narrative will likely generate.

If you still feel too fragile to deal with your own emotions, much less others' reactions, consider waiting to release your story until you're emotionally stronger. The more clear-minded, confident and guilt-free you are about the process, the better your writing will be, the more capable you'll be in dealing with the aftermath and the more likely the feedback will be positive.

2. For Better, For Worse, For Publication

Lisa Romeo

I once wrote a 26-page essay about postpartum depression, and my writing mentor at the time, Ann Hood, pointed out that not until page 23 did I mention a husband. Knowing I was still married to my kids' father, what, Ann asked, was going on? I had an excuse. Postpartum depression was uniquely female, a singularly maternal experience; it was *my story*. Ann didn't buy it. Revision, please, said she.

But when it came to putting my husband on the page, I was paralyzed. So, I did what I learned at journalism school, long ago. I went right to the sources: women whose memoirs and essays included nuanced, well-rounded characters otherwise known as husbands, longtime partners, and exes, and I asked them for advice.

I picked a handful of writers whose brains I wanted to pick, and called my project (satisfying my MFA program's research requirement): *To Love, Honor and Omit: How Married Women Nonfiction Writers Grapple with the Perils and Pleasures(?) of Putting Their Husbands on the Page.*

For Peggy Orenstein, scaling this particular literary hill was a challenge in writing her memoir, *Waiting for Daisy*. Others I talked to included Pulitzer-prize winning former *New York Times* columnist Anna Quindlen, literary essayist Mimi Schwartz (*Thoughts From a Queen-Sized Bed*), memoirists Jill Smolowe, (*An Empty Lap*) and Meredith Hall, (*Without A Map*), writers Joan Anderson, (*An Unfinished Marriage*), Ilene Beckerman, (*Love, Loss and What I Wore*), and Ayelet Waldman, who landed on Oprah over a *New York Times* essay about loving her husband more than her children.

Here are some of the tips and advice I garnered for navigating the minefield of representing the spouse in essay and memoir.

First, decide if he is even a part of the story. It is possible to write a meaningful literary work of very personal memoir or essay with nary a husband mention. Think Anne Morrow Lindbergh's *Gift From The Sea*. Hall's ex-husband seems somehow present in spite of his literary absence in her memoir. The trick is to acknowledge the absence of the mate's viewpoint.

If the material demands the mate, determine if he cares about his portrayal in print. Sounds unbelievable, but some husbands really don't care what's written, whether in an obscure newsletter or best-seller. If that's your situation, congratulations, and turn the page. Otherwise....

Know his privacy policy. On the way home from a party, my husband will know how much Mitch earns, what Suzanne's house cost, and will have disclosed those same details, since he sees life as an open, interesting book. What about yours?

And his public one. You may think you know–I did, but then a writer friend asked my husband if he "minded" being written about, and he said *yes*. That sure got us talking. Then there is Waldman's husband, best-selling novelist Michael Chabon, who stoically accepts any public airing of private matters as part of being married to a writer of personal nonfiction.

Get a go-ahead or go ahead anyway? Some writers have formal discussions with their spouses about what's on-or off-limits for a future book or essay. I heard about wives who will drop a project cold if a husband says so. Quindlen's hundreds of columns about family quietly resisted discussing her husband in much detail, at his request.

Got ground rules? Most couples do, though more than one writer, including Waldman said, he's *married to a writer, tough luck*. Another writer's husband has complete veto power if he's mentioned; he's never used it, but the agreement guides her writing choices. In general however, common sense trumps literary license. Play fair. Don't be vengeful in print.

Media matters. His feelings might vary with the venue. An essay in a niche magazine about despising his favorite sport is less threatening than a marriage memoir. Unless it's on the front page of the sports section, I could probably publish anything and my husband would never know. I don't and I wouldn't, but I could.

Test the Terrain. My approach to letting my husband know what I'm up to is usually oblique and casual, over a meal or when the DVD is too boring to finish: *Honey, remember in Bermuda when we fought over tennis?* I take only mental notes. Others are more direct: *I'm writing about our fights over how to spend vacation time. Objections?*

Write first, ask questions later? Smolowe wrote her complete manuscript before discussing any of it with her husband, who it turned out, had a lot to say, much of it negative, but she changed hardly anything.

Play reporter. Especially when the experience you are writing about is a shared one—adoption, moving abroad, a spouse's illness—consider your husband as a source. Sometimes, Shwartz will formally interview her husband, tape running, which she finds can change her perspective. Orenstein interviewed hers too, though a little less formally, and except for details in one chapter, ultimately went with her original instincts.

Understand why you are asking. Do you want your husband's input to help shape the story, or like me, just to learn more about the issue or time period you are writing about? While writing, I keep a running list of questions, and get his "answers" eventually, but do this strictly to help me write a better, more emotionally well-rounded essay, not because I want him to have his say. But that's just me.

Editing happens. Will you ask your husband to read over your work before submitting? When you hand over pages, will you also give him a short turn-around time and a pencil (like me)—or a red Sharpie and weeks to deliberate? Some writers find this a good time to step back and reconsider their draft with the input a spouse provides. Others are content to get a grunt from a spouse simply acknowledging he has seen it.

Is a thumbs up necessary? I've heard of only one case where a writer shipped off a final, very personal manuscript, without the spouse having read it. Brave or stupid? Depends on the marriage. In your partnership, is approval or disapproval a condition for publication? For staying married?

Heads-up! Some think it's basic courtesy to let a loved one know they are going to appear in print, and how. Within a marriage, nearly every writer I asked said it's probably a survival tactic.

Fallout plan. Once published, a reviewer thinks your marriage is a divorce waiting to happen. An in-law thinks hubby's been wronged. Together, decide if reader reaction should matter. On your own, decide how much that one special reader's reaction does matter.

3. Interview with Meredith Hall

Lisa Romeo

Meredith Hall is the author of the memoir *Without A Map* (Beacon Press, 2007), which spans three decades beginning with her emotional and physical distancing from her family in the 1960s when she became pregnant at age 16. Now the memoirist-in-residence at the University of New Hampshire, Hall has earned a Pushcart Prize and the Gift of Freedom from the Room of Her Own Foundation. Her book and personal essays—published in literary journals, *The New York Times* and major magazines—focus intimately on family relationships. She talked with me about how husbands and other loved ones figure into memoirs.

Lisa Romeo: In *Without A Map*, you barely mention your ex-husband. Is his absence telling us as much as if he were on every page?

Meredith Hall: I have often been asked about this, and readers tell me that he is, in fact, very present. I hadn't intended that. It might be very effective as a writing technique—absence as statement—but I can't claim I did that with any awareness of its effect.

LR: Did you decide in advance not to include him, or did his character just not find a way into the narrative?

MH: There is always that difficult question for the memoirist of, what is my story and what is someone else's? I was very aware as I wrote of exposing my oldest son to a very bright public light. He understood, and encouraged me to write him into my story. But this made me very aware of wanting to protect everyone in my family as much as I could. My sister and brother, for example, might have played a much more significant role than they do, but I wanted to give them cover. In deciding how much to write about my husband, giving him cover or not was not my concern. But there were two issues: one was our children. I didn't want them to have to read about their father or about their parents' marriage. Then, I had to decide if I really had anything to say about that part of my life, anything larger than the events themselves. I couldn't make that larger meaning, and so I left the marriage out.

LR: You've said that you wrote each section around "obsessive images." No such images about the marriage, then?

MH: Even if I decided that I was going to include the marriage, I would not have had a lot to say. It feels transparent, not complex. Although I was married for many years, as a sort of artifact it does not take up a lot of room. The biggest issue is the children: the responsibility must be to them, I think.

LR: What advice might you have for writers who want to, or feel they need to, make the spouse a central character?

MH: I tell writers—do not bother to write if you are not willing to be absolutely honest with your readers. The one thing you offer is insight, and it must be earned, not feigned. Does anyone dare to be completely honest about their mate? We are not (so honest) in our lives. How can we be on the page? At what cost to that loved mate, and to the relationship?

LR: I've noticed that memoirs in which a female writer puts a husband on the page in a complex three-dimensional way are rare, and they are often written by widows.

MH: Well, here is a telling fact: I can't even think of a memoir in which the current mate is present. They are invisible, because of this issue. Think about how much attention is paid to our childhoods, our early family life. We gain perspective, and have authority over our observations and questions. A current marriage? You might have one or two friends to whom you lay bare your life, but you carefully edit and secret away most of your thoughts and actions regarding that marriage from everyone else. A published book is not your confidant, not your journal, not your best and closest friend. It is the stranger, listening.

For me, the great responsibility is to write our characters with love, and that means allowing our readers to love even those who are far from perfect. I want that complexity, that wisdom and maturity from a writer. An adored husband is an icon; the person is imperfect and complex. I don't care much about the icon. It is the imperfect person, loved in a much deeper way by the writer, who holds me.

LR: Writing a husband as a complex character, including flaws, reflects back on the writer. If he's a jerk on paper, I suppose she's the idiot living with a jerk.

MH: Every word we write exposes a memoirist's Self, defines us, identifies us, reveals us to the world and to ourselves. I also think there are very, very clear rules in our culture: we speak well of our mates. If we don't, we appear superficial, critical, self-serving. Unkind. So in that way, writing some sort of "truth" would reveal us, on the page, as a rule-breaker. The problem is in justifying why we might write that intimate, alive and breathing and—married to us—character!

Regarding my memoir, readers always ask, "But what about your husband?" Readers are greedy, beyond the bounds. But I think it is enough to say, "There was/is a husband. But this is my story." Acknowledge his presence—one or two sentences—and then claim your own ground. Some readers will object, but smart readers will understand what you are up to.

4. Keeping Your Distance: Avoiding Sentimentality in Family-Centered Writing

Jenn Brisendine

Emotion—love and loneliness, joy and pain, celebration and grief—is the blood in the veins of family writing. In both fiction and nonfiction, emotion sparks relationships, increases conflict, and drives characters' actions. Most crucially, it prompts readers to invest their own feelings in a story. Emotionally-charged writing, however, can be risky. In an effort to express all those passions, the writer might send emotion rushing out in a reckless stream, trapping the story in the floodwaters of sentimentality.

Avoiding overly sentimental storytelling—especially clichés, melodrama, and generalizations—allows emotion to surface through a natural voice and style. Eliciting a strong emotional response in your reader depends on sincere and subtle expression of feelings.

Wipe Out Clichés

A cliché is a phrase that has become well-known through overuse. We should always strive to eliminate clichés in written work, but it's especially important to avoid them in descriptions of emotions:

> *Carla's heart was breaking. Tears welled up in her eyes and rolled down her face.*

These clichés express sadness, but they don't deliver the depth of emotion you intend. They cannot ignite feeling in your reader, because the words lack any ember of newness.

To recognize a cliché, analyze how easily an expression comes to mind. Often, the imagination will offer a cliché because it's an easily-generated, prepackaged description. Additionally, task a critique partner to read your draft and hunt down clichés.

To revise a cliché, use fresh comparisons and descriptions. Seek language you've never used or read before. Instead of stating that a character's heart broke, try comparing that sadness to something universal—*Carla's sadness made her feel heavy and waterlogged, like she'd fallen fully clothed in a pool of grief*—or create double-duty description that shows character backstory:

> *On a mission trip in college, Carla had witnessed grieving mothers swaying and wailing. Now she wanted to open her mouth and let that same wail go careening out.*

Skip the Melodrama

Melodramatic writing is the literary equivalent of old-time movie moments in which the heroine flings a forearm up to her burdened brow:

> *It was the most terrifying moment of my life.*
> *Greta thought she might die, she was so mortified.*

Over-the-top statements like these may come across as inflated and insincere to the reader.

To recognize a melodramatic phrase, search emotional passages for sentences that make exaggerated claims about feelings. Are you stretching the truth or relying on superlatives (*most astonishing, best day, worst mood*) to describe emotions?

To revise a melodramatic phrase, describe the scene and the character's role in it. Write with a tight focus on the situation and let the reader's imagination generate the emotion:

> *The truck accelerated toward me, and the only sound in the silent car was my own gasp.*

Instead of grand declarations about a feeling, show the physical effect of the emotion on the character: *Greta forced her shaky legs to stand. The stares of hundreds of coworkers who had seen her fall pressed on her like gym weights.* Allow the reader to feel the emotion with a vivid comparison.

Feel the Feeling

How does a feeling feel on your face, in your stomach, on your skin? If it had a sound or a smell, what would it be? Close scrutiny of an emotion's physical effect can provide ideas for your writing.

> Fear—Have respirations slowed, or quickened? Is sensory input more acute, or dulled?

> Embarrassment—Is skin heating up, or crawling with chill?

> Anger—Does it burn? Prick? Stab? Jab?

> Worry—Is it like gnats buzzing, a laundry stain, an odor that won't wash off?

> Grief—Is it like the solidity of lead, or the emptiness of a cloud?

Strive for Specificity

Ever study propaganda techniques? One method advertisers use to sway consumers is known as the "glittering generality": "Buy our detergent and you'll *never* see stains again!" "Make *every* night a good sleep night with our chamomile tea!" In family writing, it's tempting to invoke a generalization, especially while communicating emotion:

> *Walter had never felt so happy.*
> *Angela was always very embarrassed to walk into church late.*

You might intend for words like *always, never, so,* and *very* to have a strong impact, but ironically, these words tend to generalize and weaken.

To seek out words that generalize in your draft, use the Find feature on your word processing program. In addition to pinpointing and reconsidering uses of *never* and *always,* search for *very, so, every, any, all, almost,* and *some.*

To revise generalizations, use details to paint a clearer image:

> *The muscles in Walter's face stretched and quivered, unused to the challenge of a smile.*

Instead of making the unrealistic claim that a character always or never feels a certain way, describe the scene with sensory imagery:

> *A familiar heat brushed Angela's cheekbones as the ladies in the last pew turned to witness her late entrance.*

If you eliminate clichés, melodrama, and generalizations, your draft will be free of the biggest dangers of sentimentality, and your voice will demonstrate authenticity by conveying a larger emotional reality. In family writing, the strongest emotions emerge through subtlety and sincerity.

5. Killing the Phantom

Corbin Lewars

After teaching memoir classes for several years, I started offering a workshop entitled "How to Kill Your Mother." No, I am not changing careers and becoming a hit woman, I am merely addressing the, "I don't want my mother (ex-boyfriend, employer, etc.) to read my memoir" conundrum. This fear not only dictates what the student writes, it sometimes prevents her from writing at all. To prevent this from happening, I offer several ways to silence that negative voice.

Silence

Although it is exciting to say you are working on a book, the first rule of thumb when writing a memoir is silence. Other peoples' narcissism may cause them to be more offended that they aren't in your book, than worried if they are. You can share your drafts and ideas with an impartial writing group or mentor, but the fewer people you tell the better.

A writer faces innumerable barriers such as lack of time, fear of inadequacy, or multiple interruptions when they try to focus. It is difficult enough to overcome your own hurdles without adding the extra burden of eliciting other people's opinions. Sharing your ideas and drafts with friends and family members will not only slow you down, it may even derail you from your original ideas and themes.

Hold Off on Research

Memoir is the one form of non-fiction in which research is not necessarily recommended, especially in the beginning stages of writing. Too much, if any, research can encumber your flow.

The story doesn't need to be precise with dates and locales in the draft phases. Your main objective is to write as much and as frequently as you can. This won't happen if you spend a week researching the average temperature in Atlanta during the summer of 1977. The reality is, no one is going to mind if you are off a few degrees.

An even more dangerous, ill-advised type of research is asking anyone who may be in your book for his or her recollection of events. Memories vary for people, especially if the event was an emotional one. In order for your memoir to remain your memoir, it needs to be your account of situations, not others'. Asking other people for clarification usually ends up muddling the writer more than aiding her.

What is Truth?

One of the most succinct and useful books on the craft of writing a memoir is Judith Barrington's, *Writing the Memoir.* She writes about the subjective nature of truth and states that as in life, there may not be an absolute truth in memoir. She also explores the notion of emotional truth, reminding us that people's feelings vary and each person's memory will be altered by their particular feelings. Therefore, each person may have a different "emotional truth" when recalling the same occurrence.

A certain amount of creative freedom is allowed in memoir. In order for the story to flow, you may need to rearrange some events chronologically. Perhaps you vividly remember your childhood front porch being vast, yet in pictures it looks small. If it is an important memory for your story, go ahead and leave it as a large porch. If you find it difficult to recall details about certain places or events, concentrate on what you do remember and write as many of these details as you can. This exercise may help you to remember more. If it doesn't, it could be because the details you don't remember aren't pertinent to your story.

Memoir is a story *from* your life, not the story *of* your life. In order to differentiate between the two, make sure your memoir is based on a theme and adhere to this theme throughout your entire book. Several authors have gotten into trouble when they made up their backgrounds or large portions of their lives to enhance their memoir. James Frey's *Million Little Pieces* is a perfect example of this. If your theme is a rags to riches story, at one time, you really need to have lived close to poverty. Your writing should be compelling enough to draw the reader in without relying on over-dramatizations and fictional scenarios.

The Beauty of Drafts

The prospect of writing several drafts of a manuscript can feel overwhelming and daunting, but instead I advise you to view it as liberating. Telling yourself no one will read your first draft silences all of the "thems," the people you don't want to read your memoir. It also allows you to free yourself up with your writing and use it as catharsis. Spend a day writing about all of the ways you feel your mother caused you emotional trauma. Tell us about the affair you had, even if it was only imaginary. Complain about all of the people who you feel have mistreated you and reveal all of your family's secrets. Although none of this material needs to remain in the final draft, it is crucial to let it out at some time. By writing about what you don't want to write, you can more easily access and assess what you do want to write about.

Memoirs need time to percolate. If what you are choosing to write about is a recent or reoccurring issue for you, you won't be able to gain the perspective and distance from it that you need until the second, third or even the fourth draft. Unfortunately, you won't be able to get to the other drafts until you complete the first messy one. Once you have a complete draft, take some time away from your memoir. During this break, you will be able to gain clarity on where the gaps in your story are and what can be eliminated all together. Again, being clear on your theme will help with this process.

Diplomacy

Writing numerous drafts allows you to become more diplomatic in your telling of the story. View the first draft as the telephone call you make to a girlfriend after a hardship, which may be full of profanities and offers very little self-awareness of your contribution to the scenario. In time, you will start to see the other person's point of view and your perspective on the situation may broaden.

During a third revision, a student of mine redirected all of her blame and anger towards her father and placed it on her parent's divorce instead. By changing, "I hated what my father had done to my mother," to "I hated what the divorce had done to my mother," she no longer feared family members reading her memoir. The tone of the book also changed from a tirade about her father to a more mass appealing, in depth look at the effects of the divorce on her family.

Almost any tone is acceptable for memoir except retaliation or whining. Anger is fine, but a two hundred-page rant about one's ex-husband is not going to appeal to many people. A great example of this is Jeanette Walls' *The Glass Castle*. Her upbringing with two mentally unstable parents could be full of pity and rage, but instead she uses her journalistic background to describe her tumultuous childhood in a removed and nonjudgmental way. In doing so, she allows the reader to form her own opinions and feelings about the situation, rather than become consumed by Walls' sentiments.

What is Not Said, Says a Lot

If after several drafts you cannot move past your bitterness about a certain person, make their presence in your memoir very minor or even obsolete. Sometimes, the absence of a character says a lot. The savvy reader will be able to read between the lines; you don't have to spell it out for them. Perhaps, as more time passes, you will gain more perspective regarding this person or situation and can base your second memoir on this expanded awareness.

In a recent essay, "The Weight of Like," I described some of my earliest memories of rolling around in the back of our station wagon with my sister. My father was driving us to a birthday party with his usual cigarette in one hand and martini glass tucked between his legs. When I read this aloud in class, one of the students said, "That says so much, without giving anything away." My intention was to offer the reader a glimpse into my childhood without directly complaining about or insulting my parents. The paragraph offers this, while allowing my still smoking and drinking (as well as avid opponent of seat belts) father to laugh and say, "Those were the days."

Who Cares?

"Is my story interesting to anyone?" is the main concern of many of my students. The rise in "Reality" television proves that many people are voyeuristic. Twenty of the top twenty-five highest rated shows in 2002 were Reality shows and they continue to excel in popularity (Balkan). Some of the shows are based on famous people, but many are not.

Your memoir will probably not have the action and drama displayed on a show such as "Survivor," so it will need to pique people's interest by being a revealing account of a situation others can relate to. In order to do so, you will need to delve deeply into your theme. A daily account of what you did that day will not hold people's interest, but a comprehensive musing and narration of an event or time that greatly impacted you will most likely gain you a readership.

Often the writer is her own biggest critic. It is her own voice that she needs to silence when thinking her writing isn't interesting to others. Sometimes, it is difficult for her to access her true voice because she is too worried about being nice. Virginia Woolf addressed this dilemma as battling a phantom in her essay "Professions for Women." She claimed the "phantom" was the voice inside women's heads that told us to be sympathetic and tender, especially when referring to men and their work. In order to be a premium book reviewer, Woolf claimed she had to kill that voice. If she didn't, it would have "plucked the heart" out of her writing.

A writer needs to learn how to silence her self-depre-cation and need to please so her story can be told in the most optimal and riveting fashion. As long as you are being true to yourself, are willing to reveal areas of your life, and do not do so in retaliation, you can feel confident that your story is worth telling.

Anonymity: Theirs and Yours

Writing your memoir under a pseudonym is one way to si-lence the phantom. It allows the writer access to an alter ego who is not afraid to be honest in disclosing her story. Publish-ing under this pseudonym is always an option, but even if you don't, the act of writing drafts under an alias can be liberating.

Writing in the third person also allows a writer to dis-tance herself enough from her experiences to be able to access her story without being encumbered by her emotions. Say-ing "she" rather than "I" allows for a buffer when describing something painful or difficult. After suffering from writer's block for years, a student of mine chose to write her memoir in the third person. By the time she was half way through her first draft, she had unwittingly slipped into saying "I" rather than "she." Once this occurred, she realized narrating her hardships no longer caused her to feel as if she was reliv-ing them; she was merely writing about them.

Changing people's names also removes the "what will she think?" fear for some writers. Try modifying people's physical characteristics or other identifying details as well. Again, you may only need to do this in your drafts, but it would be acceptable even in the final version as long as it doesn't substantially alter your story. Stating someone has blonde hair rather than red and being vague about where they live and work is fine, but stating someone was Obama's press secretary when she was actually an intern is not acceptable.

By following these basic guidelines, you will hopefully be able to remove many, if not all, of the barriers standing between you and your memoir. These are not steadfast rules, rather suggestions of how to stay motivated to write. I am frequently asked, "How do I become a writer?" and my answer is quite simple, "Write." Find a way to incorporate writing into your routine. Even devoting an hour a day two times a week will transform you from someone who wants to write, to someone who is writing.

References

Balkin, Karen F. "Introduction." *At Issue: Reality TV*. San Diego: Greenhaven Press, 2003.

Barrington, Judith. *Writing the Memoir,* 2nd ed. Portland, Oregon: The Eighth Mountain Press, 2002.

Frey, James. *A Million Little Pieces*. New York: Anchor Books, 2004.

Lewars, Corbin. "The Weight of Like." *The Seattle PI* (2010). blog.seattlepi.com/singlewritermama/

Walls, Jeannette. *The Glass Castle: A Memoir*. New York: Scribner, 2006.

Woolf, Virginia. "Professions for Women" in *The Death of a Moth and Other Essays*. New York: Harcourt Brace & Company, 1942.

6. The Parent Trap: Five Mistakes to Avoid When Writing Essays about Family

Anne Witkavitch

Write about what you know. Every writer has heard this advice but often finds it is not so easy to follow when writing about a subject close to the heart—family.

As writers, we're wired to pay attention to and observe the big and small things that make up our daily lives, to look for those experiences that would make a great story, and share them through words on a page.

The easy part is finding material to write about. Life with family produces an endless stream of story possibilities. Our relationships serve up wonderful tales to share with readers that many of them can relate to in their own lives.

The hard part is translating an event or experience into a story that has universal appeal. A personal essay that's publishable needs to portray intimacy but also appeal to a wide readership—an audience of strangers who do not know anything about you and must be persuaded (through your talent as a writer) to care. Family stories must be written in a way that keeps the audience engaged and maintains their interest from beginning to end.

Writing About Family

When writing about family, we must approach our subjects from three distinct perspectives. First, as family members who have an interesting or humorous personal experience to share; second, as writers who want to tell a compelling story; and third, as editors who must assess the writing from an outside-in point-of-view to ensure it will sustain the interest of a broad audience.

We must move away from simply telling anecdotal stories that relay information about something that has happened *to* us—whether it is cute, heartwarming, humorous, or tragic—and instead, translate that tale into a captivating story that shares something intimate and personal *about* us. As we do this, we must use our skills as writers to develop universal themes, create identifiable characters, develop strong plots, describe rich settings, and produce believable conflict in order to be credible and authentic.

Five Mistakes and How to Avoid Them

It is no surprise, then, that five common mistakes we make when writing about family are rooted in our inability to step outside of the action, distance ourselves from our subjects, and, as writers, use our technical skills to turn personal experiences into good, compelling storytelling.

Mistake 1: No universal theme.

Stories need a reason that moves beyond the "what" and identifies the "why." A universal theme gives purpose to our essays without getting preachy or making a deliberate point. It provides the thread that holds together the action and leaves behind a lesson or "so what" for the reader.

Mistake 2: Fear of getting too personal.

Sometimes writing about families is difficult, especially when tackling sensitive or difficult topics. However it is too easy to play it safe and stick to the details on the surface, the ones that are easiest to share. As writers we need to force ourselves past our "safety zones" and challenge ourselves to go deeper into our own lives in order to gain credibility. For example, if writing about a mother and daughter experience, the story will be more powerful if we reach back into our pasts and identify a similar memory we can share from our experiences with our own mothers, even if doing so stirs up emotions difficult to write about.

Mistake 3: Nice story but no plot.

As writers we must connect the dots for our readers and structure our writing to move them forward through the story from point A to point B to point C. By doing so we create an effect between the actions, build tension, and set a pace that keeps them reading. Without plot and pace stories go flat—and we lose our readers' attention before they reach the end.

Mistake 4: Tell, not show, what is happening.

When writing about family experiences, we have the distinct advantage of having lived the "real story." Present and in the moment, we observe first-hand the scene, hear the dialogue, and feel the emotions. But our readers are at a disadvantage. They are not there with us as the event is happening and it is our job to paint an accurate and vivid picture that puts them in the experience. By showing and not telling, we build trust with our readers and invite them into our personal worlds.

Mistake 5: Write only in the past tense.

Because we write about events and experiences that have already happened, we tend to write personal essays in the past tense. This is usually fine and is perfectly acceptable. However, writing a personal essay in the present tense can have a surprisingly positive effect on the reader's experience. Present tense connects us with readers in a powerful way and on a more intimate level by letting them participate with us, not merely as third party observers after the fact. It's the difference between watching a live stage performance and seeing the movie. The experience is immediate.

The good news is that all five of these literary "parent traps" are easy to spring, releasing us to transform good stories into great essays about the people most important to us—and in doing so creating publishable material that not only satisfies our calling as artists, but resonates with readers as well.

7. Rattling Family Skeletons

Arlene L. Mandell

Ever since Sappho penned some lines on the island of Lesbos, poetry lovers and literary sleuths have been examining every fragment of writing to discover clues to the person behind the poem. Since poetry lends itself to varying interpretations, and misinterpretations, this sleuthing is one of its many intriguing aspects. Poetry, by its very nature, is both allusive—filled with similes and metaphors and images—and elusive—what does Poetess X mean by the word "dark" in line 17 in her poem about lilacs?

As poets, none of this need concern us. We should, theoretically, write whatever we want about husbands, ex-husbands, dictatorial fathers (see Sylvia Plath), lecherous uncles, and stingy aunts. And why not expose the mother who doted on your brother, shortchanging you, the clearly superior sibling?

Confessional poetry can be a sneaky way of telling the world what you don't want to confront directly: a son who calls only when he needs money, or a daughter whose life is so much more interesting and important than yours that she cuts you off in mid-sentence. Is this poetry or therapy? And does it matter?

On a gentler note, we can also write in detail about our adorable grandchildren and our intimate relationship with our pets (see Emily Dickinson, Elizabeth Barrett Browning, etc.). These human/dog relationships can be such a major factor that Maureen Adams, a clinical psychologist and professor at the University of San Francisco, recently published a study, *Shaggy Muses*, which delves into the lives of five esteemed women poets and writers and the inspiration and contributions of their pets.

Some of the loftiest poets seem to write "only" about

nature, but we know that deeply symbolic meaning may lie beneath the most placid lily pond. Mary Oliver, beloved by hundreds of thousands of readers, revels in nature. We follow her on her daily walks, observing birds and grasses through her eyes and graceful words, and don't really need to know about her personal life. But, if we wish, we can intuit certain things from the dedications in each volume.

Back in the 1960s, confessional poets like Sylvia Plath and Anne Sexton, both of whom committed suicide, sometimes made oblique and confusing references to their parents, husbands and children. Plath, in her famous poem "Daddy," writes: "Daddy, I have had to kill you. You died before I had time" which she does not mean literally, but means nevertheless. Sexton wrote some disturbing verse regarding her young daughter, which implied improper sexual activity. Was it true? Written for shock value? We will never know, but she did say, "It doesn't matter who my father was; it matters who I remember he was." That sort of lets her off the hook, or does it?

Since we spend most of our lives interacting with our families, it makes sense to use this rich material in our writing. Sometimes women poets are "accused" of writing about family as if we disdain loftier subjects like eternity. But that first day of school, when your child bravely steps into the kindergarten classroom, and doesn't even wave goodbye, can feel like a small eternity until he returns, with nametag askew and red crayon on his new white shirt.

If there's a secret to writing effective poems about one's family, it must lie in finding those specific telling details which can, for example, describe your mother as a young woman as revealed in a black and white photo.

Marge Piercy, a poet who is both prolific and profound, takes us to a Pittsburgh slum in her poem, "Photograph of my mother sitting on the steps." It begins:

My mother who isn't anyone's
just her own intact and yearning
self complete as a birch tree
sits on the tenement steps

We learn about her mother's life, not all of it pretty, see her wearing her only good dress, longing to be "luminous and visible." We're drawn into the story, which reveals a powerful family secret. And we're encouraged to examine the old photos in our own family albums, to tell the stories barely concealed in them.

Another poet who uses specific details to define a turning point in her life and her daughter's is Linda Pastan, who describes the experience of watching her daughter learning to ride a bike. The poem, "To a Daughter Leaving Home," is full of the poignancy of seeing the girl on both a physical and metaphorical journey away from her mother. It ends with these words,

> the hair flapping
> behind you like a
> handkerchief waving
> goodbye

What parent hasn't felt that collision of emotions, the pride in your child becoming independent, and the sorrow that she is learning how to leave you? And how many of us won't recall our own specific details. Did he leave a teddy bear on his closet shelf when he went off to basic training?

One of Emily Dickinson's famous lines addresses the issue of revealing/concealing: "Tell the truth but tell it slant." This is excellent advice. Taken to its extreme, we might describe our paternal grandfathers as smiling teddy bears or slimy toads.

Let's discuss sex for a moment. Even though the persona in the poem is not actually you (though so often it is), how specific do you want to be? Some poets are nonchalant and straightforward about describing such intimate matters as sleeping arrangements. Ellen Bass, an accomplished teacher and prolific poet who lives in Santa Cruz, CA, in her poem "Winter Solstice," describes the scene in "an overheated apartment on the Upper West Side." She reports:

I roll over and over like a rotisseried hen
while Janet's breath softly rises and falls
and our son sleeping soundly on the floor,
his broken leg silently knitting bone to bone.

In the next stanza, she adds her newly widowed mother-in-law, the mother-in-law's friend and even an ancient wheezing schnauzer to the scene.

As someone who has attended one of Ellen's workshops at Esalen in Big Sur and also slept in overheated apartments on the Upper West Side of Manhattan, I feel privileged to be invited into this scene from her life, which *seems* true.

Another brilliant California poet whose readings I've attended is the much-honored Jane Hirshfield, whose poems appear regularly in the Best American Poetry and Pushcart Prize anthologies. She lives somewhere north of the Golden Gate Bridge in Marin County. There is nothing in her luminous poems which mentions a cat, dog, or significant other. That aspect of her life remains private.

There's an ever-growing body of poetry about illness and death, from the sadness of a miscarriage to the slow loss of one's parent through Alzheimer's disease. Sharon Olds wrote an entire volume, *The Gold Cell*, about her father's final days. Others choose to allude to a life-threatening medical condition in more subtle, yet no less moving ways. One example comes from Carol Smallwood, a Michigan poet and author of *On the Way to Wendy's*, who is one of the editors of this anthology:

A Spider in January

Was on Wendy's wall so I slipped it
an empty cup

My table was near a divider wall
where sun crept and remembered early
man's monuments to measure time

The sun slid down my neck, the slant
on the table widened. As a decoy for

cold from opened doors I swallowed
pills, post-chemo the last

I'd put the spider in my plant at home.
It wasn't moving–but maybe it would
come spring

We learn of the poet's illness first through the words
"post-chemo" and then, by inference, with the metaphor of the
spider.

The links between any poet's writing and her actual life
may be as gossamer as that spider's thread or as concrete as
the information on her driver's license. Since the only poetry
I can discuss with absolute authority is my own, I've selected
four samples, starting with "Creamsicle Lover," about my first
boyfriend, who shall remain nameless:

Creamsicle Lover

Standing in front
of the frozen food case
I see Creamsicles
and remember
the way you'd suck
the breath out of my body
with your wet kisses

and remember the first time
outside the candy store
you in tight jeans
and a T-shirt rolled
above bulging biceps
and me in white shorts
legs already suntanned in May
licking my Creamsicle hard
to keep the sweet syrup
from running down my arm,

poking my tongue
in its creamy center

and you with a portable radio
on your shoulder
harmonizing with the Platters
— "Earth Angel, Earth Angel,
will you be mi-ine" —

your hot eyes
and those black eyelashes
brushing your olive cheeks
while you slid
down my body

and me an innocent 12-year-old
tossing my ponytail
sauntering down Hemlock Street
knowing you'd follow.

Okay, I admit I was 13, not 12, but otherwise the poem is reasonably accurate.

Now let's fast forward 30 years to a short poem about my ex-husband, which was published in a divorce anthology, *We Used to Be Wives*:

The Ex

He has grown smaller
his dark curls no more
than a few greasy wires
pressed across his scalp
but that voice is the same–
deep, genial–a voice
that could sell snake oil
to a snake.

Perhaps you can see why no family member, not even my second husband, has been privy to this charming description.

For contrast, here's a "nicer" poem about my daughter, which was published in "The Metropolitan Diary" section of *The New York Times*:

Little Girl Grown

Monday I tied blue ribbons in her hair
before she went to school.
Tuesday I packed her teddy bear
and she was off to camp.
Friday I drove her to college
with her silver flute.
Sunday she moved to Manhattan
with her fiancé.

Will the neighbors on East 35th Street
please see that she doesn't dawdle
on her way to work?
She's the one with the flute
and the teddy bear
and blue ribbons
in her hair.

Though I don't mention her name, I'm telling the world–to a New Yorker, *The Times* is the world–that she's living with her boyfriend. At her engagement party, the poem was set to music and sung by two of her friends. And yes, dear readers, they did marry.

The fruit of that union, my beloved grandson, has been the subject of a number of poems, including "For Derek in the Spring of His Second Year":

Holding tight to his father's hand
the small boy slips into a woods
filled with screeching crows.

When brambles tear at his clothes,
his father shows him how to bypass
the tangled patches.

At the stream they toss twigs
in the surging water and he wants
to wade in. His father pulls him back.

Now he is tired, stumbling,
rubbing his eyes, so his father
hoists him up on his shoulders.

Together they made their way back
to the house where the boy lies down
on his soft quilt and dreams.

I read "For Derek" at his bar mitzvah and he seemed pleased. But now that he's almost 17, I must be careful not to invade his privacy, or at the very least, not send him copies of any poems till he's 25 . . . or 30?

From the four poems of mine included in this essay, selected from 300 or so poems I've written in the past 20 years, you may already have learned far more than you care to know about me. And I haven't even included a single cat or dog poem. Most of my work is not "confessional" in nature, however, though bits of me are no doubt revealed in my work.

Therefore, my advice is similar to Emily's: Tell all...well, tell almost all...but be cautious in using proper names...and make every effort not to share...unless it's that first "Creamsicle Lover" boyfriend, who seemed quite moved when I located him recently in Long Island, though his shrill second wife could be heard in the background saying, "Who is she? What does she want?"

References

Bass, Ellen. *The Human Line*. Port Townsend, Washington: Copper Canyon Press, 2007.

Pastan, Linda. *The Imperfect Paradise.* New York: WW. Norton & Company, 1988.

Piercy, Marge. *Colors Passing Through Us.* New York: Alfred A. Knopf, 2003

Smallwood, Carol. "A Spider in January," *On the Way to Wendy's.* Columbus, Ohio: Pudding House Publications, 2008.

8. Writing About Religion Requires Pseudonyms

Rosemary Moeller

My writing is mostly about my family or comes from experiences I have living on the Plains. One area I'm reluctant to write about is religious beliefs. I live in a very conservative Christian area of the country that is content with its worldview of salvation and damnation. I share none of these beliefs being non-Christian by choice. This hasn't kept me from playing music at church or singing in choirs, volunteering at fundraisers, teaching Sunday school or vacation Bible school. It does make me uncomfortable at writers' meetings because I can't share many of my ideas and themes I'd like to write about, and I find myself censoring my own expressions. I don't like that.

I want to explore how I see the faith base of people around me in characters and images but I don't want to hurt the feelings of many really wonderful people. I'm not talking about hypocrisy here. It is the foundations of their faith that I cannot agree with. But I struggle to approach the themes without too much pain for anyone.

There are times when I'm affronted by someone's behavior but just file it away for a scene in a story. Like the civic meeting when we had to vote on whether or not to sponsor a tour of homes for the holidays, and the President informed us that she had prayed and received a positive answer from Jesus so no more discussion was necessary. We would be doing it.

Teachers are personally insulted if they are asked to refrain from using coloring pages of nativity scenes in class, having Christmas trees in the school, making Santas and angels for every corner of the halls and singing carols to calm the kids before holidays. They really don't think any sane person could be more than a humbug for not wanting all the joy of the season to fill the classrooms. For most people culture and religion are intertwined so much that they cannot separate them. But I have goals to work on in stories that do just that.

I've had teachers explain to me how Hitler was a twentieth century instrument of God's punishment, and how boys from here would have died in a farm accident or car crash if they hadn't gone to Iraq because their time was up, and I did have a friend apologize for jewing me down at a book sale. These attitudes leave me with a vile taste in my mouth and an inability to challenge their statements. I feel the chasm is too deep, too wide to be worth the effort, but in stories I can carefully climb down and cross barriers that in conversation are impossible to overcome. It is the power of storytelling, narration of voice in poetry, to be heard and control the tone of the speaker and the comfort of the listener.

I don't know where all this casual intolerance comes from. I've yet to hear a priest or pastor not preach about Jews, Muslims or Hindus in the most negative terms. And still I'm asked which church I belong to. When I respond that I don't go anymore, there's the look to the side, the sigh and the "Oh." Belonging to a church is like watching high school sports. Out here, it's expected of everyone. The unchurched are frowned upon at church and in circle meetings, and assumed to be lazy because they obviously don't want to help make sandwiches for funerals. I have no problem making a dozen sandwiches. I just don't want to go to church. It's either boring or stressful, compared to baking bread or doing embroidery on a Sunday morning. But I try to find a voice that can be patiently listened to for a reasonable period of time to present a totally different worldview. It isn't usually accepted without an argument, but I believe in the value of confrontation. I just don't know when to give up and back off , and when to plow ahead.

It's hard to tell friends that you just don't believe what they believe in. I must be lying to myself because what sane person isn't Christian, doesn't believe in the God of Nazareth.

There's so much disagreement among Christians that it seems frivolous to be a complete outsider. I could still be contrary, argumentative, disrespectful, undisciplined and Christian. But not a Christian? What's wrong?

I can have reasonable, intelligent conversations with believers of immaculate conceptions, creationism, heavenly assumptions, transubstantiations and transfigurations. I don't doubt their faith; I just don't feel the need for it. It's not that I'm impatient, but I'm not waiting for the Messiah or Elijah or any meteor to strike. I am waiting for the opportunity to honestly press for peace while many are eagerly anticipating the coming rapture. These images of end time are forceful and powerful and should be able to live metaphorically but I want to challenge them politically.

I am spiritually "in the day", kind of like my mother in the nursing home. Mortality is a condition, not a sentence from some celestial court of angels in dresses, mostly musicians playing boring hymns. That heaven is so unattractive to me. Mine is undesirable, which is okay, the transparent nothingness of soundless, unbeating emptiness.

I cannot desire an abusive father for a godhead that wants to destroy his creations out of distaste and disgust, but needs an alter ego to restrain Him from damning all but those who're on the good side of the shielding second personality. Most of my deeply religious friends are spiritually self-loathing, repressing most of their impulses for an assurance of lasting peace in heaven. I don't get it. I don't like abusive parents, and don't see the human condition as based on the irresponsible whims of a parent who would save only the family of an alcoholic father. But then maybe the Noah story does make sense. Two of a kind. This would be impossible to discuss with people decorating the church nursery with rainbows and doves and paired mammals, this story of mass genocide and unforgiving horror. But the attempt to retell, revise and reevaluate is too important to abandon because of righteous indignation. There's too much at stake in today's multi-cultural global village.

Give me God, undressed, inhuman, unfathomable, omniscient and let me wallow like a happy pig in this earthly mud of today, grateful and in awe, but not in church.

Part II

Finding Time to Write With Career and Family

9. Balancing Act: How to Devote Time to Your Craft Without Neglecting Your Kids or Your Day Job

Kezia Willingham

I have three kids, a husband, and a full time job. I go to the gym every weekday morning at 5:30am. So when do I find time to write?

On the weekends, I get up at five or six o'clock in the morning, turn on the coffee machine, and get started. Sometimes I read for about 15 minutes first, while sipping coffee. Other mornings the passion to write is so strong that I come downstairs and immediately plunge into recording my thoughts. I've dedicated myself to the task of becoming a writer. In order to do that, I must make the time. Weekend mornings I am able to devote a few hours to writing. It is only then that I have both the quiet and mental space to devote to my craft.

I think about writing much more frequently than I actually do it. Fortunately, I have a good memory. The gym tends to be a place where I can sort through my dreams and analyze them in the context of my daily life, to see where they fit into what I am writing about. By fully giving mental space to my thoughts, they are less easily forgotten. If it is a weekday, I occasionally send myself emails to remember ideas, deadlines, or drafts. I consciously revisit ideas, revelations, and story ideas so that they become temporarily hard wired in my brain. I probably should carry around a little notebook, I am sure they come in handy, but I worry there is a good chance that I would lose it or fear other people reading it.

During the week, my day job is non-negotiable. It pays the bills and provides health insurance. In the evenings, I devote the remaining few hours to my children who are hungry for their time with me. I have eliminated volunteer and extra-curricular work because I feel that my schedule is full. In order to be the kind of mother, employee, writer, and wife that I want to be, I have to set boundaries and limit other involvement. Years ago, when I was single mother, a friend of mine shared some very good advice in regards to the demands of others. She told me, "Your job, other people, will always ask for more of your time. The person who needs your time the most is your daughter, who will only be young once." She was right, and I've prioritized my time accordingly while still allowing some for myself.

Reading the words of other women writers has allowed me to see that we *can* and do find time to devote to our work. Whether during the wee hours of the morning, late at night, perhaps a lunch break at work, or when the children are visiting a friend, we choose to write before doing laundry, sleeping, shopping, or talking on the phone.

One does not need fancy equipment, or a room of one's own to do this work. I sit at my laptop, in the common living space, while everyone else sleeps. I told my husband that writing is very important to me and I would like him to get up with our toddler on the weekends. My laptop is dirty, the chair cuts off the blood flow to my legs, but it works for me. I tell myself that if I ever get paid for something I write, then perhaps I can invest in an ergonomically correct writing space. Until then, I will use the tools available. I do not have a printer at home. I send emails of my work to the library when I need to print. Fortunately, many publications accept online submissions, eliminating the necessity of a printer.

I know some women who are lucky enough not to have to work outside of the home, who are able to devote time during the day to writing while their children are at school. In the past, I wasted time envying them. I made excuses about not being as privileged and prevented myself from actively pursuing my goals. Once I quit feeling sorry for myself, I was able to stop making excuses not to write. Once you set your mind to achieving a goal, you look for reasons to make it happen, not for quitting before you get started. The only things you really need to write are a few hours and writing utensils, whether a computer, or a pen and paper. The rest is up to you. Your story is uniquely yours. Most likely, someone, somewhere, will want to read it. Day jobs and children need not be impediments to the writing life; you must make time wherever you can in order to fulfill your dreams.

10. It's Not a Hobby: Writing and the Value of Non-paid Work

Kate Hopper

A frequent lament of my students is the challenge of carving out time to write. There is the tower of laundry on the sofa in the living room, the dinner that needs to be made, the sick child home from school, the co-worker calling to find out why you haven't e-mailed the report that was due two minutes ago. With all of the work/home/family responsibilities spread before you, how could you take an hour (or even twenty minutes) to sit down in front of the computer and write?

In her essay "5 A.M.: Writing as Ritual," Judith Ortiz Cofer describes how she began her habit of writing for two hours every morning. She had the urge to write, but couldn't find the time until she began getting up before her family was awake. She writes, "If I waited until I had the time, I would still be waiting to write my novel." She goes on to say that the "initial sense of urgency to create can easily be dissipated because it entails making the one choice that many people, especially women, in our society with its emphasis on the 'acceptable' priorities, feel selfish about making: taking the time to create, stealing it from yourself if that's the only way."

Sadly, the jobs for which people earn the most respect are usually those that earn the most money. The work that has been historically women's work—keeping a home, raising children, feeding a family—is, still, often not valued as "real" work. Similarly, writing is often unpaid, which sometimes makes it seem less valuable, less important.

But if you don't value your writing or writing time, it's easy to allow that precious time to be the first thing to go when your life becomes too busy. (And when aren't you too busy?) If you want to make writing a priority in your life, you may need to change how you think about it.

Writing as Work

If you are committed to writing and want to make sure it doesn't become "the thing you want to do but never do," you need to ensure that you (and your family members) value both your writing and the *time* you spend writing. One way to do this is to start thinking about your writing as work.

If you were starting a career in business administration, it wouldn't be unusual to have one or two (or more) internships before you landed your first "real" job. These months, though often unpaid, are invaluable, helping you learn the ropes of the business world. The same goes for your writing. You need time and space—and many months—to make headway with your writing, to learn the craft of your trade. If you're not making money from your writing yet, think of it as a long-term unpaid internship.

Once you reframe your writing as work (whether you're working on a paid freelance article or a short story that's unlikely to ever make you a cent), you will be more likely to treat it as work. Set a schedule that's realistic, and on those days, show up for work and log in your hours. (This may be only once a week or even once every two weeks. Don't set yourself up for failure by planning to write every day if that's not feasible.)

Stick to Your Schedule

Even with the best intentions, sometimes things (a sick child, a dying dog, etc.) land in our laps and make writing for a week or two impossible. It's important to be flexible, especially as a mother-writer. Have faith that you will eventually get back to your work. But make sure you're really valuing your writing time and not letting other tasks and responsibilities infringe upon it. You wouldn't skip a meeting or church or your grandmother's 100th birthday party because your sofa was covered with laundry and the kitchen floor was filthy, would you? Probably not. So don't skip your writing time because of these things either.

Because I work at home, I've developed a high tolerance for household mess. As soon as I get my younger daughter down for her nap, I head straight to my office and open my laptop. I don't stop on the way to unload the dishwasher or clean the clutter from the dining room table.

If you have time at home when there are no children underfoot, don't spend it with housework. Go directly to your computer. Folding laundry and making dinner are activities that can be done with the help of little hands. But crafting a sentence is much more difficult with someone tugging on your pant leg.

Communicate

Reframing your writing as work and setting a realistic schedule for getting it done are great first steps, but unless you have the support of your family, the obstacles between you and finishing that essay might become insurmountable. It's important that the people in your life understand how important writing is to you so they can support you. If you have a partner, talk to him or her about what writing means in your life and work out a schedule. If you are home with kids during the day, maybe Saturday mornings become your writing time. Or maybe your partner takes the kids to the park and gets them ready for bed one evening a week, so you can head to the library to write.

Writing is hard work, but when you've decided it's part of who you are, you have to find a way to fit it into your life. Doing this begins when you give it the value and time in your life that it deserves.

References

Kallet, Marilyn and Judith Ortiz Cofer, eds. *Sleeping with One Eye Open: Women Writers and the Art of Survival*. Athens, Georgia: University of Georgia Press, 1999.

11. Laundry, Life, and Writing: Making the Most of Short Sessions and Stolen Moments

Lela Davidson

Women who write also hold down day jobs, feed families, schedule social engagements, and wash clothes. We often feel we have no right to take time away from these productive tasks for something so selfish as writing. If you want balance the writing life on top of other obligations, you must learn to make the most of tiny pockets of time.

Psych Yourself Out

First, create the right mental state:
- Pretend you're a real writer.
- Give yourself permission to write.
- Accept that short writing sessions add up.
- Don't grieve time that's already lost.
- Prepare to write on the bus, in the bathroom, or during PTA meetings.
- Be gentle with yourself. Making the most of your time takes practice.
- Relax. Stop taking yourself so seriously and have fun.
- Have faith. Enjoy the process, knowing it all works out in the end.

Choose Writing

The first step to finding time to write is to identify how you currently spend your days. For one week, keep a running list of activities with tally marks for each fifteen-minute increment. Once you have the facts, you can make intentional choices. Look for opportunities to squeeze in writing. How about ten minutes while the kids brush their teeth? What about fifteen minutes of your lunch? Could you wake thirty minutes earlier? Ask yourself if you give up half the time you talk to friends, check email, or watch TV. All it takes is a decision to start the creation of a new habit. Schedule longer blocks on time, but also plan to sneak writing into cracks and crevices of your day.

Let Your Subconscious Write For You

Relying on your subconscious may seem silly, but short writing sessions prod the hidden part of your mind into action. Writing for even five minutes makes a positive statement that you're serious about making time to write. The subconscious then gets to work finding more time. The words that result from all those short spurts of writing percolate while you're busy grooming the dog and matching socks.

Don't discount your daydreams. Writing is more than putting pen to paper or fingers to keyboard. Plot lines and character arcs can be worked out while clearing the garden of fallen leaves. Archetypal patterns can be mulled over while ironing. Notes scribbled while listening to your mother on the phone may become a short story.

Write Faster and Better

Sometimes you end up getting more done in a few minutes of focused effort than in a longer session because your concentration is more intense. After thinking, creating, and synthesizing your words subconsciously, be single-purposed when you sit down to write. Resist the urge to do writing-related activities such as research and surfing the web. Put words to paper. Most importantly, separate the writing and editing phase. Shorter blocks of time pay off when you learn to write fast. Not only will your quantity of writing increase, but you also develop focus and efficiency. Another benefit of writing fast is that it frees your creativity, resulting in an improved finished product.

One way to get words down quickly is to give up all aspirations of getting it right the first time. Practice free-writing with no expectations. Here are the rules:

- Time yourself and keep the pen or keys moving until the end.
- If you don't feel like writing, do it anyway.
- If you don't know what to write about, make a list.
- No thinking allowed! Just write.

Put words on paper as fast as you can, letting all those fragments of thought hit the page before they slip away. You'll fix it later.

Shorter Blocks Let You Write Anywhere

The best thing about short writing periods is that they empower you to write anywhere. Waiting for kids to get out of school or activities is captured as writing time. Even a long line at the post office needn't be wasted. Keep paper and pen available always. Carry index cards or post-its in your pocket.

Write amid distraction. For many women there is no quiet time. Will you use this as an excuse not to write or a reason to write? Actively practice writing in noisy or active environments like track meets and crowded fast food restaurants.

To stay organized try one or more of the following:

- Keep index cards on hand and then transfer notes to a notebook or computer file.
- Write everything in one spiral bound notebook. Use the perforated kind so you can take out individual pages to sort or file later.
- Keep a running list of projects and their various stages of completion.
- Create a file on your computer for jotting down quick thoughts.
- Send e-mail and voice mail messages to yourself.
- Keep printed drafts of works in progress handy so

you can grab one whenever you're off to a place where you might have a few minutes of down time.

Having a system in place to take advantage of tiny pockets of time pays off even more when you have an hour or two. You won't waste any time rifling through drafts and files.

Women Write Anyway

Once the urge to write has found you, there's no going back. You must write, just as you must eat, sleep, work, and tend the family. Yes, women are busy, but we write anyway. Over time, recognizing and using small blocks of time will become a habit. Gradually, you will find time stretching around all those other tasks to make room for writing, life, and the odd load of laundry.

12. Mother Professor: Going Back for the PhD

Geri Lipschultz

Say you've just put your son or daughter through college, and you've been bitten by the bug. Perhaps you've got yourself an empty nest, or maybe there's a second or third child yet to raise. As if being a mother and a writer isn't enough, something tells you that it's time to immerse yourself in academia, return to school. Perhaps it's your stagnant career, your stagnant marriage, or your stagnant sense of self. Maybe it's all of the above. You've tried everything to boost your morale—you've applied for jobs of various sorts, but you can find nothing full-time. Perhaps it's this personal malaise that's spilling into your marriage. So, you take a deep breath, and you do some research—for yourself. You look at colleges, and you consider both the low residency and the universities, their programs.

At first, you might feel like the proverbial child in a toy store, but then you settle down, and you find a program of study that pleases you, that you can count on to alleviate at least two out of the three dilemmas listed above. Low residency programs offer graduate programs whose credit hours come with distance learning and a brief week or two stint on campus. Degree programs range from one to three years, as a rule. The price tag on the low residency programs is high, as opposed to the financial package (either a teaching stipend or the coveted fellowships) you will invariably get from the college that asks you to relocate. You ponder whether you, yourself, can live with all the repercussions. You discuss it with your significant other, who gives you his/her blessing. If the GRE's are called for, you map out a time to study as you never did when you were of the appropriate age, and you painstakingly fill out applications, gather recommendations—the works.

Within months you find yourself with an invitation to change your life, knowing that this will also cause changes in the lives of those you love. This is especially true if your college requires you to re-locate, and it may be compounded if you have children who will accompany you, but it's all possible in this postmodern world. Long distance relationships can extend into familial territory, but if you take your children with you, you will have to scout out schools, doctors, dentists, day-care, and the like—but it's doable. Some colleges offer more of a community than others, so this will be among your criteria when you settle on one, the one among all those who've extended their invitations, who've welcomed you into the fold.

In both the full-time and low residency programs, you can expect to find dedicated students. You will find competitiveness. You will find challenges the likes of which you may not have seen since your late teens and early twenties. You may find age-ism. You will find yourself aching physically and mentally, but as for the rest, prepare for a wonderful ride.

Remember this, that although it may be years since you were on the other side of the desk, you are a writer, and you will be able to count on your writing skills. One might think that all the information is at one's fingertips, but the real beauty of going back to school for someone who has been writing all along is that the decisions have been narrowed down. You can put yourself in the hands of your department, and you can still write on the side, although this will take time. It might not happen the first semester, or even the first year, but sooner or later, you feel that you are in your element.

Prepare for all the contingencies of moving to a new place. Know your grocery habits (health food, whole food), your clothing habits (and your children's clothing habits... which become more serious if you're coming from a city or suburbia and heading toward rural America where the closest mall (something you might actually be grateful for, even if your daughter is not] may be seventy miles away). As for finances—make your calculations. For furniture, consider thrift stores, tag sales, and prepare to have your own tag sale—or three—when you graduate. This may be cheaper than hauling anything. If you have children, remember they need to have a home, even if it's a second home; you may want to bring the dog, the cat. Make sure there is a plan intact for monthly visits to and from your spouse, their father. Other considerations include finding a medical team, both for you and your child.

Once you're fully settled and in school, you may find technological challenges, so take, advantage of all the free classes in navigating the ever-growing landscape of computers. You may find your memory is not what it was, so you will have to find ways of compensating. You may have to be the best note-taker in your classes. But where you have the advantage is in the social department. You won't be doing the drinking that your younger counterparts will be doing. I do recommend making room in your budget, however, for an occasional glass of wine and a bottle of champagne for the day you graduate.

It's true that you'll spend more time than you think helping your child get accustomed to a new place and living without his/her siblings and a full-time father...but perhaps your husband/significant other will give her more quality time when he comes to stay for the week, while you (and not he) are going to the conferences, attending meetings, reading your work, or simply holed up in another room writing your brains out.

Understand that while others may look at this as a grand act of selfishness, and to some extent it is: your self-nurturing will benefit your family in ways you cannot conceive of, as you happily find yourself, diploma in hand (or framed on your studio wall), re-entering the job-market, re-establishing yourself as a writer who is significantly much stronger, wiser, if older, but happier and having, as a result, much more to offer your family and the world.

13. Penciling It In

Cassie Premo Steele

Long before I became pregnant, when I wasn't even thinking of it, I went to see a movie with my mother-in-law and Karen, a woman friend of mine. At the time, Karen was the mother of a delightful toddler daughter and was also eight months pregnant. After the film, Karen and my mother-in-law were talking about "staying home," and my mother-in-law said, "It's the same thing every day. Pick up this, fold that, put this away. Over and over. But you don't mind it."

Karen nodded.

At the time I thought this comment mostly reflected my mother-in-law's peculiar obsessive-compulsive nature—but I also thought that there was truth in it—that being a mother might just be this repetitive, this mindless, this boring. This filled with constant cleaning and housework. And so I put off getting pregnant for several more years.

As young women writers, we sometimes feel we have a heavy burden to carry and a hard choice to make. In the past, we are told, most successful women writers were not mothers. Emily Dickinson and Virginia Woolf come to mind. Hermits and suicides—these are our role models.

So often young women writers put off having children in order to focus first on their craft. I waited until I was 32 to try to get pregnant; by then, I had received my Ph.D. and published my first book. Order, plans, schedules—these ruled my life, and I wasn't quite sure how motherhood would fit in with that.

When my daughter was a baby, I found myself, just as my mother-in-law predicted, repeating the same activities over and over. Groceries on Monday. Laundry on Tuesday. Vacuum on Thursday. Pick up toys at 8:00 each night after the baby went to bed. I stuck to my plan like a general, as if the life of my army, the foot soldiers in my mind, depended on it. I felt fulfilled, gratified, truly at peace when my house was clean and orderly. I savored my cleaning supplies like perfumes, keeping them locked up in a cabinet, and using them sparingly, endowing them with the power to make my life beautiful. I knew this was slightly—crazy. But I couldn't stop.

There is a Goddess of Order, and it comes as no surprise that she is also a mother. According to Chinese mythology, the mother of all creation is Nu Kua, who first created humans out of clay and then got to work bringing the universe out of chaos by cleaning up. Putting up some pillars to hold up the sky. Decorating the clouds with jewels so rain would come. Straightening the land so crops could be sown.

But this is all that is known about her. I look in book after book and can find no further stories about her. There is no plot to her life. She tidied up. Then disappeared. End of story. My need for order was almost the end of a story in my life.

I have a writer friend who, though far away, sustains me through her letters. She is also a writer mother, her boy having been born two weeks before my girl.

Sometimes she goes away. A blackness takes her. She falls into a hole. Or a redness takes her. Something I've said. She retreats, and then-after weeks, or months, or, once, a year— she comes back.

One time, when my daughter was a toddler, I had not heard from her in three weeks. Three weeks and three days. 24 days. Almost a month. I'd been counting.

The reason, that time, was my need for order. I had asked her if another woman friend of mine could stay with her overnight on a journey west. My writer friend said no, her house was a mess. And she had felt such shame and incompetence about this that she fell silent. It took her almost a month to find the courage to tell me this.

I was reading her letter, on the day when it finally arrived, while my toddler daughter Lily played nearby, and I had a sudden urge to rush to my stationery, wanting to explain.

"First, she isn't that close to me. She asked me to ask you, and it really did not matter to me. I felt no judgment at all toward you. I wouldn't want a stranger in my house. I was just being polite. I shouldn't have even asked."

This is what I would have written. But I didn't. Lily brought me a book and wanted me to read, sat down in my lap, and so I put the pen down, and I read.

And hours went by, and I made dinner and cleaned up from dinner, and put Lily to bed, and straightened the house, and slept, and woke up, and did the breakfast dishes, and mopped the kitchen floor, and—

Suddenly it hit me. My writer friend is right. I am— what? obsessed? frenzied? dictatorial? crazy?—about order and cleanliness.

And it almost pushed my beloved friend completely away from me. This image she had of me, of my house, haunted her and spooked her out of meeting an interesting woman who was on her way to live in an ashram, which would have been wonderful fodder for a character, and kept her from sharing her feelings with me—all because she feared what the friend would report back to me about the cleanliness of her house.

Many middle-class white women have been brainwashed into becoming Cleaning Police. When we go into each other's homes, we either exclaim, "Oh, how nice!" when we see cleanliness and order, or we stay silent and judge while the other woman apologizes.

I think back to my pre-mothering past. I was in a women's group and we would meet at each other's houses every other week. Each woman's house was spotless. Beautiful. You could eat off the floors. Literally. One woman vacuumed every day. Every day. She once spent so much money on a new vacuum that she was afraid her husband would be angry, so she kept it in her neighbor's garage and went to get it each day after her husband left for work.

This group eventually ended.

As soon as one begins to divide things up,
*   there are names;*

Once there are names,
       one should know when to stop;
Knowing when to stop,
       one thereby avoids peril.
                              —Tao Te Ching

I needed to know when to stop. In that letter, my writer friend had asked me, "How do you work, keep your home clean, write, mother, and wife all at once?" The truth is I didn't. I did one thing at a time, when I had planned to do it, gave it all my attention, and then left it behind.

And this made me, certainly, somewhat rigid. Organized, competent, and clear-headed, yes. But hard, stiff, unyielding. Women friends did not "stop by" my house. Karen used to, the one with two young children, but I asked her to stop. I didn't like being surprised. My house was a mess. Or I was writing. Busy. My day was planned.

But over the years, as my daughter grew, so did I. The seeds of my growth could be seen in that moment—when I had the impulse to write to my friend and defend and explain my position, but then Lily asked me to read a book, and I took her in my lap, and read.

This is akin to the Taoist philosophy of Lao Tzu from China, which the West has often misinterpreted as passivity and "doing nothing." Was I really "doing nothing" when I read to my daughter in that moment? There are many people in our culture, men and women alike, who might say yes. But as mother-women-writers, we must have the courage to say no.

Our growth as mothers and as women writers comes from learning to bend and sway with the seasons, to pay attention to what—and who—is right in front of us at the moment.

Yes, we plan. Yes, we clean. Yes, we organize. Yes, we pencil things in. But once all that is done, we find ways to leave the arranging behind and drop deeply into a kind of presence from which all creation and all love comes.

Without exception, every woman I know who mothers and also makes time for her creativity—writing, art, music, dance, yoga—had to decide at some point in their lives to *let the house go. To let go.*

They relaxed their standards. They stopped trying to be perfect. They learned not to rearrange the dishes in the dishwasher after the husband had already loaded it. They allowed the teenager's room to be a pigsty and got into the habit of shutting the door.

I sometimes wonder about Nu Kua. I wonder if she didn't know when to stop. If there are no stories about her because she cleans, still. Not very much narrative action in that. "And now the drapes are hung. And now the floor is mopped. And now the windows are done." Or if there are no stories about her because she stopped too suddenly. Broke down. Fell apart. Couldn't take it anymore.

As women writers, the legacy of Sylvia Plath haunts us. The way she put out breakfast for the children before doing it. Something deep within us nods at this gesture. We know the well of love she felt for them even as the love she felt for herself ran dry.

So much has changed since then, since the only role models we had were Dickinson and Woolf and Plath. The writings of so many women of color, women who historically have always had to balance work and family, have given us new pathways to follow. Women scholars such as Paula Feldman and Beverly Guy-Sheftall have unearthed the work of Black and White American women from before the 20th century who were mothers and successful writers at the same time—women such as Anne Bradstreet, E.D.E.N. Southworth, Lydia Huntley Sigourney, and Frances Ellen Watkins Harper. And the work of contemporary mother writers continues to inspire us in ways our foremothers couldn't have imagined—as we e-mail and blog and Skype and connect through web-based publications like *Literary Mama* and *MamaVerse*.

Other things have changed, as well. My mother-in-law passed away this past December, and every time I fold laundry or make a list for groceries or smile at my daughter who carries her name, I miss her. I miss her and I honor her memory by being lovingly present with the task at hand.

Over the last few generations of women, we have seen the pendulum swing back and forth between domesticity and career. When I am present and aware enough to appreciate what and who is right in front of me, I think that perhaps we are reaching a middle point, a point of peace with ourselves as women and writers and mothers.

And peace cannot be penciled in. It must be attended to again and again. Like picking up this. And folding that. And putting the other thing away.

But you don't mind it.

Because you do it all with love.

And love is really the point of it all, at the end of a life or at the end of each day.

14. Today's Freelancing Momma: A Look Into the Dual Career of Writing and Motherhood

Daphne Butas

Mothers as Part of America's Freelance Nation

You all know someone who is a new mother, or perhaps you are a new mother yourself. You probably also know a woman who works from home in some capacity. Perhaps she is a part-time consultant or graphic designer looking to earn a little extra money on the side. Or maybe she is a freelance writer because she needs to have something to call her own that is different than her role as a mother. Well if it seems like more and more women that you meet at carpool, spinning class, or playgroup are blogging for bucks, freelancing for magazines, or penning book proposals, it's probably because they are.

Motherhood and Something Missing

Many women today are finding that when they take time off from work or their careers for motherhood that they are missing something. For some women that void is about not being able to contribute financially to their household. Others feel unfulfilled because they have opinions and advice to share and no outlet for expressing them. And for some it's about feeling appreciated and capable of more than laundry and changing diapers.

Whatever the reasons fueling their motivation, mothers are becoming a large part of today's freelance workforce; doing everything from copyediting and proofreading to publishing and feature writing, squeezing their writing lives into their hectic motherhood lives.

Motherhood is Work

Only other mothers know firsthand just how grueling parenting can be as a job. It is constant and there is always something to be done. Being a mother demands 100 percent of your attention, 100 percent of the time, and it consumes you in every way—emotionally, mentally, and physically. It is a job that you anticipate will be challenging, but fun. And it is also a job that you don't really fully understand until you are in the trenches of the everyday cycle of parenting.

Being A Writer is Work Too

Being a writer is similar to parenting in that it too is all consuming. Writing as an act or profession, for the true writer, is neither a pastime, nor something that she just likes to do, but a need; something that she must do each and every day in order to feel balanced and centered. It too appears easy on the surface and slightly glamorous as professions go, but it is challenging in every way once you commit to working at it constantly.

Can You Balance Both?

So, can it be done? Is it feasible for one woman to balance two fulltime jobs simultaneously, and still do them both justice? Can she fulfill herself and her own needs while meeting the needs and demands of others who depend on her in one of these other roles?

The answer is, YES. You can do both. You can be an excellent mother and an exceptional writer all at the same time, while not losing sight of yourself and getting the satisfaction that you require from each endeavor. The question you should be asking then is not *if* it can be accomplished, but *how* can it be accomplished?

How to Balance Motherhood with Your Writing: Real Writing Mommas Offer Advice

"I was at home with a nine-month old, and I felt like I had something to say so I started writing essays," remembers Ellen Pober Rittberg. Ellen's first piece was picked up and published in *The New York Times* humor section, and that just fed her desire to write even more. She turned to writing initially as an outlet from motherhood, describing herself as not being able to, "even imagine putting all her eggs in the mommy basket," but somehow always found a way to do both; take care of her children, and nurture her writing career at the same time. "I had three kids in three years, and then I hired a babysitter so I could write outside of the home," confesses Ellen.

Even if you consider it pure luck that her first piece was published in *The New York Times*, you have to acknowledge the dedication that Ellen showed by continuing to write. Because she wanted to experience both careers, Ellen always found ways to make the workload of both motherhood and writing manageable. "Being a lawyer and getting a law degree was just something that I always wanted to do. It was a personal goal I had set for myself. I didn't want to give up my writing (freelancing), so I had one day when I wasn't in law school and I kept my writing up that way," says Ellen.

Ellen's best advice for mothers trying to balance their dual careers is:

- Be disciplined. You don't have to write at the same time everyday, but try to make it a point to write some-thing everyday.
- Look at writing as a discipline. If you love it enough, it's no longer a choice. It becomes second nature.

Leslie Truex says that the attraction for her to the world of freelancing was because of her desire to be a mother. "I wanted to stay at home with my kids so I tried to be a writer in the mid-1990s, but none of my freelance pieces, nor my book proposal got picked up because I was writing too much like I was still in school."

Slightly deterred, Leslie began doing research about book ideas that she had. As a tool, she created a marketing website and was able to get her book sold in 2007.

With two kids, Leslie is the first to admit that when they were little and she was just starting out as a freelance writer it was much harder. "They are teenagers now so it's a little easier, but it's still difficult at times. Sometimes I have to do work at night, and it can be distracting with everyone home for holiday break. But the flip side is that sometimes I get so involved in my writing that my kids are calling me and I don't respond."

Persistence encouraged Leslie to stay with her writing career while mothering, and from her experiences the advice she offers is:

- Select something that you are interested in.
- Learn the market.
- You have to be able to pitch yourself to people. "Not a lot of writers know how to sell themselves to get hired, but you have to learn to do that." A perfect example is blogging. You can write all the free blogs you want, but if no one buys it, you are not going to make any money.
- You have to be organized because it takes a while to submit queries and hear back about them. It is a lot of logistics.
- Always be marketing. Whether you have a book you are trying to sell, or you just want to publicize your services to more people, always be marketing yourself, your ideas, and your work.

Lorraine E. Fisher of Off Ramp Publishing is a perfect example of someone who took the road less traveled. She had a stable job at a reputable nonprofit that she enjoyed. Then she got pregnant and things changed.

Her writing career basically began by accident. "Any job I had I always ended up being the in-house editor or writer. The joke in my family became that I was born with a red pen in my hand," says Lorraine. But what really sealed the deal for this writer and made her launch her freelance career right as she entered motherhood was her desire to do her own thing. She found that once she became a mother, her life as a career writer in corporate America was just not the right fit anymore, and she bucked the system, opting for the "off ramp" instead.

"I was working at a nonprofit organization that did work with children and you would think that that was the perfect place to take maternity leave, but when I had my daughter and went back to work I realized it wasn't the right fit for me (anymore) and I ended up quitting to stay home with my kid."

With extra time on her hands, Lorraine began to write a book, but was unable to get it signed by a major publishing house, so like Leslie, she went about things a bit differently. Lorraine founded her own publishing house and self-published her book as a means to an end.

It worked. Quite well, in fact. Lorraine's book came out in 2006 and then in 2008 she began to expand her company's services to include freelance writing, copyediting, and transcription services to help further build her credentials, and really solidify her legitimacy as both a writer and a publisher.

Now, Lorraine spends about 50 percent of her time generating new business and clients through meetings, workshops, writing seminars, and personal contacts, and the other 50 percent of her time doing the actual work for which she gets paid.

Lorraine admits that if she had it to do over again, she "would have asked for more help initially. Both financially and in terms of knowledge and information," so she is happy to share her advice with others:

- Ask for help. There are countless organizations out there that offer free advice and help.
- Seek out a mentor and ask specific questions, whether it is in your writing role or your role as a mother.
- Be assertive and confident in your abilities. "Initially I was not very confident because I had not worked at a major publishing house, but I can do this and I am good at it. I am confident of that now."

- Do your research. Find out who the competition is, and what the competition charges so you can establish your own worth and rates accordingly.
- Be flexible to a point. "For example, I have two published rates online so that I have some wiggle room with what I charge."

What you can learn from these freelancing mommas is that there is not set way to do things. There is no written rule that says that you have to be a writer before entering motherhood or vice versa, just as there are no rules that say it has to be one role or the other.

The message of value here is that many women perform both roles, and often say that one feeds the other. They write because they need something separate from their motherhood role, but they also continue to freelance to show their children that hard work pays off. A break from the breastfeeding and carpooling of motherhood is an opportunity to write, and a break from the pressure of deadlines and headaches of writer's block comes in the form of reading books, and playing trains with your two-year old.

Being able to recognize that you need something unrelated to your role as a mother, makes you wise, and provides you with the opportunity to be a better mother when you are on duty. In the same vein, part of being a great writer is being able to draw on your real life experiences when you channel your creativity through your writing, and there is no greater source of life experience than parenting.

When you think of today's freelancing mothers, think of pregnancy. It is sometimes hard for the baby and mother to co-exist in one small body, but despite the ups and downs of pregnancy, the child that you create is a true labor of love.

Things are the same for a momma who writes. It can be challenging and frustrating at times to juggle all the demands of your life—grocery shopping, laundry, babies, deadlines, meetings, writing groups, and more. But the words that you write, and the kids that you raise are proof of your ability to endure that labor of love and do both with success.

References

Lorraine E. Fisher, phone interview with author, January 4, 2011.

Ellen Pober Rittberg, phone interview with author, December 28, 2010.

Leslie Truex, phone interview with author, December 23, 2010.

Part III

Making the Most of Your Family Experience

15. Making Up Grandma: How to Blend History and Imagination Into Powerful Family Narratives

Lela Davidson

The best family histories are rich with detail. Dry reports of events, dates, and places are more likely to be filed in a scrapbook than read by future generations. The problem is that family stories may have been passed around for so long that only the highlights have endured. Even if all you have is a fragment of a tale, you can capture the essence of someone's life. A little imagination creates a narrative that is more than the sum of its parts.

Don't worry about embellishing events. All history is subjective. The alternative is that stories are lost forever. You can always include an appendix of factual information sources so that interested readers can separate the hard facts from your imagined tale.

Getting Started

Think of your ancestor or family member as a character in a story. Begin with what you know. Then concentrate on building your character with as much information as possible, including facts, inferences, and other imagined particulars.

Maybe all you've got is a bit of family gossip, a name on a ship's passage record, or a childhood memory. Perhaps you're interviewing living relatives who don't provide enough substance for a readable account. Personal bias and memory problems can also be an issue. Starting with what you know gives your research and imagination a jumping off point.

Consider these questions:
- What year was it?
- Who was present?
- Where were they?
- How did they get there?
- How old was the character at the time?

Say your grandmother tells you about the time she fell off the rear end of a horse at her grandfather's Missouri farm. Although she related the incident clearly, the details never got much beyond the sweaty horse's behind and her cousins' mocking laughter. The challenge is to translate her anecdote into a readable story.

Harnessing the power of imagination follows a logical progression. First, place the story in history, starting with known facts. Next, make educated guesses about the emotional state of your character. Finally, consult your imagination to create states of mind, events and conversations to give your reader a better idea of what this person may have been like.

Life in Olden Days—Setting Your Story in Time & Place

Written portraits are more complete when they are set at specific moments in time. National events, weather phenomena, politics, and celebrities all made their impression on your character. Visit the library for reference material. Books written for historical fiction writers are especially rich sources. The Internet is also a good source for preliminary research. Use what you know from birth and death documents, land deeds, and church documents to place your character in time. Incorporate specific details about family life, occupations, foods, fashions, and regional politics into your story.

If your grandmother was about twelve when the horse incident occurred and she was born in 1915, the year is 1927. Assume it was spring or summer. A quick Internet search informs you that on June 13th New York City honored Charles Lindbergh for his solo trip across the Atlantic with a ticker tape parade down 5th Avenue. How would this event have affected the day of a twelve-year-old girl on a Missouri farm?

Every place has a story. How people came to be at a particular place reveals much about them. Maybe your grandmother spent her entire life in Missouri. But how did her grandfather come to settle there? How did he acquire his land and meet his wife? Providing background about place allows the story to stand alone for someone who knows nothing about you or your family.

Use Intuition to Find Emotion

Adding emotional depth to your stories makes them more interesting. Diaries from the period your character lived give a glimpse into daily routines and emotional lives of people who lived in similar circumstances. These add tangible details, but your gut already knows how your character felt.

What if your grandmother once told you about how the girls always visited her grandfather's two-holer outhouse in pairs? Putting this detail together with the horse anecdote, we paint a richer picture. Think of the jokes that would have followed her. A fall into the outhouse hole would have been much worse than the fall off the back of that horse. Did her cousins' teasing haunt her at the supper table? Follow her to school? Was it charming or humiliating?

Going All the Way Into Imagined Territory

After setting a character in time and place, and imagining her emotions, conjure up supporting surroundings, conversations, and even events. In her book *Discovering the New Autobiography and Writing Memoir as Literature*, Tristine Rainer teaches the method of reverie. Grab a notebook and use a relaxation technique such as deep breathing or muscle contraction and release to get comfortable.

Once you feel relaxed, put yourself in your character's setting and start asking questions. Think about and visualize answers for all senses. What do you see, hear, smell, taste, feel on your skin? What is the weather like? What do you want? What are you thinking of? Write freely and in present tense. Then turn the picture in your mind into a movie by moving through the scene mentally (and even physically) to bring more images and ideas to mind. Ask yourself what happens next? Put all this on paper without worrying that you're making it up. You'll choose later what to keep and what to discard.

Even the Shortest Stories Deserve to Be Written

Something happens when we think about putting ink to paper. We become fixated on getting everything right. But this isn't what stories are about, especially family stories. Even if we're just writing a short description to accompany a photo, the richer the sensory detail, the more valuable the story becomes to our family and beyond. So tell your stories with courage and imagination. Because it's a shame to let a story die just because it's only a snippet.

References

Rainer, Tristine. *Your Life As Story: Discovering the "New Auto-biography" and Writing Memoir As Literature*. New York: Jeremy P. Tarcher/Putnam, 1998.

16. Teaching Writers to See Family

Diane LeBlanc

I grew up in a house whose kitchen windows looked across a narrow strip of lawn into the Robinsons' neighboring window. We thought nothing of seeing Mr. Robinson standing at the sink in his V-neck undershirt while we sat in our pajamas eating cereal. Neither family pretended not to see the other.

When I began to write about family, I found it useful to imagine what the Robinsons saw from their window. Verlyn Klinkenborg confirmed my instinct in his introduction to *Turning Toward Home*. Klinkenborg predicts, "What strangeness have I become habituated to? You would ask if you could see your family as you see your neighbors." It's easier to say that meals brought my family close than to explore my ambivalence toward the intimacy of thighs rubbing and elbows knocking at every meal, not to mention the survival-of-the-fittest speed at which I learned to eat.

To encourage authenticity and complexity, writing teachers may guide writers to look at family as anthropologists study cultures or as neighbors see each other. The following generating and revision exercises offer practice to that end.

Generation

Brainstorming

Mention "the first hunting trip" or "learning to drive" to a group of writing teachers and you're likely to hear a collective groan. These experiences are not in themselves cliché. They become cliché through generic descriptions of "piling into the pickup on a crisp October morning" and "Mom hanging on to the passenger's door for dear life." Before writers gravitate to obvious stories, I invite them to choose at least three topics from this list and write several paragraphs of action, description, and dialogue about each. Although these paragraphs may not lead to an essay, they serve the practice of writing about family.

- A time when a family tradition failed/succeeded
- A visit from a "legend" in your family
- An incident involving illness or injury and your family's response to it
- The role of food in your family
- The role of pet(s) in your family
- The role of sports or physical activity in your family
- A time when power shifted
- An incident in which faith was challenged or strengthened
- An event that exposes your family's attitude toward race, class, sexual identity
- An event that reveals the significance of television within your family culture
- The power of language, or who speaks for the family
- An event that involves art and its place in family culture

Finding Story
In *The Situation and the Story: The Art of Personal Narrative*, Vivian Gornick distinguishes between situation and story. Situation is the physical action or subject, such as learning to drive. The story, in contrast, is the writer's mediated construction of events, what we discover through writing. For example, the subject of my essay "Voices" is Lester, the Black ventriloquist dummy I received for Christmas in the early 1970s, when I was nine or ten. As the essay chronicles my ventriloquism lessons and living room performance, it explores Lester's place in my White, working class family and community. The essay's story is how I learned race.

With the goal of moving beyond generic description, writers may test their exercise paragraphs for situation and story using these questions:

- What moments excite you? What makes these moments exciting? Excitement may indicate that you are not just reporting memory; you are exploring a new way of seeing a situation.

- What moments bore you? Are you plodding through narrative for the sake of conveying information? If so, situation, not story, is controlling your writing. For now, write episodes that interest you. You can clarify and connect as you revise.

Sustaining Story
After starting, committing to, or abandoning several drafts, writers may need additional strategies to move an essay forward.

- Reposition the narrator and the scope of vision. Go inside or outside. Sit on a stair that overlooks a room. Look through the mail slot or a key hole. When vision and focus shift, what do we hear, smell, touch, taste?
- Change the age of the narrator. Experiment with differences in detail, language, and complexity of understanding when you are ten, fourteen, eighteen, and so on.
- Bring in additional voices. Rewrite an entire scene in dialogue. Let family speak.
- Take a single paragraph and double its length with fresh detail. Now reduce it by half. What happened to the original paragraph?

Revising & Editing

Thinking about Audience
After generating enough material to identify their stories, writers may begin to imagine readers. Whether they imagine "JUST my family" or "NOT my family," the following questions may help writers conceive audience.

- If your imagined audience is exclusively family, do you need to describe the kitchen in which you grew up? Tell your audience something they don't know.
- If you can't imagine family reading your work, con-

sider why. Does your essay reveal more about family members than about you? If so, you may be appropriating someone else's story. Have you invested enough of your experience to claim the story?

With audience in mind, writers may revisit exercises in "Sustaining Story" to experiment further with level of detail and perspective.

Editing

Family writing tends to enlist familiar verbs. With family, we *cuddle, shed* tears, and *beam* with pride. We *tuck in, take after,* and *stomp away.* We *pile* into cars and *get* bear hugs from grandpa. We *go* on vacation and *attend* funerals and weddings. While functional, these verbs have little muscle. Likewise, vague adjectives can lessen a subject's distinction. This revision exercise appeals to writers who benefit from seeing patterns in their writing.

- Circle or highlight in one color all of the verbs in at least three paragraphs. How precise is the physical action? Take a sentence in which someone performs a common action—sneezing, crying, walking. Elaborate into a full description, appealing to as many senses as possible. Now return to your original sentence and experiment with the fresh verbs you generated.
- Write a list of questions, to share with a group, about certain actions in your essay. For example, what does the "family walk" look like? To what animal's movement can it be compared? How does this walk wear on shoes? What is the length of a step? A question exchange may provide new ways of seeing the familiar.
- Underline or highlight in a different color the adjectives. Then remove every one. What's left? Rebuild with new details generated from the previous activities.

This article has proposed that teachers introduce a few basic concepts as touchstones:

- See family as we see neighbors, or as neighbors see us

- Distinguish between situation and story
- Identify relationships between story and audience *after* generating material.

These concepts provide a common language for encouraging and responding to writers throughout the writing process.

References

Klinkenborg, Verlyn. Introduction. *Turning Toward Home: Reflections on the Family from Harper's Magazine*. 1st ed. Ed. Katharine Whittemore and Ilena Silverman. New York: Franklin Square Press, 1993. Print.

Gornick, Vivian. *The Situation and The Story: The Art of Personal Narrative*. New York: Farrar, Straus and Giroux, 2001. Print.

17. Telling Our Truth: Writing the Legacy of the Dead

Carol Hawkins

I never wanted to tell you about all that, didn't want to say hard things about your daddy, but not talking about him, I never got to tell you the other part. How much we loved each other. How much pleasure he took in (his children). How it was for a while, loving him and trusting him. Everything that was broken and mean cannot erase what was good.
—Dorothy Allison, *Cavedweller*

How do we, as writers, tell our truth about the disappointments and failings of family members who have died and also honor their humanity? This question came up for me while writing a memoir about my dead husband. He died in 1996 but he continued to stay with me in my mind. Some days I recalled the love and passion we shared, and then there were those days when I recalled the lies and addictions that drove us to divorce ten years prior to his death.

Relationships become confusing when we examine the impact they have on our lives. The relationships that matter are those we learn from, but the lessons are not always recognizable, easy, or timely. How do we begin to sort out the meaning of a relationship with a family member who has died, especially when that person brings back moments of conflict and struggle, like my relationship with my husband? For me the answer was to write my way to understanding and compassion.

I suggest that we begin by asking ourselves some key questions, knowing that they will lead us to other questions. These questions will begin our inquiry into a life and will serve as helpful guideposts for our writing:

1. Who do we consider when writing about a dead family member?
2. How do we take a larger audience into account?
3. What point of view will we use when narrating our stories?
4. Which stories matter most among the many lived with that person?

Sometimes the toughest question is the most obvious, where do we start? I began simply, in a fashion I learned as a child: Once upon a time . . .

Waiting For My Prince to Come

I waited up all night for him. He went out just after dinner to meet a friend for a "quick beer," but his beers were never quick, and I never knew his friends. We were living in Spokane at the time, the fourth state and second country we attempted to call home in our then ten-year marriage. My life progressed from home to school to him. I was twenty-eight years old when one word from his lips shattered my world forever. After he came home drunk one morning after not coming home from work the night before, I asked him if he had been with another woman. He answered, "Yes."

Audience and Accountability

What would my husband think if he read this memoir, which goes on to describe events that followed his admission? Would he object to my telling that he drank too much and cheated? Would my children be surprised by these admissions? Would my writing hurt my children by revealing their father's drinking and womanizing, and the anger and rage I expressed towards him that kept them up all night?

I can only speculate what my husband would say. My guess is that he may not want me to mention his behavior, but this is only speculation, I really can't know for sure. I write of drinking and infidelity because they are the central conflicts in the story, but I also write to discover some meaning that will help me let it go, some understanding and compassion for both of us.

I recall my husband's early wounding, when his father died. He was twelve. I write about his anger at his mother for dating a Black man shortly afterwards. I provide the time frame and the larger context, to explain how a white woman dating a black man was still a taboo in our time of questionable segregation, especially in Cleveland in 1969, where racial unrest during the Civil Rights Movement erupted into riots.

The reader must always be taken into account, if we choose to have an audience for our story. Readers need to know the story beyond the story, the cultural background in which the story takes place. My husband eventually ran away from home and joined the Marines. He never finished high school. He managed to avoid Viet Nam, on a drug discharge, but it left him suffering from survivor guilt, making it especially difficult for him when he ended up in detox at a V.A. hospital with vets who served in Viet Nam.

My children, on the other hand, would not be surprised by this story. They already know these details—that their father never went to Viet Nam and that he professed racist attitudes, but would they become upset if I aired this in public? I decided to ask them. Both seemed reluctant to read what I wrote. My youngest told me she had to set a boundary between her healing process and mine. Just because I was ready to write about her father didn't mean that she was prepared to read what I wrote. However, neither of my daughters has censored me. Many family members do not pay much attention to my writing nor do they wish to read my recollections, especially about hard times. Yet, they never ask me not to write about family, nor do they seem concerned. I wonder if it's an issue of trust or disinterest or avoidance. Perhaps if I wrote a bestseller and ended up on Oprah they'd all pay attention, but the bottom line is that a writer is accountable to herself and her own story. I keep my children in mind. I would not want to surprise them. No secrets divulged. There were no secrets. Unfortunately, my children got sucked into the chaos of their parents. They witnessed everything.

Point of View

Writers must become the protagonists of their own stories. Sometimes combatant, writers must reveal their struggles with the departed to reveal the impact on their lives. We must narrate to an intimate audience, as if in conversation, using an engaging tone. For example, in my memoir about my dead husband, I try to explain how love slips into hate when relationships fall victim to addiction and betrayal. I remember the reader, who may be my child or a family member, and the larger audience that may have their own experiences with addiction and betrayal. I keep the focus on my intentions and how my husband's behavior made me feel. I choose scenes that convey a central theme. The writer must identify and describe the essence of the relationship without judgment, aware of prejudice or bias. The writer must hold back from making any assumptions, but step forward and describe both sides of the story. I loved my husband, but there were times when I felt like I hated him too. Addiction often results in a love/hate paradox. I now understand that I never wanted my relationship with my husband to end; I just want the hurtful behavior to stop.

Choosing Stories

Writers must come up with concrete scenes as well as the big picture that may provide the historical backdrop. They must show as well as explain how these stories shaped their lives and their relationship with the deceased. They must examine their own motives for telling these stories and stay focused on their intentions, which in my case, is to explain the reasons why I found it so difficult to let the departed go. I realize that few relationships are perfect, but mine shifted between extremes. I couldn't just write about the hate. I also had to write about the love.

Teen Lover
I first saw him in the school parking lot. He sat there in his 1964 baby blue GTO with his elbow hanging out the window, his chin on

his forearm, behind aviator sunglasses, with the mirror lenses, yet I knew he was staring at me. I was walking my dog, Nicky, a toy poodle I thought represented someone with class, something I needed as a young girl who grew up relatively poor among my working-class (their fathers had jobs, mine didn't) and middle class schoolmates. I had on my faux fur leopard jacket. My hair sat on top of my head like the puffball Nicky strutted on top of his. I must have looked ridiculous. I was seventeen.

I loved his good looks—chiseled jaw, olive skin, broad shoulders, slender waist, long legs, and unsettling hazel green eyes, but he wasn't a handsome boy when I first met him-- pimples, thick glasses, hair oily and slicked back, but he always had charm. He put himself right out there, professing his love for me, right from the beginning. No playing hard to get. No tough guy routine. His baby blue 1964 GTO was no steed, but what could I expect…he even dueled for my affection with an old boyfriend who was abusive. How does a young girl with romantic notions of love ever forget the prince who rescued her?

Locating Our Humanity

I write to challenge my own truth and to find meaning in my relationship with my husband as I attempt to connect my experiences with a larger audience. I write to render a portrait of a man who was not just a drunk and womanizer, but a loving husband and father. I discover that what I most appreciate about my memories of him are our adventures in the outdoors, and how he taught our children and me to love and respect nature. We find solace in the mountains where we used to camp and fish. We sought peace in the arms of Mother Nature after his death. Still, his alcoholism and sexual exploits hurt terribly, as did my responses to them, and his behavior at times brought up familiar feelings of distrust and abandonment.

Conflicted relationships often carry strong sentiments of love and hate. Some find it hard to reconcile these feelings. Many close to me would get impatient with my ruminations over my husband, so I would try to keep them silent. The author, Fran

Dorf, who wrote a book to deal with the death of her four-year-old son, takes on those who tell us to "get over it already" when our grief persists, even after years of mourning:

> I hated all the suggestions, those people who mean well but whom I've come to call the de-legitimizers of grief: the babblers (*Let's talk about anything, anything except your horror*); advice givers (*Concentrate on your other children; Adopt another child; It's time to get past it now, why don't you?*); pain-minimizers (*God must have wanted him; He's in a better place; You did everything you could*); lesson-learners (*Everything happens for a reason*); and pseudo-empathizers (*I know just how you feel*).

Writing the legacy of the dead does not guarantee the end of grief, but it does allow for different perspectives, and the realization that whatever the legacy, it is a product of the writer's own creation.

Living Legacy

Writing the legacy of a dead family member reveals how I swung the emotional pendulum between extremes of love and hate. What did I love about him in the first place? How did he hurt me? What about his hurt? I come to realize that we were both already wounded when we met. No one's to blame. No one could fix what hurt the other.

Writers must inquire into their own lives to write about the dead. We must tell our own truth about our relationship with the departed. We must take responsibility for those in our care who were also affected by the relationship, and we must write for a larger audience by filling in the blanks as we acknowledge how our experiences are not unique. We begin by asking questions, developing a moral stance, and carefully choosing which stories to tell. We name our intentions: compassion and understanding. We begin in a fashion that we learned as children, "Once upon a time," but we end suspicious of fairy tale romances, and hopefully, resolution.

References

Allison, Dorothy. *Cavedweller.* Penguin Press, New York: 1998.

Dorf, Fran. "My Son's Name Was Not Elijah." *Wellness & Writing Connections: Writing for Better Physical, Mental, and Spiritual Health.* Ed. John F. Evans. Enumclaw, Washington: Idyll Arbor, 2010.

18. To Everything There Is a Season: Or What to Expect When You're a Writer Expecting a Baby

Geri Lipschultz

Having a baby is nature's miracle, no doubt about it. For a writer, the changes can be monumental, from the way she structures her writing time to her sense of self, but knowing this is half the battle. Depending on your temperament and writing style, you will want to make the best use of the pre-birth time. Before the baby arrives, you will want to get everything squared away, knowing you will have to let some things go. It's a good idea to know what those things are. Depending upon the kind of writer you are, it can range from work that doesn't pay to that long, ponderous novel you've been puttering on. On the other hand, this might be the perfect moment to invest in marketing research. While it's true a writer stands to lose a fair amount of writing time, she may gain new subjects to write about. Not only do different markets open up, but a writer who is also a mother-to-be should prepare herself for a change in point-of-view. If the writer can allow herself to be malleable, she may find that what she loses in time, she will gain in inspiration.

That said, prepare for an increase of work the size of a mother-load. Not only will the writer's hackles be raised at the encroachment upon her time, but she will find herself stretched bodily and emotionally, which is to say she will be pinched and poked and prodded. She will never be the same. Although it's as foolish to generalize about motherhood as it is about writing, one can safely assume that both are as demanding as they are rewarding. Reflect on thyself as a writer, I would caution the mother-to-be. Prioritize your habits, requirements, and desires. Without the rudiments of a structure, it is likely that one's writing time will find itself ground down to a literally screaming halt.

It might not happen immediately, but sooner or later, the writer within the mother will demand her space. She would do well to make use of those nine months (or eight-and a half and counting) to prepare not only for the full-time task of caring for her breathtakingly gorgeous if helpless infant, but also for structuring physical time and creating emotional/mental space, as well as a location—literally—for her writing. That place might be close to or distant from the sleeping baby (thank capitalism for the blessing of a monitor) depending upon the writer, depending upon the mother. Some mothers set up easels or workstations right in the studio, setting the stage for the child's taste of independence, one hopes, in life after toddlerhood.

There are as many books about mothering as there are about writing. The road is wide. One would assume the writerly mother-to-be is someone well read on the subject, but she may not know what kind of mother she wants to be. Or, she may decide what kind of mother she wants to be only to find out when the infant arrives that she has changed her mind, and this back and forth can continue indefinitely. Which is to say that motherhood is a creative act. Not all that different from writing.

Does she want to be thinking of her writing when she is nursing, or does she want to dote on her baby; does she want to look into those sloe eyes or take in the never-ending waterfall-like rhythms of the sound of sucking. Take notes, I say! Take notes for a later time,

Or don't. Sooner or later, these notes might—with a little help—bloom into articles to send to parenting or family magazines, or newspapers, or they may be creative endeavors, metamorphosed into fiction or poetry or creative nonfiction. Subjects run the gamut—from nutrition, entertainment, and stories about stages of development—to descriptions of perfect moments, family outings. These subjects and opportunities will continue to grow as your child grows.

Creativity will guide you, and do be creative about childcare. Some mothers hire tweens or teens to provide caretaking in the studio itself, freeing up the mother-writer who will know that there's another set of eyes and arms attending to the beloved child. Some mothers set their children up to the television or even a computer; others don't dare.

As I say, it's foolish to generalize. Every decision, about nursing, clothing, bedding, (later it will be schooling, music/art/athletics...and even later it will be colleges...) is up for grabs.

The point is a new baby is a powerful life-changer. It is a time of reckoning. The writer is wise to allow for this, to allow for a sea change, because this is a time she will never get back. Not only will she have to answer to herself, but she may have to answer to the child, the person her child will become. Nevertheless, it's her decision, and it's a decision that some cannot make ahead of time.

That said, forewarned is forearmed, and there are ways for the writer to keep it going, and these suggestions primarily have to do with structure, with time and place and space.

I think it's safe to say that most writers are fiercely protective of their time, because it takes time to press an idea into being. Much of that time is spent waiting, but all writing is a function of time. The greatest task, I would have to say, is accounting for time, and disciplining oneself to write during nap-times, for example, although many advice givers (usually they are mothers or mothers-in-laws) will tell you to sleep when the baby sleeps. The second greatest challenge is allowing for a change in identity. The third, and I make it third because for some, this is not an issue, but there is the small possibility of what has come to be known as "mommybrain." Not every woman experiences this, but women who do must understand that sometimes the best writing comes after refraining from writing.

Key are awareness and preparation and support, even if that support comes from within the woman (writing journals), although many women, if they have the wherewithal to get literal help, will pay for childcare, housekeeping, laundry, diapering service, and the list continues.

Some writers are single mothers; some are married with partners/husbands who will help. Still, to wear the hat of mother and writer is no easy task, but with diligence and discipline, a woman may be successful at both. I suspect that for most writers, there is no greater joy than motherhood, such that even seeing one's name in print pales in comparison. But there's no reason to forego that smaller joy. That motherhood changes a woman has been well documented. For a writer, these changes may open up the world in more ways than she can imagine.

19. Using Family in Writing for Chicken Soup for the Soul

Diana M. Amadeo

Chicken Soup for the Soul's website calls itself a world leader in life improvement. The website goes on to say that, *Chicken Soup for the Soul* anthologies have been helping real people share real stories for fifteen years, bringing hope, courage, inspiration and love to hundreds of millions of people around the world.

There are well over 100 *Chicken Soup for the Soul* books in print. With 101 stories per book, that leaves over ten thousand true stories to wrap your mind around. Most of the *Chicken Soup* stories are ordinary stories told by average people, crafted in a meaningful way. The vast majority of these stories are not shocking, tragic, groundbreaking or even hilarious. But they do tug at your heart. I have been fortunate to have stories within seven of these books. God willing, there will be more acceptances in the future. Like most writers, I have many stories to tell. Hopefully some of those stories will find a place in a new *Chicken Soup for the Soul* anthology.

I came out of the womb with a pen in my hand. Well, that's a slight exaggeration, but I can't recall ever not writing. I grew up scribbling my thoughts on paper and my parents, thank heavens, encouraged it. As a child, I had a favorite writing spot in the girls' bedroom behind the dresser next to the heating vent. I could completely shut out all the sounds of the noisy busy household, while writing in my journal. After many calls for supper, my parents knew just where to look when I failed to come to the table.

It's no surprise that my first acceptance for *Chicken Soup for the Soul* was a story about my childhood. This piece came from a place where I felt safe, secure and creative. The greatest challenge I had writing this story, included within *Chicken Soup for Brother and Sister's Soul,* was keeping it within the suggested word count of 1200 words (magazines and anthologies are requiring much shorter essays these days). Having read many *Chicken Soup for the Soul* books, I was familiar with the simple, folksy style that seems to land acceptances with the editors. Usually with short pieces like this, I'll put all my words on paper and then edit. Outlines are only used on larger manuscripts.

My first acceptance at this publisher was not my first submission. I had sent nearly a dozen stories to *Chicken Soup for the Soul* before my manuscripts were finally accepted. What took so long? I am not really sure, as my style hadn't changed much. So I advise writers who want to publish in this or any other venue to be persistent. It is wise to never give up on your craft and never destroy (or delete) your hard work. Eventually, with a little tweaking and editing, that story just may find a home. One of the best responses I ever received from an editor was, "We are not publishing this book even though it is needed and well done. Be patient and persistent...it *will* get published." That book did get published – 15 years later.

If you follow that age-old writer's code to write what you know, eventually family stories are written. My entry into *Chicken Soup for Wine Lover's Soul* was a funny little ditty that I put together while preparing a big Thanksgiving meal. I wanted to bring a type of wine to the holiday table that my three adult children, spouse and I would enjoy. So my husband and I had a little private wine tasting. We had been to both formal and informal wine tasting events in the past. Our private wine tasting was haphazardly concocted with a protocol uniquely our own. The experience was fun and quirky...and romantic, too. It fit nicely into the tiny book that was one of a set of *Chicken Soup* books for the holidays.

Twenty-four years of my life were spent as a registered nurse caring for sick babies in the Neonatal Intensive Care Unit. Nurses are privy to the most heartrending stories of people facing the most difficult moments in their lives. The NICU is one of the most emotionally charged units in a hospital. In the NICU entire families: babies, siblings, parents, aunts, uncles, grandparents and other relatives, as well as medical personnel, face challenges, tragedies and triumphs. Sometimes all these circumstances are met in one eight-hour shift. *Chicken Soup for the Soul Celebrates Nurses* and *Chicken Soup for the Adopted Soul* retell some of the harrowing but wonderful experiences in my nursing career. Being a registered nurse as well as wife, mother, sister and daughter allowed me to write from a well-rounded perspective. Parental worries, sibling angst, grandparent assistance and helpful, supportive nursing staff all found a place in these stories as well the trauma a baby goes through during premature birth. The editors were more than helpful in navigating the legal and confidential aspects in telling stories of this genre.

These weren't the first publications of my nursing career as I had written for many nursing journals during this time. I also wrote some books. My children's book *My Sister Amy is a Preemie* was published by Zondervan and told the fictionalized account of family's rollercoaster experience after delivering a premature infant. Earlier, the children's book *There's a Little Bit of Me in Jamey* was published by Albert Whitman and Company. It was the first children's book of its kind dealing with childhood leukemia and bone marrow transplantation. This book was on the American Cancer Society's suggested reading list. There is an interesting side note about *Jamey* also. I was approached at my son's T-ball game by one of his teammate's parents. The mother of the teammate wanted to know if I had written the book. You see, her son had childhood cancer and went through similar experiences as I had detailed in the book. She said the book had really helped them through the trauma. It is little moments like this that stay in a writer's heart forever. Your words truly make a difference in people's lives.

Family stories can be funny, nostalgic, serious and unique. I have lived with multiple sclerosis for nearly two decades. Twelve of those years were in a wheelchair. During this life's journey I have met many extraordinary people who cope with their disabilities in deeply personal ways. These marvelous people felt a certain kinship with me and openly shared their stories without reservations. *Chicken Soup for the Soul Tough Times, Tough People* and *Chicken Soup for the Soul Celebrating People Who Make a Difference* touches upon some of my brave and heroic family and friends. All these stories have met with friends' and families' preapproval. *Chicken Soup for the Soul* not only insists that every person mentioned in their stories approve of their use in the book, they also must give written permission to use their name before the book goes to print. Using family for your stories can be a very touching, loving experience. Just always make sure that person wants his story to be told...and don't promise publication unless the contract is in your hands.

Along those same lines, my youngest daughter wrote about growing up with a handicapped mother as part of her application essay for college. During her second year at MIT, a call out was issued for the *Chicken Soup for the Soul Thanks, Mom* book to be published for Mother's Day. She dusted off her old manuscript, revised it and sent it in. Her unusual story about her thoughts of me in a wheelchair while she was running in a race was accepted. Here's the kicker – my story about my saintly mother who raised ten children didn't make the cut. Oops. My daughter likes to remind me that her writing in this particular instance outshined mine. And it certainly did. I was glad that no promises were made to my mother that her story would be published.

TV personality, Art Linkletter, used to say "kids say the darndest things". Yes they do. Write those cute things down. Keep a journal. You never know when these little pearls of wisdom are going to come in handy. Do your kids fight like cats and dogs? Remember that for future reference. You never know what memories may be useful later on. My brother and I used to argue incessantly. We refused to work or play together. We were so bad that my mother often wished aloud that we would someday have children just like us to return the headaches that she endured raising us. There were ten children in our god-fearing family, yet it was just my brother and I that were used as bad examples of what not to say or do. Imagine my mother's surprise, fifty years later, that the story of my brother and me (as adults in cooperation caring for a victim of a car crash) would grace the pages of *Chicken Soup for the Soul: A Book of Miracles*. She's proud of us now. And Mom looks upon our childhoods with a sense of humor. Reminiscing on our childhoods always leads to a wisecrack from Mom. Now I know where my youngest gets her sarcastic wit. Grandma laughs that my story about her for the Mother's Day book didn't make the cut, just like her granddaughter teases me that hers did.

Publishing in *Chicken Soup for the Soul* books definitely has its perks for writers. In the midst of acceptances from *Chicken Soup for the Soul*, I was approached by Pauline Books and Media to write a book about the new saints canonized by Pope John Paul II. *Holy Friends: Thirty Saints and Blesseds of the Americas* with its beautiful colorful illustrations was published in 2005. It became an award-winning book the following year and still sells well.

Writing for *Chicken Soup for the Soul* has taught me to write from the heart for myself and those that I love. For me, technical pieces have no soul and it shows in my writing. I'd rather draw you to tears, make you sigh or find you speechless after reading my piece, than attempt to dazzle you with my perceived intelligence. In a world of chaos, I wish to convey peace and hope through my actions and words. *Chicken Soup for the Soul* helps spread this message across the world.

What is next? I am moving into my autumn years. Autumn with its brilliant colors, delightful chill and garden rewards has always been my favorite time of year. There are places to see, experiences to have and emotions to feel. I do believe that there will be a bountiful harvest of stories begging to be written. Oh…and have I told you about my grandchildren? Maybe you will read about them, soon.

20. Using Writing as a Means of Surviving and Transgressing Family Violence and Trauma

Anna Saini

You are not the only one. Yes, your story is unique, your voice birthed of a singular experience, but you may take comfort in the knowledge that you are not alone. Not everyone's family life is a product of white picket fences. This is something we can appreciate because although we are not alone, our twisted journey through childhood or marriage, whatever the site of family violence, ensures that our experiences inherently reside beyond cliché. We are well equipped with raw material that makes great art – drama, struggle, conflict – these elements that are painful relics of our past, often even difficult parts of our present, is the stuff that many writers crave. However, it's not enough, because as I already noted, you are far from the first person who has experienced family violence; this does not a writer make. Here we will explore how we can use writing not only as a mode of surviving family violence but as a way of creating something beautiful from what is, outside of the artistic world, a perversion. Here we will look at how we can use writing to heal from violence, retell our stories creatively yet truthfully and how we can move from purely confessional catharsis writing to work products of literary merit.

Survival Comes First

Write everything. Write the expressions reflected on faces in mirrors, actions that incite anger, write the grip on the weapon and the posture of the fist. Write down the details as well as the broad arc of events serving as the undercurrents to violence, even if seemingly unrelated to the central theme of your story.

You do not yet know the theme. Family violence is not the theme, it is the consequence. Your story cannot revolve solely around the violence, it will use the violence as an instrument to reveal something of meaning or perhaps the meaningless of it all. You will resolve that later, for now write everything to save the trouble of having to return to these memories that often become reclusive out of necessity, a mis-guided effort toward self-protection. Resist the urge to suppress these experiences with the silence of your pen. Survival comes first. As much as you want to murder the remembrance of these difficult times you must nurture them by insistently recording them. Keeping a journal is indispensable in this regard.

No one can fault you for failing to keep a journal or otherwise keeping track of the violence, trying to bury these demons, but you will seldom find success burying the undead. You will want to excavate your history of violence because in the absence of such expression it will take root and fester. It can cripple you mentally, emotionally and often physically in the form of chronic pain or illness. It may cost you a great deal in sick days or psychotherapy bills. It is not a replacement for other forms of treatment but it can assist you in accomplishing what other means cannot. Writing as a form of therapy is as cheap and efficient as it gets, it is self-directed and allows you to turn inward to process your experiences and make sense of them. It may constitute your next opus. It may liberate you from an albatross of guilt.

It may also harm you. This harm is likely temporary, but it is good reason to move with caution when writing down past events that attempt to evade you or that you attempt to evade. Your escapism is a natural form of protection and you should respond to it with due respect, treat it with dignity. Challenge it, gentle, revisit, gradually.

Ask yourself probing questions:
- When did it hurt the most? What color was the hurt, how did it smell, what did it sound like?
- What is the event you least want to write about? What happened one day prior? One week after?

- How did it begin and how does it end?
- Who saved you? Who failed you?
- When did you fail yourself and when did you save yourself?
- What don't you remember?

Brainstorm more questions that speak to the particularities of your experience while remaining decidedly vague, therefore allowing you the space to release your memory without judgment.

In these initial stages write in a stream of conscious style, do not edit your thoughts and do not fear the unpolished appearance of your writing product. You are collecting raw material, dusting off fossils that resist revisiting, that coward amongst your artistic insecurities. It is a good start to write everything down that you have the bravery to recall. Let go and be free to write everything, even when it fails to meet your standards, which it likely will not, at this point.

Truthful not Truth

Abandon your sense of objectivity. Writing is not the realm of objectivity and this is even more pertinent when writing down painful memories of family violence. When working with your raw material you should aim for truthfulness rather than arriving at an indisputable truth.

You may want to name one the villain and other the innocent, but this will rob your work of depth. The characters you construct, imbued with your righteous sense of good and evil, will sink with an air of implausibility. Worse, you will marry yourself to a dichotomous perception of your past, you will skip over the complexity of your experience, and you will oversimplify at the expense of your own learning and growth. Ultimately you and your well being, your artistry, will lose in this game of labeling trajectory of blame. Succumb to the reality that truth, in this context is subjective. Commit yourself to conveying truthfulness without engaging in a false attainment of Truth.

Meticulously describe the events, the people and the environment that compose your world. Tell of the violence but do not skimp on the delicate moments, the peaceful times, the kindness and simple beauty. Explore the innocent qualities of villains and villainous qualities of innocents. Blur the lines between victims and wrong doers, just as in real life, where the lines are decidedly blurred. The more that you are willing to reflect the confusion of reality in your story, the more credibility you will earn with your audience. Trust your reader in recognizing the veracity of your claims. Your aim is not to tell, but to show your side in the most compelling manner possible and allow your readership to make whatever conclusions they see fit. You cannot write with a vendetta. You must abandon efforts to set the record straight. Accepting room for interpretation will do you well.

You will find in writing of family violence, as with other creative endeavors, that your truth competes with the truth of others, that these competing truths are not mutually exclusive. Especially in the case of abuse in the family, others will dispute your recollection or flatly deny your memories, memories that they treat as allegations. They may go as far as to discredit you publicly and attack your work. The best offense is a defense of strong writing that effectively communicates your truth even when it reflects badly on you or well on your abuser. Exhibit magnanimity in your work by considering the motivations of those who have meted out violence on you and incorporating the best possible interpretation of their viewpoint into your story. Resist the impulse to canonize yourself and demonize the Other. Resist the impulse to respond to violence by doing violence to your own integrity and that of your writing.

Similarly avoid the pitfalls of protecting those implicated in your story even though they are likely your loved ones and you are likely exposing some of their most private times of their lives. At least in your first drafts you should write with an eye for unfailing accuracy. Censoring yourself will compromise your writing process during these initial stages. Consider obscuring identities by changing non-essential character traits or creating composite characters, omitting events that are not vital to the plot and modifying the narrative to exclude unnecessary indictments while making revisions. You can fictionalize your work, or write poetry employing language that makes your exact subject matter unrecognizable.

There are measures you can take to lighten the blows if you have negative things to say about others, but it is highly inadvisable to submit your draft, at any stage, to others for approval even if you comment on aspects of their lives in your work. You are telling your story through your perspective, which is your right and you must take ownership of this.

Beyond Confession

This is your story, but ultimately you want it to reach other people. You may argue that you are writing only for yourself; if this is true then you may as well confine your work to your journal where it need not matter how you craft it to speak to a broader audience. There is nothing wrong with pursuing writing as means to survive violence through expression. However, when your writing becomes bigger than yourself, when it extends to reveal larger truths that are relevant to others despite their differing backgrounds and experiences, to access the universal, this is when your art becomes a means to not only survive but to transgress violence. When you use writing to transform one of the most base, cruel and unfortunate elements of our humanity, violence in the family, to a personal triumph, this is when writing resembles alchemy.

There is no clear answer of how this is accomplished but you will go a long way toward this goal by following the above recommendations: writing truthfully with out spelling out your intentions and digging deep to uncover your most reluctant past. This is necessary yet insufficient progress. To create a work of literary merit you must engage in revision. Keep in mind the truism that relatively few will show interest in your work simply because it actually happened or because it actually happened to you. The former puts your work in the genre of true-life drama that is at best mundane and at worst sensationalized or visa versa. The latter will preoccupy only those who know you personally and care enough to fuel gossip mills with a reading of your work.

Ensure that your writing upholds the tenets of the craft including plot and character. Your story should have an arc and your characters should have depth. Your work is not exempt from these tenets simply because it is true to your life. Hold your writing to the same standards of a work of fiction because when read by some one unknown to you, it may as well be fiction. Tease out the meaning in your work that is relevant to others despite socio-economic, age, gender or any other difference while avoiding heavy handedness. Accomplishing this will invest in the longevity and profundity of your writing product.

This said, write for yourself first and foremost. Write something that speaks to your experience, your values and conveys insight into your world. Create something that reveals something poignant about your life and derives from it meaning. In doing so you will likely create something that says something not only about your life but about life in general. Because your life and the lives of those who intersect yours is the fabric of existence. Your story is rife with the violence and harmony inherent in the balance of history. Your story is your story and therefore only yours to tell.

21. Writing About Family and Illness

Aubrey Hirsch

The task of writing about family often involves confronting illness, since, at some point; every family deals with one kind of illness or another. This type of writing must accomplish the same goals as all good writing, while contending with the extra difficulty the illness itself presents. Regardless of subject matter, most writers of poetry and prose want to reveal a character or persona to the world, to express the emotional truths of that character's journey, and to present these elements within a well-crafted narrative. Typically, however, the topic of illness brings with it at least a pair of additional goals:

1. To inform the reader (to varying extents) about the illness's objective characteristics—its causes, treatment, diagnostic procedures, and so on.
2. To fairly represent the subjective aspects of the illness—its symptoms, the feelings that accompany it, its psychological consequences, and the effects it can have on outsiders.

These goals, in turn, carry with them special challenges and rewards. In this article, I seek to help you both identify the challenges and develop techniques that you can use to overcome them.

Covering the Basics

When first writing about illness, many writers make the same common mistakes: using loaded words carelessly, getting lazy about research, and falling back on shocking images. The advice below addresses these basic issues.

- **Watch your language.** For many kinds of illness, a rich vocabulary of degradation exists in our culture. This is particularly true for mental illnesses. If you choose to use any words that might be offensive in everyday speech, do so with care. To avoid alienating your readers, make sure the contentious language fits with the speaker's voice so that your readers will know it belongs to the character and not to the author.

- **Do your research.** Don't cut corners by inventing facts. Even though your characters may be wholly fictional, you need to put in the time and effort to learn about the symptoms, signs, diagnostic tests, treatments, side effects, etc., of the actual disease. Your readers expect that you're writing about a fictional situation in their real world, and you should honor that expectation. With the rise of the Internet, good information about practically any condition is easy enough to come by that finding it won't eat up too much of your valuable writing time.

- **Don't rely too heavily on the gross-out factor.** A few well-placed details will help your reader get into the body of your suffering character. But too many vivid descriptions will make it seem like you're neglecting strong writing in favor of sensationalism. Taking this shortcut to getting a visceral reaction will leave your readers unsatisfied in the end. Let their reactions come from the emotional content of your piece, rather than trying to shock them into feeling something.

Making it Fresh

Because the topic of illness is so common in creative writing, stories, essays, and poems in this arena risk coming off as tired and cliché. Illness touches everyone at some time or another, so at least some of your readers are likely already familiar with the situation you're portraying. This familiarity among readers forces writers tackling illness to work harder to make their pieces feel new. Some ways to preserve your originality:

- **Be specific.** You can examine a common topic in a fresh way by sticking closely to the unique journey of your character. Avoid broad statements like "Breast cancer patients often feel x, y and z," which writers can find tempting as easy ways to convey the results of their research. But you can do better by talking about your character's individual experience instead of relying on generalities. By using your character's experience as a vehicle for presenting the illness, you can make the universal elements of your piece more affecting through their specificity.

- **Resist clichés**. Idioms like "strong as an ox" and "avoid it like the plague" have lost their power with readers, who have heard them again and again. Likewise, some descriptions have been used so often that they, too, have become cliché. For example, hospital rooms are too of ten described as being white, sterile, or uncomfortable, and doctors as brash diagnosticians or bespectacled nerds. Instead of rehashing these common adjectives and characterizations, surprise your readers with new descriptions or quirky details that will make your settings and characters seem three-dimensional rather than stereotypical.

- **Take advantage of cultural knowledge.** Be aware of what most of us, as your potential readers, will already know about the situations you're describing. For example, almost all of us have had blood drawn, so you don't need to tell us that it hurts. Given the goal of efficiency for any piece of writing, it's to your advantage as the writer to skip over any information you can trust your reader will already have. As soon you mention the syringe, your readers will conjure up the pain of being stuck with a needle all on their own, without you having to make it explicit. Spend your precious words instead on the important task of conveying information and perspectives that might be new to your audience.

Keeping it Focused

One of the biggest challenges of writing about illness is to narrow the tremendous amount of information about any given condition to just those facts, images, and reflections that will be most useful and poignant. To help you decide what to keep and what to let go, you can take inspiration from another art form. Photographers use a lens is used to crop and focus an image, selecting the contents of the picture, removing irrelevant data, and bringing certain objects into sharper view. Creating a narrative "lens" can work the same way. Your lens should reduce the scope of the creative piece and allow your readers to focus on a specific facet of your topic. Use the techniques below to find an appropriate, effective lens to work with.

- **Connect character to illness.** What defines your character? Whether he or she is real or imagined, take a few moments to write out a brief character sketch. Focus on the details and be as specific as possible. What do her hands look like? What is the first thing he does when he gets out of bed? Does he have a favorite tie? A beloved pet? Are there any hobbies or pastimes that you associate closely with this character? Choose one angle of his or her personality that seems the most rich and telling to you. Then think about how to present the illness in ways that tie into this aspect of the character's persona. For example, if your character restores antique cars, you might compare his heart surgery to the process of putting a new transmission into a '67 Mustang. If she's an avid gardener, you might liken the journey to a diagnosis to the way she carefully watches the green things in her garden to identify them as weeds or flowers

- **Let your research inspire you.** How does the literature associated with the illness make you feel? Patients with acute and chronic diseases are often buried in brochures, website FAQs, self-help books and the like. These voices, which are often overly flowery or overly mechanical, make great jumping off points for writing about illness. Similarly, the information contained in these sources can inspire your presentation of the material to your own readers. What surprises you about the way the illness is presented in a brochure? Do you feel comforted by it? Do you want to rebel against it? Are there any particularly cloying sentences you might be able to parody in your own piece? Imagine you were writing a self-help guide for someone just diagnosed with this illness. What would you say? What would you not say?

- **Construct an emotional lens.** Is there a single day, scene or moment that best captures the emotions you are trying to convey? Try to identify the three emotions you feel most strongly when thinking about your character's illness (be it fear, anger, sadness, guilt, or relief, for example). Write a scene that best captures each emotion. Maybe the car ride when you drove your mother to her first cancer treatment perfectly conveys fear, or perhaps the phone call when you heard the news shows your surprise. Choose the most compelling scene and rework it into a story or poem, focusing only on that single scene. If you attempt to render the entire experience of the illness, you are likely to end up with a bloated summary that spans too much time and "tells" instead of "showing." If you can home in on a single revealing moment, you will allow yourself more room on the page for concrete imagery and reflection.

Letting Go of Guilt

Guilt often plays a big role in the process of writing about family and illness, especially if the illness is not your own. Writing about someone else's condition can feel inappropriate or exploitive. A loved one may even accuse you of overstepping personal boundaries when he or she hears about your project. These pointers can help you let go of any guilt you might be feeling so that you can focus on the writing:

- **Remind yourself why you're writing this piece.** What inspired you to invent this character or tell this person's story? What do you hope to accomplish while writing it? What do you want your readers to take away from the piece? Make a list of your inspirations and motivations and keep it nearby as you write. This list will help you remind yourself what's really behind your words.

- **Take ownership of the story.** If you are writing about someone close to you, bear in mind that their story is your story, too; illness never affects only one person. If the story has stuck with you enough to make you want to write about it, chances are you were affected by someone else's struggle in some important way. The sooner you can start thinking of the experience as your story, too, the sooner you will start chasing away any guilty thoughts or feelings.

- **Write for yourself first.** Sometimes writers block themselves by thinking about what other people would say if they saw the work in progress. In the early stages of your writing, it's best to imagine the work as existing only for you. After all, it's in your notebook or on your computer screen, and no one can see it except for you. For many writers, this kind of enforced privacy is the only way to ensure a truly honest first draft. Later, if you're thinking about publishing the piece, you can consider how others might react, whether you want to change names, or if you want to edit out any very personal material, and so on. But for now it's just for you, so don't be afraid to tell the truth!

This might seem like a lot of advice to take in all at once, and it may help to proceed through your revisions in layers. Look first for the basics, then think about issues of freshness, and so on. Or, start with high-level, structural concerns like finding a lens, and then zoom in on the language. Writing about family and illness can be difficult, but when you've finished a polished draft, you'll be rewarded by writing that is both challenging and inspirational, that resonates with readers' own experiences while showing them something new. You will also have honored yourself or your loved one by giving a lasting voice to the experience of illness.

Part IV

Writing Exercises & Strategies

22. Create the Mother Lode: Journal About Yourself, Your Family and Memories

Sheila Bender

Even when life seems too busy to "really" write, you can work on gathering and storing images, details, and reflections about family life, personal experiences and memories. The brief pieces you journal during the busy times in your life are a rich vein of valuable ore integral to future writing. Not only will journaling keep you from lapsing into writer's block and convincing yourself that you have forgotten how to write, it will help you produce prose poems, sudden fiction, sudden nonfiction, and fragmentary writing, short forms in fashion. As you find more time in your life for writing, you can assay your journal for elements about your spouses, parents, in-laws, children and daily tasks to include in longer projects, and they are reusable. Just because you wrote a poem about the way a child has taught you much about life doesn't mean you can't write an essay or a story or a novel about it, too.

Five Exercises for Rich Easy-to-Do Journaling That Leads to More Writing

You can use these exercises again and again, and you will create different pieces each time.

Use Artifacts to Write
Sit in a room, a garden, a yard or in a museum, gallery, cafe gift shop or park. Even your car will do when you are running errands or taking kids to events. Notice five objects from where you are. Write down their names. Next, whether in that spot or at home, write a passage for each object, selecting from the following menu items (mix it up!):

1. The most important memory from recent or past family life that comes to you when you name this object
2. A fantasy you have when you look at the object
3. Why you wish this object wasn't there
4. If you were to name the object after a person you are related to or close to, who would it be and why
5. What seeing or having this object makes you miss about the way your life used to be

After you've written all the parts, find a title that seems to pull them together—for instance, "What Remains," "Writing To Find Out," "Objects," or "Today."

Use Recipes to Write
Take a recipe and pair it up with a time in your life. List each ingredient and each direction, and then after each one, write part of a story from your life at the time you associate with the recipe. Alternatively, find a new recipe and write about why you are choosing it today. Then do the exercise of writing between the ingredients and directions using current stories of your life.

Write Postcards and Letters
Choose a person living or dead with whom you want very much to communicate. Write a series of "post cards" from one place or from several places, over one day, a few days, or a few weeks or months. Describe those places especially for that person. Or write letters to this person—each time imagine you are choosing different printed materials to write on. Imagine that you are writing on the backs of things: food labels, checks, Visa receipts, take out menus, old letters from someone else, etc. Describe what you are writing on the back of to the person and integrate words from that paper's other side. If you pretend you are writing on materials other than paper, make sure a description of that material enters into your letter.

Break Other Writing Apart to Find More to Say
Take a poem you like and break it into stanzas, leaving white space between the stanzas that you will fill in with your own

writing. Or take some prose—a shopping or to-do list, a report card, a report, a notice you have received, or a letter you have found, received or sent—and divide the sentences with white space in which you'll write. What you write will bounce off the lines you've taken from the other material. You'll include descriptions and questions from your life that resonate for you with the writing you have copied out.

Find Topics to Write About by Making Strange Lists
I like the number seven when I make lists — 7 Things I Think About When I Think About You, 7 Places I May Never See But Feel As If I Have Seen, 7 Places I Would Like You to See, 7 Places I Would Like to See Before I Die, 7 Dresses I've Worn Since We Were Married, 7 Dresses I Gave Away, 7 Gifts I'd Give You If I Could, 7 Things That You Have Brought Me, 7 Insults I Take Seriously, 7 Insults I'd Like to Blow Off, 7 Things You've Said That I Really Heard, 7 Things I Forgot to Tell You. You get the idea. After you have listed the items in the list you are making, write about each one of the items; remember to use specifics that appeal to the five senses. One or two of the items will interest you more than the others and you may write pages!

Six Sources for Reading Short Forms Online

Reading the work on these sites will encourage the idea that what you are putting in your journal is not far from being what editors of short forms like. Each of the following websites has easy to access readings as well as easy online submission processes should you find something in your journal to work on and send in. Part of building that mother lode is building a publication history and it isn't hard with so many publications looking for material:

Frag Lit, An online magazine of fragmentary writing devoted to publishing journal entries among other forms.
fraglit.com

Tiny Lights: A Journal of Personal Narrative's Flash in the Pan posts short, often poetic, pieces of prose that soar.
tiny-lights.com/flash.php

Brevity, A journal of nonfiction 750 words or less.
creativenonfiction.org/brevity.index.htm

Flash Fiction Online, A source of short, short stories.
flashfictiononline.com

One Sentence, an online journal dedicated to fiction and nonfiction stories in one sentence.
onesentence.org

Narrative Magazine offers traditional short stories as well as other forms of literature, including iStories, a very short form.
narrativemagazine.com

Write, read, write some more. Send some pieces out for publication. You will be creating the mother lode and teaching yourself how to stay engaged in the writer's life.

23. Don't Forget the Story: Implementing Fiction Techniques in Creative Non-fiction

Jenn Brisendine

Imagine a father character in a play. He sits and writes in a diary while a voiceover tells you how angry he feels because his teenage daughter took his credit card without asking. Now imagine the same conflict shown through an active scene: the father character slams the fridge, skips a bottle cap across the room, and argues with the daughter about her mall trip.

In a challenge for the audience's interest, the second, more active method of storytelling would beat the first every time. As writers, we want our creative nonfiction to have the same vitality as a lively stage play or a scene of riveting fiction.

Whether your current family-oriented work is a memoir, blog, essay, or piece of literary journalism, it might benefit from the fiction technique of scene writing. Incorporating real-time scenes can boost the appeal of your non-fiction in several ways:

- You'll promote increased reader involvement in your text.
- You'll achieve a variety of paragraph lengths and eye-attracting white space.
- You'll provide readers an opportunity to reflect at the scene's end.

Show a Real-time Scene

A standard recommendation for fiction writers, "show, don't tell" is also great advice for writers of creative non-fiction. Showing a scene is like offering readers a magic passageway into an event instead of sitting them down to listen to a tale. Allow readers to draw conclusions and elicit themes based on the pieces of the story (scenes) you show them. The result is a more fulfilling reading experience for them, and a greater likelihood that they'll select your work again. When you show instead of tell, you enhance action, setting, and conflict. This sentence is simple narration:

I remember how, on a beach trip last September, a sea gull took my son's hot dog right out of my hand.

But a real-time scene can hook and hold readers more effectively than a recounting of circumstances:

I stretched my hand toward my son. Suddenly an explosion of gray wings erupted on the sand near my feet. A whush-whush of air brushed me as a gull flew between us, clipped the hot dog from my fingers, and soared away.

Employ the Senses

Paint your real-time scene with sensory imagery. Let your reader see the view, hear the wind, smell dinner cooking. Instead of telling them *The hospital room was bleak*, show readers the bleakness: the color of the walls (*like pale mint jelly*), the scents (*lemon, chemicals, soap*), the emptiness (*not one magazine or framed print to draw attention away from the exam table*).

Emotions can be shown through sensory imagery, too. Instead of *I was afraid* or *My husband looked worried*, describe how your fear amplified the silence or how you saw new wrinkles coat your husband's face.

Reveal with Conversation

The use of dialogue contributes great interest value to your scene. Dialogue can convey conflict (through arguments or confessions), demonstrate character (through word choice, tone, and pace), and advance your "plot" (through revelations of complications and discoveries).

While your tone and personal style will greatly affect the composition of your dialogue, consider these pointers often utilized by fiction writers:

- Use *Dylan said* instead of *said Dylan.*
- Instead of a *he said (-ly adverb)* construction, skip the adverb and show the emotion another way.
- Stick with *said* almost exclusively when you tag the spoken line. On the rare occasion when you choose another verb, make sure it's a verb of speech (*muttered, whispered, murmured*).
- Omit tags when the speaker is evident.
- Instead of *said*, consider an action tag: *"I'm leaving." Peyton let the door slam behind her.*
- Use *grinned, smiled, laughed,* and other "mouth actions" as action tags: *"Stop with the jokes." He grinned.* Don't use them as verbs of speech: *"Stop with the jokes," he grinned* isn't correct.
- Avoid info dumping, in which a long spoken passage informs the reader on necessary but uninteresting exposition.
- Choose punctuation with care.

Picky with Punctuation

Correct dialogue punctuation is vital in displaying a scene's subtext:

Comma: *"I'm going, and you're coming with me."* (There's barely a pause.)

Period: *"I'm going. And you're coming with me."* (Now there's a much stronger pause.)

Question mark: *"I'm going? And you're coming with me?"* (The speaker's vocal inflection has changed, and so has the meaning.)

Exclamation mark: *"I'm going! And you're coming with me!"* (Inflection and meaning have changed again.)

Points of ellipse: *"I'm going. And you're..."* (The speaker trails off, indicating uncertainty.)

Dash: *"I'm going. And you're—"* (The speaker is interrupted.)

To see how fiction-writing techniques like show-don't-tell, sensory details, and dialogue work together to create a high-interest reading experience, first consider this journal-style passage of non-fiction:

> *All day I chastised Aidan to demonstrate good "zoo manners" at the expense of his enthusiasm. At the deer park, he begged to pet the deer like he saw others doing, and I hesitated. The hand sanitizer dispenser seemed a paltry weapon against germs. This could become the story we'd tell in future years about a scar. But I figured I'd issued enough negative responses that day. The thrill on his face when I told him to go ahead diminished my tension. Aidan got a lion sippee that day, but I get to keep and cherish the memory of his smile forever.*

Now try the story revealed in a real-time scene:

> *I grabbed a handful of the back of my preschooler's shirt and clutched it. "Aidan. Get off the railing."*
>
> *"Mommy! Did you see that leopard sleeping?"*
>
> *Minutes later, I tugged his hand. "Aidan. Let someone else have a look."*
>
> *"Mommy! Aren't the elephants cool?"*
>
> *Minutes after that, I turned up the You've Been Warned voice. "Aidan. Keep your feet away from the fence."*
>
> *"It's okay, Mommy, the giraffes don't mind."*
>
> *No climbing. Wait your turn. Don't jump. Be careful. By the*

time we got to the deer park, we could've run for a "Zoo Manners of the Year" Award.

"Mommy! Can I pet the deer, like they're doing?"

I hesitated. The hand sanitizer station looked grungier than the deer themselves. My mom-alarm had a crystal ball moment, complete with my own future words: "Remember when the zoo deer went nuts on Aidan? He still has the scar..."

I let out a breath, and it was like taking off pinching shoes. "Yes. Of course you can."

His smile was the best souvenir I could've found.

Ultimately, in a real-time scene, your message is uncovered by the reader instead of stated by the writer. Best of all, you allow the story to take center stage.

24. Family in Nonfiction: Making the Familiar Strange

Yelizaveta P. Renfro

One of the challenges in writing about your own family is that you know the people so well. Where do you even begin? How do you describe them to a reader who's never met them? How do you make them seem vibrant and alive? By distancing yourself from your subject matter—by thinking like a stranger who has just met your family for the first time—you can gain a new perspective that will bring freshness to your writing.

Be an Ethnographer

In 1936, James Agee lived among Southern sharecroppers and later wrote about his experiences in his book, *Let Us Now Praise Famous Men*. By living with families, observing them, and taking careful notes, he was able to create a compelling portrait of the men and women he met. In describing them, he often employs striking details, using unexpected metaphors that express the uniqueness and wonder in each human being. For example, he describes "George's red body, already a little squat with the burden of thirty years, knotted like oak wood, in its clean white cotton summer union suit" and "his wife's beside him, Annie Mae's, slender, and sharpened through with bone" (51). Agee seeks out details that stand out in the reader's mind.

In his research, Agee uses ethnographic techniques: observing a culture firsthand over a long period of time and conducting in-depth interviews. As an outsider, Agee does not need to create distance between himself and his subjects. In writing about your own family, you can employ many of the same techniques, but you will need to work at gaining distance and perspective. Imagine that your family is a community and that you are an outsider. Try writing descriptions of your family members based entirely on what you can observe—not what you know. Try to think about how your family members appear and sound to others. Can you recreate their speech on the page? Can you describe their appearances and mannerisms?

View the World through a Child's Eyes

To children, the world is a fresh and amazing place. They often notice details that are lost to adults, and they approach new situations without preconceived ideas or judgments. In a sense, they are the best ethnographers. In her memoir *An American Childhood*, Annie Dillard is able to make the familiar and mundane seem strange and remarkable by capturing her view of the world as a child. In the following passage, she describes her parents' shinbones: "The bones were flat and curved, like the slats in a Venetian blind. The long edges were sharp as swords...Loose under their shinbones, as in a hammock, hung the relaxed flesh of their calves. You could push and swing this like a baby in a sling. Their heels were dry and hard, sharp at the curved edge. The bottoms of their toes had flattened, holding the imprint of life's smooth floors even when they were lying down" (26).

Think back to some of the discoveries that you made as a child. Select a mundane object, and make it seem remarkable by viewing it through a child's eyes. Write a detailed description of it. Next, select a family member you would like to write about. Concentrate on just one physical attribute—her eyes, her hands, her hair, her voice, even her shinbones. Imagine how a child might view that one characteristic. How can you make it seem fresh and amazing? Write a description of it. Select other physical characteristics and describe them as well. Piece together the descriptions and see if a portrait of your subject is beginning to emerge.

Focus on a Cultural Artifact

Think of an object that has great significance for your family. This could be a piece of jewelry, a book, a tool, a musical instrument, a food, an article of clothing, a piece of art, etc. If you have the object, place it near you while you write. If you don't have the object, visualize it. Now write down everything you can about its physical appearance: size, shape, color, weight, smell, taste, sound, etc.

Once you have described the object, go beyond its appearance. Explain why it's important to your family. Describe where it came from, how it's been used, and who has owned it. Describe the people for whom the object has meaning. What does the object say about the culture that it comes from? Keep writing until you've exhausted the subject. Try selecting another artifact and doing the exercise again. A whole series of essays could be framed this way. You might select a different object to focus on for each member of your family.

Conduct an Interview

Interviewing is an important tool for ethnographers. Even though you know your family well, interviewing can still be useful as you reconstruct your family's story. You might think you know exactly how something happened, but you'll likely be surprised if you talk with other family members. Everyone has his own perspective and story. Gathering these details from others can make your writing richer and more accurate. Interviewing family members does not have to be a formal affair. You can, of course, prepare detailed questions in advance and take notes or record the interview. But if your family member is reticent about a formal interview, have an informal chat. You can begin the conversation by saying, "Remember the time that...."

Conducting interviews is also useful when you are writing parts of your family's story that you did not experience yourself. In telling my family's story in an essay, for example,

I interviewed my parents to learn about the day they met. The material you gather in interviews can help to fill in gaps where you lack first-hand knowledge. It also allows you to see your material through another's eyes; the additional perspectives will help make your family come alive on the page.

References

Agee, James. *Let Us Now Praise Famous Men*. Boston: Houghton Mifflin, 2001.

Dillard, Annie. *An American Childhood*. New York: HarperPerennial, 1987.

25. How to Write a Childhood Memoir

Catherine Gildiner

First of all, I want to clarify what a memoir is and is not. It is not an autobiography, which demands more external accuracy than a memoir. A memoir should be *your* memories of your past. In order to write a memoir, you must trust your memory and not second-guess it. You need to be able to recall things as you remembered them in childhood. Capturing the childhood feeling is the most crucial part of the memoir. If, for example, you remember your childhood home as huge and rambling and then as an adult you go on a research trip and find the house smaller and less elegant than you remembered it in childhood, you should describe the home as you remembered it—not as it exists today. That rule goes for the entire memoir; or else it will read as an adult reminiscence, which is different from a childhood memoir.

Secondly, writing a memoir takes nerves of steel and you need to have ice in your veins. What you have to say is not always complimentary about yourself or others. I am amazed by how often people say they desperately want to write a memoir but they have to wait for their relatives to die. Guess what? You may die before they do. You need to write what is in your heart. If you are true to your memory, then you have done the job. Writing a memoir is not a popularity contest. If others remember things differently from you, so be it. Memory is not a ticker tape of reality. It is what is left after your unconscious is finished distorting it. It is what gets kicked around in your mind for years. Usually, if you have retained a childhood memory, it is significant and it is up to you to figure out what it means and how to fit it into your book.

The question most often asked of me is how I have remembered so much of my childhood. Did I keep diaries, etc.? The truth is that my entire childhood memoir has only ten episodes in it. Everyone can remember ten episodes from their childhood. The trick is to find a way to expand on them and then to string them together in a memoir.

Memory is associative, so what you need to do is remember something from childhood and then everyday when you go over the memory on your computer, you will expand it slightly as one idea in your brain taps another into being. The brain is like a pinball machine; the more times the ball goes around, the more it will light up associative memories. You must expand the memory into a vignette and then into a chapter of your memoir.

When I taught memoir courses, I was surprised by how often people came to the course saying they had no childhood memories! This left us with no raw material. Fortunately, I was a psychologist for twenty-five years before I became a writer. I had taken thousands of case histories over those years and had a pretty good idea what types of events are important in childhood. I call these developmental moments. They are moments in time when you grow one step further along the continuum toward adulthood. In order to get people started on their childhood memoir, I list several of these points in time and then I have everyone in the class write about those moments. I will list them below and then describe how they have been used in my memoir, *Too Close to the Falls*, and by some of my students in the past.

- start from your most traumatic or most salient memory and work around it
- first time you realized that the world was not like your home
- first time you realized that your parents were not always right
- first sexual memory
- first aggressive memory when you were bullied or bullied another

- memory of winning or losing a contest or event
- unfair treatment
- caught for wrongdoing
- first time you confronted death
- first sexual attraction

I call this my ten-point guide to writing a childhood memoir. If you can answer these questions, then you can write a memoir. It is only a matter of filling in the details. In order to give you an idea of what I mean, I will explain how I used some of these points in my book.

Use the most traumatic memory and work around it.
Usually the most vivid memory you have is the one you should write about. That memory is probably the nexus of a lot of other memories. As you write this memory, keep track of others that arise as you describe this one. Darwin said that we keep traumatic memories in several places in our brain so that we can access them quickly when in danger. For example, if you are a caveman and herd of stampeding elephants almost crushes you, you have the memory of their thundering footsteps in your brain so that you know you must run. Remembering danger or trauma is crucial to our survival so our memory may skip over day-to-day activities and focus on the past trauma. Write it all down even if you don't know if you will use it or not. It will be like gold mining. One vein opens up other veins. When you are writing this big episode, I guarantee that more memories will surface than you ever thought you could possibly remember.

In *Too Close to the Falls*, I was frightened when I went to a psychiatrist for having stabbed a boy. That episode tapped into the idea that my parents were not always right, bullying and the idea that I was different from other people.

The first time you realize that the entire world is not like your home.
Teasing out this memory is crucial in writing a childhood memoir. It is the first step in growing up and seeing the world

as broader than your immediate surroundings. To give you an idea how this works, I will give you three examples. In *Too Close to the Falls*, my mother never cooked a meal so I was shocked when I went to a friend's house and noticed uncooked meat on the counter. When I ate dinner at my friend's home when I was five, I asked for a menu and was shocked the mother was the waitress.

When I taught memoir writing at a bookstore the management served coffee and cookies after the class. Several homeless men came to the class for the coffee and cookies and were taken aback when I made them write memoirs before dining. One man wrote that he thought kindergarten was a place where everyone learned to make up 'happy stories' about their home life. If you made them up successfully you went to first grade. When his classmates said they went to a baseball game with their dads, he said the same thing. Then once he went to another boy's house for lunch and discovered that his friend was not making up 'the happy stories.' He realized then that his home was different. He had two alcoholic parents who rarely acknowledged the children.

Another of my students was an orthodox Jew who was told never to eat meat and dairy at the same time. Otherwise she would be smote. She went to a Christian friend's home in kindergarten and was served a baloney sandwich on white bread with butter on it and a glass of milk. Fearing death, she didn't eat it; however, she was very frightened that she would be surrounded by dead people and no one would be able to drive her home. By evening when the family was still alive, she realized for the first time that religion was an idea and not a reality.

The first time you realize your parents are not always right.
This is another moment of growth away from the family when you begin to see that your parents are not perfect, but are flawed human beings. That comes as a shock to most children and tends to frighten them. In *Too Close to the Falls* I turn to my parents when I am bullied. (More on bullying below) I am in

grade three and I turn to my mother for help. There is a boy pulling out my hair and I need strategies for getting him to stop. She suggests inviting him to our home and making him a friend. Even in grade three, I knew that advice was off the mark. I asked my father and he, believing in law and order, said "take your concerns to your teacher." When she didn't help, he suggested I go to the principal who was the chief nun, mother superior. She said I should offer up my sufferings for the lost souls in limbo. I had confronted the adult world and no one had helped me. It was my first parental disillusionment.

Many of my students have written about their parents' alcoholism or their abuse or other family secrets. It is a painful exercise realizing that your parents are not perfect and fertile ground for the memoir.

First sexual memory.
This memory is not to be confused with your first sexual attraction, but is really part of that inchoate memory that something is going on in the world that you, as a child, are not privy to. It is in fact your first discovery that sex exists in the world at large. Freud is not exactly crazy when he says that the two basic instincts are sex and aggression. We have to suppress them in order for civilization to work as planned. These two emotions are sublimated, denied or repressed. Therefore sexuality is confusing for children. The child may say or do something sexual and then be reprimanded for it. Then there is an incident that let' the child know that sexuality exists everywhere in the world and it is being kept from you. For almost any child this discovery is shocking.

In *Too Close to the Falls*, when I was in the second or third grade, I delivered medicine to Marilyn Monroe from my father's drug store. The delivery car driver named Roy accompanied me. Marilyn answered the door in her slip and I was appalled by this indecency and later ask Roy if he was offended and he informed me that he liked it! It was at that moment that I learned that although Catholic school and society in general were warning girls not to be immodest, people lined up to see

Marilyn Monroe. I had no idea why she was so popular, but I did know that as the song goes "Something's happenin' here."

In the best memoirs I have read this moment is always captured. Sometimes it is a brutal shock, (See Mary Karr *The Liar's Club*) or sometimes it is much more subtle. (See Joyce's Dubliner's "An Encounter" where a man exposing himself disrupts the innocence of childhood.)

First time you are bullied or bully another.
The pecking order of childhood is crucial and its sorting itself out is one of the most painful lessons of childhood. In my book, I am bullied by a boy and my parents give me ineffective advice. Ultimately Roy, the delivery car driver, suggests I hit him with something hard when he is unaware of any tension. I stab him with a compass, am sent to a psychiatrist and all hell breaks loose. Yet, I still remember the fine moment when that boy backed down and I rose triumphant. Nearly all of my male students have very vivid memories about the pecking order, which entails bullying, or being bullied.

First time you confront death.
The moment you realize that someone has died and will not return is the moment that you realize you too will eventually die. It is a shocking revelation and you should try and recreate the situation that helped you to realize this sad truth. Usually it is through the death of an animal, or a relative.

When writing your memoir, include all of your own wrongdoing and your bizarre notions of reality. I can assure you that everyone who reads your childhood memoir will remember his or her own strange notions. After all it is the job of the child to try and figure out the machinations of the world and the interesting part of the memoir is your childhood understanding of society.

26. Mothers and Daughters: Telling Shared Stories

Diane LeBlanc

The last three words I wrote for a recent collection of poetry became the first three: for my mother. But if I had written those words first, I might not have written the poems.

Many of us write about our mothers because our stories are inseparable from theirs. For example, former U.S. poet laureate Louise Glück opens *Ararat*, a collection of poems involving family, with the line, "Long ago, I was wounded." Emotional distance within family casts the book's speaker into the role of witness and listener, which informs her vocation as writer and reflective witness in a larger, often combative world. To tell her story, Glück must write about family, particularly her mother.

So, how can we write shared stories in ways that both reveal *and* respect?

Writing is the first action. These exercises are designed to stimulate ideas, to quiet censoring voices that keep us from telling our stories, and to encourage revision with an audience in mind. Then we may begin to choose which stories we'll share within and beyond family.

Getting Started

Take inventory. Create lists of people, places, objects, events, and other "landmarks" that characterize your relationship to your mother. No detail is too small or too ambiguous. My lists include a green station wagon, Jack LaLanne exercise records, hair curlers, scars, the smell of Camphor Ice, Lake Groton, paper dolls, and dried paint tubes. Get the picture? Drawings and photographs may help clarify details.

Begin like a journalist. Don't take facts for granted. Ask "who," "what," "where," "why," and "how" to get the details of a story you think you know. Your sources may include your own journals, interviews with family, and research through local historical archives.

Write to discover. Writing to discover, rather than to say what we think we know, may yield surprising work. For years, images of a scar on my mother's leg kept appearing in my poems. It's her scar, and I felt reluctant to expose it. Eventually my reluctance became my guiding question: how many family scars have we exposed? And what have they taught us? The resulting poem, "Scars," portrays me as a child studying my mother's scar as she sits in the sun one afternoon. I connect the scar to her brother and the accident that caused the scar, a story I heard often as a child. I was surprised to realize that I wasn't really writing about the scar. It was a vehicle for the larger idea that in family we sometimes hurt each other by accident.

Writing Around Obstacles

Assume a persona. If you get stuck while telling your own story, borrow a mother/daughter story from literature, myth, or fairy tale, such as the myth of Demeter and Persephone or the tale of Three Spinning Fairies. Imagine you are the daughter of one of these mothers. Try telling her story in a contemporary context. Or use elements of the time-tested story to tell your own. Tapping into a larger story sometimes reveals that our experiences, while unique, may have a universal source.

Write, cut, paste. Writing can be a liberating activity, even if you have no intention of sharing your work with an audience. I hesitate to recommend the old "write then burn it" advice as a means to free forbidden stories. You never know what you may want to salvage. If you reach a point where your work is surprising you to the point of discomfort, don't stop writing. I paste material cut from live drafts into electronic folders titled

"Dumped Lines" and "Dumped Prose." If you share a computer, you may look into password protection, simulating the locked diaries many of us kept as adolescents. There's also the option of hiding printed work in places no one will suspect. Cut material can be a rich source of material when you want to expand a work or write further about a topic.

Experiment with points of view. Shifting the narrative position of a poem or essay may allow new details to emerge. Review a poem or essay that is currently told through the first person, "I." What happens if the point of view shifts to "she"? Given this shift, what details can the narrator know or not know? Finally, try again, this time directly addressing the person you are writing about. This experiment can reveal whose voice is best situated to tell a certain story.

Revising for an Audience

Create a companion. Sometimes a poem or essay that feels complete tells only part of a larger story. In that case, write a companion. Months after writing "Scars," I wrote "Glass and Snow," a poem that observes my body's similarity to my mother's:

> These are her bones:
> clavicles like cedar hangers
> holding our slack designs,
>
> toes bullied sideways
> by shoes we regret
> and can't take back.

The poem ends as my mother and I talk across darkness from separate bedrooms, a scene that signifies our reluctance to waste any precious time when I visit her for one week each summer. We talk until we fall asleep. The later poem does not eclipse the child's ambivalence in "Scars," but it confirms that

I've grown beyond it. I don't present one poem without the other.

Be fair. The poet's role as witness deepens throughout Louise Glück's *Ararat*. The midpoint poem "New World" begins with this qualified observation:

> As I saw it,
> all my mother's life, my father
> held her down, like
> lead strapped to her ankles.

The poem develops by contrasting the speaker's once "buoyant" mother with a father who preferred sinking to living. After the father's death, the mother drifts weightlessly "like an astronaut/who somehow loses the ship," free but "without relation to the earth" (39). Glück takes responsibility for the unflattering portrait by presenting the image as an observation, not the truth of her parents' marriage. It is *her* truth, not *the* truth. And that's your goal, to tell *your* stories.

References

Gluck, Louise. *Ararat*. New York: The Ecco Press, 1990. Print.

LeBlanc, Diane. *Dancer with Good Sow*. Georgetown: Finishing Line Press, 2008. Print.

27. Now and Then: Using the Retrospective Narrator in Memoir

Christin Geall

I've already lost touch with a couple of people I used to be.
—Joan Didion, "Keeping a Notebook"

Using only one voice in a personal essay or memoir is like kneading dough with one hand; it makes the job tougher than it needs to be. To get the emotional tension we want in a work of nonfiction our main job is to convince the reader that the narrator is working towards understanding their past. To do that, it helps to have two voices: one voice for *now,* and one for *then.*

Think of it this way: you've got a protagonist and a narrator—both you. But, there's a difference between them, if you consider that the protagonist is engaged in the action of your story—she's making choices and mistakes, bumbling through family life—and the narrator, she's there too, but she's commenting on the decisions of the protagonist. She can step aside from the story and tell us what she thinks. Here's how Elizabeth Gilbert makes the shift in the second section of *Eat Pray Love*:

"I had actively participated in every moment of the creation of this life—so why did I feel like none of it resembled me?" In that question, Gilbert turns the story from backstory (her previous life) to her authorial present, all on the pivot of a self-questioning 'me'.

In this chapter, I'll explore three topics related to retrospection in memoir: voice, tense and chronology.

Voice: Who's Speaking?

At the core of memoir lies one simple question: who am I? Didion's conundrum—of losing touch with our old selves, hints at the two key questions we face when writing about our past: who was I then? And, who am I now?

A reflective narrator can give you the perspective you need to answer those two questions. On the page, such a narrator might sound savvy, sophisticated or snarky. Or, their voice may be more essayistic—self-questioning, skeptical, smart. In either case, the retrospective narrator looks back in order to reflect: the reader senses they've had time to think about the past.

We all know what it's like to listen to a friend who hasn't learned from experience, a person who keeps making the same mistakes—boring at best, frustrating at worst. The same applies to nonfiction stories about family: readers want to see you make sense of your life, witness your struggle towards truth.

Still, some memoirists avoid retrospection, preferring to unfurl scene after scene with the hope that plot or conflict alone might float the narrative ship. As David Lazar says, "the memoir frequently performs memory for its audience of voyeurs." Certainly that is the case with Jeanette Wall's bestseller *The Glass Castle*. But remember the opening? When the older, wiser, wealthier Walls looks out on her dumpster-diving mother? This one scene sets up a dual perspective for the book. Wall's introductory narrator says: here we are now; we survived. It's a hook for the book, and a provocative one. Walls invites the reader into the book with a proposal: Stay with me, and I'll tell you how we got here.

Here's another instance of the retrospective voice, this time presented in parentheses in Mary Karr's latest memoir, *Lit*. In this scene, she's sitting on her porch, drinking, and thinking about her family:

"Mother fell down and pissed her pants, Daddy got into fist fights and drank himself to death. (Who but a drunk, I wonder looking back, could sit on the porch alone and get in an argument?)."

Memoir lacking such a narrator is like a museum without interpretive signs. It's like being in a vast gallery knowing that if you'd just paid the five dollars for the headset you would have learned so much more. This is how it is for our readers: they need a guide—a trustworthy narrator.

Lopate described it this way: "In personal essays and memoirs, we must rely on the subjective voice of the first person narrator to guide us, and if that voice can never explain, summarize, interpret or provide a larger sociological or historical context for the material, we are in big trouble. We are reduced to groping in a dark tunnel, able to see only two feet in front of us."

Exercise:

1. Select a scene from your work that lacks luster. Is there a moment when the narrator can step out the action and into her thoughts? Flag it.
2. Now, begin a paragraph with the phrase "Looking back now...." What do you see?
3. Consider how the meaning of the event shifted through retrospection. Push yourself further by asking: why do you remember this scene? What does your remembering say about you?

Now and Then: Present and Past

Some think the present tense adds vigor and immediacy to writing. But consider how a here-and-now voice might limit a narrator's perspective in memoir. Can such a narrator see the bigger picture? Can she supply the history needed to build pathos?

By contrast, the past tense offers two angles: the past (*I thought*) and the past perfect (*I'd thought*). The past perfect allows you to step gracefully across time. Look at difference between these two sentences:

> #1: I thought he was handsome.
> #2: I had thought he was handsome.

Which person seems wiser? The second. Why? Because just that little word 'had' inserts time into the sentence—time the narrator has had to reflect.

The past perfect can allow you to step out of your narrative and bring another related moment to light. Here's how Kathy Briccetti traverses the divide in her adoption memoir *Blood Strangers*:

> "I was proud of my youngest, the tag-along in our family, who, since he was an infant, had watched and listened. Even though he'd been privy to many of the conversations we'd had with his big brother, and of course we'd talked directly to him, too, I didn't know how much he understood about how we had made him."

Exercise:

1. Select a scene set in the past that focuses on family.
2. Ask yourself: how did those events affect me? How was I changed that day?
3. Re-write the scene in the past perfect.
4. Then, try telling the truth from today's perspective, in present tense.

Chronology

We don't think in linear terms, but we do read one word at a time, from left right, top to bottom. Beginning writers often struggle to find a framework to organize the material of memory and, by default, end up with a linear design, a straight-up chronology of events. This is arguably a solid structure, but as Sven Birkerts writes in *The Art of Time in Memoir: Then, Again*, chronology can't substitute for story. He writes: "Not only is the sequential approach a chore for the writer, but is often a deadly bore for the reader. The point is *story*, not chronology, and in memoir the story all but requires the dramatic ordering hindsight affords. The question is not what happened when, but what, for the writer, was the path of realization."

Birkert's 'path of realization' is the real work of memoir—the winnowing of memory to find understanding. If your reader doesn't think you're trying to make sense of events, why should they? As Neil Genzlinger recently wrote in 'The

Problem with Memoirs,' in the *NY Times Sunday Book Review*, "...a good memoir—it's not a regurgitation of ordinariness or ordeal, not a dart thrown desperately at a trendy topic, but a shared discovery. Maybe that's a good rule of thumb: If you didn't feel you were discovering something as you wrote your memoir, don't publish it."

Prologues often contain a hint of that discovery. The focus in a book's early pages is 'story,' not chronology, as is the case with Claire Dederer's prologue in her forty-something memoir, *Poser: My Life in Twenty-Three Yoga Poses*. The last line of her prologue reads: "Fear. I hadn't even known it was there." Fear: another great hook for a book. And who said it? A retrospective narrator.

Turning such hindsight into art takes creativity. Savvy students have asked: If I mess with multiple time periods how do I deal with chronology? With structure? What about flashbacks? Should I put them in italics? Get fancy with asterisks? Or book-end my backstory with section breaks? How can I show the narrator moving around in time? With dates?

Dates can work, as they did for Nick Flynn, in *Another Bullshit Night in Suck City*, a book arranged as a series of essays and short takes. Mary Karr's memoir, *Lit*, eschews dates, but employs multiple points-of-view, including the retrospective narrator. Here's an example of two linked paragraphs, each set in a different tense:

> I wouldn't call my pre-Warren drinking out of control because I had control. So long as I didn't leave my apartment, I didn't drink.
>
> In Cambridge, that person no longer exists. With an invisible eraser, I'm internally rubbing hard at the core of her, and Warren's steady, unwavering gaze is lasering away her external edges. Soon she'll be mist.

The Irish writer Nuala O'Faolain, in her memoir, *Are You Somebody? The Accidental Memoir of a Dublin Woman*, uses the retrospective voice to reflect on the meaning of past events. She writes:

All I know was that when I left Oxford and went back to Dublin, I faced into the future looking backwards. I was half girl still. I was half heartbroken. The place I was leaving had from beginning to end contained feelings so vehement, however silly they were, that even now it is hard to believe they don't live, still, somewhere else as well as in my memory.

Exercise:

1. Look over your paragraphs. Do you see a surfeit of 'thens'? If you do, you may have fallen into a linear chronology, forcing the reader down a shallow course of 'this happened, then this happened.'
2. Try to deepen your narrative by adding reflective pauses, pithy asides, or commentary on the mother/daughter/wife/woman you once were.

Working the Angles

As you write, consider what can't you see. Our blind spots often reveal troves of information about who we once were. Do you only recall what your mother wore, and not her expression the day she told you _____? Or, do you remember the way it rained and rained the day you found out you were pregnant/sick/learned of a parent's death? Focus on these moments in your work and pay attention to your blind spots: Note when and where your memory fails and question yourself (on the page) about the gaps in your knowledge. Not only will this lend authenticity to your narrator, (we're all fallible, after all), it might also let you shift your focus, and discover new territory for your work.

References

Birkerts, Sven. *The Art of Time in Memoir: Then, Again.* Saint Paul, Minnesota: Graywolf Press, 2008.

Shields, David. *Enough About You: Adventures in Autobiography.* New York: Simon and Schuster, 2002.

Lazar, David. *Truth in Nonfiction: Essays.* Iowa City: University of Iowa Press, 2008.

28. Teaching the Personal Essay

Anne Valente

It happens every semester. In my feature writing classes, I spend weeks teaching my students how to write an assortment of articles—profiles, event stories, general features—and watch them become more confident as burgeoning journalists. But then, when I at last introduce the personal essay near the end of the semester, I stand in front of the classroom and watch their faces go blank. It's hard to tell what they're thinking, but by the expression on their faces—slow shifts from surprise, to vague confusion, to a slight smirk on certain mouths—it's something between disappointment, and utter relief that the remainder of the semester will be smooth sailing.

Teaching the personal essay is hard work, due to the assumption that it isn't hard work—for the student, or for me.

I believe that my students understand the significance of memoirs once they write them, and that oftentimes the personal essay is their most valuable assignment. But at first, many are skeptical. Some look at me with doubt, as if their most guarded memories will be destroyed by universal criticism. Others sit back with confidence, assuming I will now overlook their writing for the pure heart they'll pour onto the page. Still others begin to treat class discussion like group therapy, focused less on the writing and more on the exchange of personal anecdotes. Such are the challenges of including the personal essay in class, and I end up feeling responsible for making sure that the assignment is taken seriously.

These challenges can be overcome, however. With some finesse, there are ways to keep the class focused, keep the writing focused, and ensure that students feel safe enough to not only write a personal essay without fear of criticism, but also treat that work as an essential form of journalistic writing.

Staying Focused

As with anything that involves some degree of self-disclosure, the choice to bring the personal essay into the classroom also brings with it the danger of class discussion veering radically off-topic. One student will mention that she's writing about the time her car stalled at a stoplight, and three others will jump in with similar tales of their cars breaking down, changing their own oil, fixing a flat. Someone may even bring up their windshield getting smashed once, which could spawn an entirely new conversation about car accidents, weather hazards while driving, anything.

Keeping the class on topic inevitably involves bringing the discussion perpetually back to the writing. Whenever I sense my students beginning to build upon each other's stories, I take the reins back by reminding them that this is exactly why writing personal essays is important. Memoirs are universal; they allow for connections. Once I've reminded them of this, it's easy to bring class discussion back to what we're actually writing about, and why.

Keeping the Writing Focused

Maintaining a collective focus in the classroom is often much easier than keeping one individual focused, especially when that individual turns in an essay that is quite literally all over the place. Harder still is when that essay deals with something particularly difficult for the student. A colleague of mine once had a student who wrote about her boyfriend's death, which had happened just one week before. The essay wasn't particularly well structured or well written, and my colleague struggled for days over how to handle the situation. Ultimately, she directed her feedback entirely toward the writing itself, with a note of personal condolence included.

Though a situation like this is rare, students are nonetheless personally tied to what they've written, and any criticism might be viewed as an individual affront. The best approach is to keep feedback centered on the writing itself, with little mention of the topic other than perhaps questions or suggestions for digging deeper. It's also important to point out what is working well in the essay, and what positives can be built upon for rewrites or second drafts.

Writing Without Fear

Feedback is reactive by nature, offered only after the essay has already been written. To ensure that students' feelings are protected even before they start writing, I also take proactive measures to ease student fears in advance.

When I first introduce the personal essay, I always remind students that they can write about whatever they choose. It is assumed that memoirs by definition are heartbreaking, and that students must scan their brains for the saddest—and often most sensitive—events in their past. It's possible to release this burden by reminding them that their essays can be whimsical, funny, ordinary, and nostalgic. Students can cover just about anything, as long as they see the purpose in what they've written. I also tell them to choose topics that haven't occurred too recently. This offers them the narrative distance to write closely, but not so close that they can no longer write clearly.

Perhaps the most successful means of avoiding hurt feelings is to organize an in-class workshop, where students' essays are read and discussed by their peers. Though this makes many students anxious, they often tell me how beneficial it is. Workshops allow students to exchange opinions that aren't mine, and to find their own vocabulary for talking about writing. They grow more comfortable with criticism, and begin to view it as support rather than censure.

Taking the Personal Essay Seriously

Ultimately, students cannot be forced to take essays seriously. I can only hope that they'll read each other's work and feel it reverberate through their own experiences, and that they'll write the truth of what matters to them. And in the end, despite their initial misgivings, I sense that they do.

By the time they've finished writing, they no longer need me to tell them that personal essays are hard work, that they're not group therapy or an easy grade, or even a terrible nightmare. They know this, without my having to tell them, because they've already done the hard work.

29. Using Your Dreams to Enrich Your Writing

Ingeborg Gubler Casey

A dream is a message from your unconscious in story form. Your dreaming mind uses images drawn from your life and from your imagination to create vignettes that shed light on your emotional conflicts. Since family relationships form the core of women's emotional lives, it is not surprising that many dreams, whether directly or indirectly, are about family. For instance, a dream may point out that you are feeling oppressed by family expectations or that you have gotten stuck in a particular role in your family or that you are experiencing emotions about a family member that you have not allowed into awareness.

To "correctly" interpret them. You are the producer of your dreams, and therefore you are the ultimate authority on their meaning. When you make a satisfying connection, when you have the "aha" experience about some aspect of a dream, you do not need to second-guess yourself. You can trust what you have learned from your dream. Yes, there may be other ways to interpret the dream—there almost always are. But it isn't necessary to understand every element in a dream to let it be useful.

A dream dialog is one way to uncover the meaning of a dream. Think of the dream as a picture of your emotional state. Everything in the dream can be taken as a symbol for some part of you, yes, even the monster chasing you. Sometimes even background elements provide rich insights.

Suppose I have just had a dream, which has in it, among other things, a large house. I could dismiss this image as trivial or I could explore it by letting myself *become* the house. As the house, I might say, *"I am a big rambling house. I'm old and need paint. I've been here a long time. Many people have lived in me, but they've moved away."* Perhaps as I let the house speak, I feel sad, and I become aware of the hidden, emotional dimension of my dream. Staying with my sadness, I may recognize how well the house represents my emotional state of the moment and I truly "own" this aspect of myself. Yes, the house is me, and it is telling me something important about my emotional state and my family relationships at present.

A dream provides a snap shot of the dreamer's emotional life at the present moment but the images have roots in the past as well. As I continue my dialog with the house by asking questions such as *"Why are you in my dream? What is your purpose?"* I will experience memories and associations that illuminate the history and meaning of the house symbol for me. All of this provides rich material for writing about family.

I may choose to use the house as a symbol in a story or poem. Or my dream about the house may reflect perfectly what I want to say and so I insert the entire dream, with or without additional comments, directly into my writing. Or I may use the insights I have gained from my dream dialog to inform other writing I may do about family.

Sometimes a mysterious dream character turns out, after reflection, to be a family member after all, only in disguise. You may have a feeling the character is familiar but you don't recognize him or her. Or the character may be an amalgam of different people. As you dialog with the character you become aware that the feelings you have toward the character resemble those you have toward a family member. Then you realize the way the character is portrayed in the dream is telling you something about your feelings about this family member. Perhaps the dream reminds you of a long standing issue or conflict that has been activated by current family events. You may chose to use this expanded understanding in your writing by using the dream imagery directly or by incorporating your insights in some other way.

Our unconscious mind is vast and full of surprises. There is no end to the characters and situations that our dreaming minds can invent. Of all the figures that appear in our dreams, those that frighten and repel us—the monsters, the crazy people, the robbers—often are the most useful. These are the characters we use to portray qualities we don't want to recognize in ourselves. The great psychologist, Carl Jung, called them "shadow figures."

Shadow figures may represent laziness, neediness, selfishness, craziness—or any quality which we judge despicable or undesirable. Our families have taught us which qualities we, as women, should particularly shun, and so we have attempted to suppress them. Of course it is impossible to rid ourselves of these qualities completely. They merely go underground and come out in dreams or other expressions.

Every human trait has a place and a value. They are needed parts of a whole. "Laziness" balances a tendency to over work; "selfishness" balances giving too much to others and not enough to self. Accepting a shadow figure that represents selfishness could be of value to many women in re-integrating this necessary quality into their lives. Get to know the shadow figures in your dreams. Ask them questions, e.g., *"Who are you, and what are you doing in my dream?"* You may be surprised at the answers.

Every family teaches different lessons about which qualities are desirable, which are tolerated, and which are despised. Most often, the qualities in each list differ for women and men. Studying your dreams, especially your shadow figures, will deepen your insights into your family's culture. If you can develop a non-judgmental attitude toward the shadow figures in your dreams, you will be stepping outside your family's emotional culture. This will increase your flexibility in writing about a greater range of human traits. You will also gain a new perspective that will help in writing about your own family.

Part V

Exploring Family in a Variety of Genres

30. Are Blogs for Real Writers? Write on Family Online, and Virtually Boost Your Career

Jen Lee

In December 2007, Technorati reported over 112 million blogs worldwide, written by individuals, companies, corporations, and media organizations. Blogging is a recent addition to the lexicon and now a household word. Jorn Barger coined the term "web log" in 1997 to describe a form that had slowly evolved from online diaries (which emerged in 1994), and shortly after, Peter Merholz shortened the term to "blog". Blogs exploded in popularity, flooding the Internet with expertise, mundane descriptions of everyday life, and everything in between. Many bloggers do not consider themselves "writers", so the most common questions serious writers have about blogging are: why should I write a blog, and how can blogging help my career? Here are the most compelling reasons to include a blog in your body of work on family.

Why should I write a blog on family?

1. Audience: The blogosphere hosts a vast readership interested in family. Working mothers, stay-at-home mothers, women whose challenges with family are exotic or mundane search the internet for voices that will encourage, inspire and inform them. Most people now use Internet search engines before visiting a library or bookstore—search engines like Google and Yahoo are the go-to source for information and resources. Creating and writing a blog is one way to ensure that when readers do a keyword search in your area, they are more likely to find your name. Add your voice to the global conversation, and find out below how to connect your new audience to your other writing projects.

2. Immediacy: Did your child just say something hilarious or profound? Did you gather humorous or tragic stories at your family holiday? The immediacy of your blog gives you a place to capture and share family moments and insights while they're fresh. Immediacy has something else to offer: balance. Many writing projects are long-term processes, and traditional publication can involve long periods of waiting. Blogging balances this with immediate gratification as you write a piece, hit "publish", and receive responses from your readers right away.

How can blogging help my career?

1. Grow your readership: a little, or a lot. Blogging is a powerful way to grow your readership—online and in traditional media. Blog readers usually find new sites and posts through search engines or referral links from other sites. Many readers use RSS (Really Simple Syndication) feeds to subscribe to daily updates of their favorite blogs.

Increasingly, editors are looking to blogs to find talented voices and compelling material, and pitching ideas for books and magazine articles. Many bloggers turned their popular blogs into book deals, like Julie Powell, the best-selling author of *Julie and Julia: My Year of Cooking Dangerously*, or Kelly Rae Roberts, mixed media artist and author of *Taking Flight: Inspiration and Techniques for Giving Your Creative Spirit Wings*. A craft acquisitions editor for North Light Books discovered Robert's blog (which chronicles her process and projects as a mixed-media artist), followed it and began a dialogue with Roberts about writing a book, published August 2008. Blogging can also create magazine opportunities. For example, *Good Housekeeping Magazine* has a monthly page that features a blog post about family that is written by a blogger, not a staff writer.

2. Network: Through blogging, you can build an online community of writers and artists whose work inspires you, or whose expertise aids you in your writing process. When you publish projects in traditional media, the same community can help you spread the word. Many writers participate in Blog Tours, in which other bloggers promote the author and her new release to their own audiences. Also, many writers and editors have blogs offering insights into their industries, like *Teen Writers Bloc*, a blog about writing and publishing literature for children and teens.

3. Self-Promote: A blog can function as an online resume. Karen Maezen Miller, author of *Momma Zen: Walking the Crooked Path of Motherhood*, has designed her blog, Cheerio Road, to showcase the books in which her writing appears and to feature samples of her most compelling writing. A well-designed blog can supplement other submissions or publications of your work.

Blogging about family has an important role to play in your body of writing on family. Writing on family finds a vast audience in the blogosphere, where readers use search engines as a primary resource and editors look for new talent. Capture and share family moments and insights as they unfold, and balance the long waiting of other writing projects with the immediate gratification of posting pieces instantly.

In addition to benefitting your writing, adding a blog to your writing on family can give your career a virtual boost. Grow your readership with an online audience, or use blogging to transition into magazine or book audiences. Network with other writers or members of your publishing niche. Use your online presentation as a showcase for writing samples that communicates to the world (and potential publishers) who you are and the contribution your voice makes.

Recommended Websites for Women Writing on Family:
- *Cheerio Road: The Blog of Author Karen Maezen Miller* karenmaezenmiller.com/blog
- *Literary Mama: A Literary Magazine for the Maternally Inclined* www.literarymama.com
- *Mother Talk: When Mothers Talk, Great Things Happen-* mother-talk.com

- *The Writers' Group:* Four women share how they encourage, give feedback, and offer critique as they create their unique literary lives. writersgroupblog. blogspot.com
- *Mamazine.com: A Feminist Publication for Mamas and People Who Love Them* mamazine.com
- *Wow! Women On Writing: An Ezine Promoting the Communication Between Women Writers, Authors, Editors, Agents, Publishers and Readers* wow-womenonwriting. com
- *Mamaphonic* mamaphonic.com
- *Motherhood and Words* motherhoodandwords.com
- *Teen Writers Bloc* teenwritersbloc.com

31. The Blogging Recipe: Instructions and Ingredients for Writing on Family Online

Jen Lee

The Chocolate Room is a chocolate, coffee and wine bar in Brooklyn, and home to a chocolate layer cake that's been voted one of the top ten desserts in New York City. The Chocolate Room's layer cake is perfection; it is a marvel. You cannot eat it without wondering: what's their secret? The right ingredients and proper execution are always a recipe for success. When adding a blog to your body of writing on family, you may wonder: what's the secret? Here is a recipe for success.

Ingredients:

access to a computer and the Internet (libraries are great if home or work aren't options)

readership

quality content

privacy

Step One: Create a web site. One option is to register a domain name (URL address) with your name in it (yourname. com, or something similar) on a site like joker.com. This is affordable (usually under $20 for an annual subscription), and you can point it to any blog location, allowing you to switch blog-hosting sites without changing your web site address. Keeping one address is the easiest way for people to find you over time.

Another option is to register a free blog through a site like wordpress.com, blogger.com, or blogspot.com. Putting your name in the URL address will increase the ability of search engines to find you. If you register at one of the above sites, your web address will look something like this: your-name.wordpress.com. The initial set up takes a little time, but is simple with predesigned themes and user-friendly customization. Most themes have a place for you to write "About Me". A small photo here is ideal, but a succinct bio is a must. Don't just list your credits, but also give a broader sense of who you are. As a writer on family, describe your current experience of family, and mention your other writing projects and interests. Be light and engaging without being unprofessional.

Step Two: Write, write, write. Three or more new posts a week will keep readers checking your site daily. The more familiar you get with using blogging software and writing online, the faster you will write and publish each post. Don't overthink your writing. Your drafts aren't public, so write in a stream-of-consciousness style at first if that helps you flush out your ideas, then after you save, go back and tidy up. Make sure there's a point—what are your readers getting out of this entry?

Increase traffic to your blog by adding hyperlinks to any person, place or thing which has its own website, and Technorati Tags (for example, *sibling rivalry* or *aging parents*) at the bottom of each post. This helps readers find your entry through keyword searches. Be strategic. Think about what keyword searches will connect your ideal reader to your other writing projects, and blog about those topics. If a news item or study comes out in your area (such as, *Birth Order Linked to College Success*), then post about it. Over time, this practice will establish you as a voice of interest in your area.

Step Three: Spread the word. Send an e-mail invitation to your online contacts (where appropriate) to visit your site. Linking to other blogger's sites and commenting on their posts (including a link back to your own site) will let them know you've joined the online conversation. They will often check out your blog, as will their readers.

A word of caution here. It can be enticing once you've begun to spend more time than you intended looking for or reading other people's sites. Don't fall into this time-waster. Let people you are interested in introduce you to each other. If you find a blog you enjoy, it will likely mention and link to others in your sphere of interest. Most bloggers who write well and write prolifically cite not reading many blogs themselves as a common secret ingredient.

As your readership grows, you may want to add something else for exposure, like reviewing books for a site like mother-talk.com. Mother Talk links to the bloggers reviewing their selections, introducing them to a broader audience.

Step Four: Final Ingredients. It's time for a brief conversation about privacy, content and quality. To safeguard your privacy on your blog, be vague about where you live. Do not name your street, your children's schools, or your employer. Only post information and photos of your family that you're comfortable entering into public domain.

Your site does not need to be formal, but it should be professional. The content should be appropriate for viewing by potential publishers. Keep overly personal anecdotes offline, between yourself and your friends. Give the same consideration to the quality of your writing. A distinguishing difference between Writer Bloggers and the rest are that writers self-edit to correct spelling and grammar, and make sure their tenses are consistent and correct.

Maximize the benefits a blog can bring to your body of work on family and to your career by following these steps. Create a web site that will help popular search engines find your name, then fill it with content that establishes you as voice of interest in your area and connects readers to your other writing projects. Invite your current contacts to your new blog, and use your blog to create new contacts and readers. Take simple measures to safeguard your privacy, and pay close attention to the quality of the content you post.

These steps and ingredients will help readers and potential publishers discover your voice and your work. Savor the delicious opportunities that emerge.

32. Creating the Fictional Family: No Character Is an Island

Yelizaveta P. Renfro

Every character comes from somewhere. Creating a family history and historical setting for your protagonists can add great depth to a piece of writing as well as make the writing process go more smoothly. This is particularly true of novel-length works that involve many characters and generations, but even short stories can benefit from the following exercises.

Picture Your Characters

Having a physical picture of your characters can help you get to know them. Find a photo or a painting of the family you are writing about. Some antique stores sell old family photos and postcards. If you are writing a historical piece, you can find images of real people who lived in the 1920s, 1930s, etc. Even if you are working on a contemporary story, these dated photos can offer you glimpses into your characters' forbears. Or look through magazines or newspapers or search online for contemporary photos or paintings. Once you have your picture, put it at your side and write everything you observe in the image; this description may well become part of your finished work. Then, begin to imagine what came before the picture was taken—and what will happen after the shutter snaps and the people get up and move on with their lives.

Visit Your Characters at Home

Families often have very specific places that are important to them: the family home, the family farm, a vacation house, a wilderness area, a family business, a neighborhood, etc. A well-drawn setting often reveals a great deal about your characters. Spend some time visiting (in your mind) the places that are important to your characters, and write down everything that you know about these places. These descriptions may work their way into your piece. Also, by being able to picture clearly the spaces in which your characters move about and live their lives, you will have an easier time envisioning scenes and selecting details as you write.

Build a Family Tree

Draw your family tree on a piece of paper. Include your protagonist's siblings, spouse, children, and parents, but also put down aunts and uncles, grandparents, great grandparents, etc. Write down full names and years of birth, marriage, and death. If some part of your character's lineage is unknown, leave it blank. Even a largely blank family tree can inform your writing; not knowing where you came from or who your ancestors are can be as significant as being able to trace your family history back to the Mayflower. You might think that Great Aunt Beatrice has nothing to do with your story; put her down anyway. The more you know, the richer your writing will be. Keep your family tree at hand while you write. Being able to see, at a glance, the year that your protagonist's parents got married can be very helpful. And a family tree can help you to avoid continuity errors. If Grandpa was born in 1926 in chapter 1, the family tree can help you make sure that he's the right age in chapter 7.

Bury Your Characters

Imagine that your fictional family has purchased a cemetery plot that will hold twelve: two rows of six, one above the other. Draw out the plot on a piece of paper and think about who will be buried where. Who is already buried there? For whom are the other spaces reserved? Who will be next to whom? Who gets the space under the oak? Who will not be buried in the family plot? Why? Think about the family politics underlying these choices. What kinds of markers and monuments will the family choose to mark the individual graves? Visiting a real cemetery can give you ideas. Imagine a scene taking place at the cemetery. Who is visiting the plot? Why? What does he or she do at the cemetery?

Summarize Your Character's Life

Imagine that one of your characters has just died. Besides deciding how and where the character will be buried, think also about how the life will be memorialized. Will there be a funeral service? What will be said? Who will say it? How will those remaining summarize the life? What kind of meaning will be found in the deceased's life? What has he left undone? A newspaper obituary is another type of summation of life. Try writing your character's obituary. What were his accomplishments? Who are his survivors? This exercise will allow you to see your character's life as a whole and to explore the impact that it has on family members.

Put Your Characters in the World

Do some research on the historical periods in which your characters live. Make note of world events and major headlines. Even people who are mainly concerned with their own lives live within the context of history. Learn about the politics, wars, economics, technology, and fashion trends of the period. Integrate these into your writing. Great Aunt Beatrice may have churned her own butter wearing a gingham apron and written letters by hand, but your protagonist might shop for organic butter in her Birkenstocks while chatting on her cell phone. Every accurate historical detail that you present adds verisimilitude to your work.

Fit All the Pieces Together

Remember that every character—even long-forgotten Great Aunt Beatrice—is the protagonist of her own life story. If you write with the belief that there is no such thing as a two-dimensional character, you will find your writing taking you in unexpected directions. You might discover that Great Aunt Beatrice actually does have an important story to tell. Doing exercises that bring to light generations of a family—not just your protagonist—will allow you to uncover some of these latent stories. If some pieces of the family tree aren't fitting for your story, remember that you can always go back and change dates or erase and add family members. Your family history is not set in stone; think of it as a guide but not a rulebook.

Creating an extended family history embedded within a specific historical milieu provides a strong foundation for fiction. Although everything generated in these exercises won't end up in the final draft, the fact that each of the characters has a specific history will make your writing more vibrant. Even works that focus on just one or two characters can benefit from this approach; every character, after all, comes from a specific time and place. To paraphrase John Donne, no man—or character—is an island.

33. From Memoir to Fiction

Dahlma Llanos-Figueroa

I'd run all the way from school so I could have my three hours of watching TV before my parents got home from work. I let the door slam behind me but stopped short as I stared at the floor. The man lay face down, still, a puddle of blood congealing around his head. When I got back to breathing again, I inched my way down the wall, making sure the blood didn't touch my new patent leather shoes. I ran all the way up to our fifth floor apartment and dialed my mother's number at work. As soon as she came to the phone, I yelled, *Mom, there's a dead guy in the hall downstairs.* The body was gone by the time I went to school the next day but our alcoholic super didn't wipe up the blood for three days. By the end of the week, the decision was made. I was sent to live with my grandparents in Puerto Rico until my parents finish saving enough money to put a down payment on a house and move us out of that neighborhood.

The change from urban New York City to rural Puerto Rico was jarring and difficult. But those two years of living with my grandparents and the many visits that followed over the years became the catalyst for my eventual career as a novelist and the basis for my first novel *Daughters of the Stone* (St. Martins, 2009).

Many writers mine their lives for the substance of their work. In fact, I would venture to say that all novelists begin their careers with their experiences of home and family. Pat Conroy is certainly one of them. In his recent book, *My Reading Life*, he acknowledges the role of family storytelling in his development as one of our most successful contemporary writers. "My childhood provided both the structure and details…I still hear my mother's voice, lovely beneath soft lamplight, whenever I sit down with a pen in my hand." Conroy is perhaps one of the most honest writers I have read regarding this issue. "All writers are both devotees and prisoners of their childhoods, and the images that accrued during those early days.... My mother's voice and my father's fists are the two bookends of my childhood, and they form the basis of my art."

The question was put to me recently during a book club discussion of my novel. *How exactly do you go from memoir, or family stories, to fiction?* I have been asked many questions in talks following my readings, but never quite that one. For me, the process was so organic, natural, that I had never really broken it down into discreet steps. But once asked, I thought about that question for weeks.

It began, of course, with story. For if there is no story there is no book. The greatest compliment I can be given is to be called a good storyteller. Technical excellence without story is an empty exercise and doesn't impress me in the least unless it is in the service of story.

So I began with story.

Those years in Puerto Rico taught me a great deal about storytelling and about listening. As a child I wasn't allowed to participate, but in the evenings I sat with the women on the porch and listened as they did their handwork, drank strong coffee and told their stories. As in many rural societies around the world, and especially in the years before televisions were ubiquitous objects in every home, storytelling was entertainment, history, family lore, and social sharing. This was especially true among the rural women in my culture. I sat back quietly and listened to every tale. This also gave me excellent training in observation, a necessity for every writer. It wasn't only *what* they said but *how* they said it.

As a child I was a sponge, absorbing everything indiscriminately. But as I grew older, during my visits, I would still sit in the dark listening, noting that much of what the women spoke about was a quickly disappearing world, a valuable world that our children would never know. I began writing down their tales and so began my journey as a storyteller.

When I first started writing, I let it be known that I was writing family stories. And I got a plethora of tales from everyone. No one I included was ever satisfied. If three people told of the same incident, I got seven different versions. So no one was ever pleased with my version of the story. If I omitted anyone, that would be a problem as well. Once my mother asked me if she was so unimportant in my life that I wouldn't include her in my tales. It became obvious that I couldn't win. So very quickly I went from memoirist to novelist out of a sense of shear self-preservation. Now the question was, how to go from family stories to the universal truths of a literary novel. How to apply narrative techniques to nonfiction? Which techniques to employ? How much to keep of the true experience and how much to change in the service of narrative flow?

I. My journey

Here are some of my givens for *Daughters of the Stone*. I decided the story would:

1. Cover about 150 years in the lives of an Afro-Puerto Rican family
2. Move from West Africa to Puerto Rico to the United States
3. Create the novel with a cyclical structure
4. Use traditional African religion as a connector between generations
5. Use elements of magic realism in the narrative
6. Use lyrical language
7. Employ the stone, moon and water as major symbols

Later on, I would have to make some modifications based on artistic needs and editorial suggestions.

8. Cut the manuscript by 250 pages
9. Follow the journey of the stone, focus on the lives of the women in the family and remove all extraneous information
10. Change the manifestation of African religion as characters move into urban America
11. Adjust the language as the story moves into modern times
12. Change some of the character names (similar names are too confusing for readers)
13. Eliminate peripheral characters making sure to keep the focus on the main characters in the story

Once my novel came out, I worried about what my family might think of the changes I made in our stories. I felt secure in that I had been true to my vision. It was no longer a story about my family and friends but a more universal story of everyone's family. It was a story of mothers and daughters who struggle with their love and resentment of each other. It was a story of women who are afraid of losing the good of the past for the unknown of the future. It was a story of the fear of loss of tradition. It was a story of immigrants trying to survive in their new home but who emotionally still live in their native land. It was a story of how we change and how we stay the same. I was confident that I had smoothed out all the seams and that the novel was something new and totally different from my memoir pieces of years ago. Nonetheless, I knew that each family member would be searching for familiar portraits.

No matter how much I explained that this was fiction, my family never let go of the idea that this was somehow their story. So my cousin Tito, an otherwise very sensible man, said Ok it's fiction. And then he kept a list of characters on hand as he read the book. And he jotted down next to each character's name, the name of the person in our family who he thought it was modeled after.

Another member of the family didn't recognize the portrait of her relative and turned to me and said, "I loved the book, especially the character Zenobia, who was such a bitch. How could you draw her so realistically?" I said nothing. Sometimes you just have to know when to keep your mouth shut.

And after all, maybe they are right. If this novel does reach the level of universal story, then it really *is* their story, as well as everyone else's. And in the end, isn't that what any author aspires to write—Everyman's story?

II. Suggestions for Mapping Your Own Journey

1. Collect stories, yours or someone else's. Remember that your aim is fiction. You may have to change names, setting, motivation, etc. Failing to do so may cost you in many ways—losing family, friends, ending up in court, etc. After trying to please family in my memoir pieces, I felt that writing fiction was incredibly liberating. I could make up whatever I wanted in the service of story and answer to no one but my own creative imagination.

2. Be fair. If you are planning to use someone else's story, make sure they understand what you are doing. If you are using a tale from a culture other than your own, check with people of that culture to make sure you aren't being offensive or insensitive. You can't please everyone but you don't want to offend your readers. Who knows, you might learn something about yourself in the process.

3. Establish your givens. If you chose to write fiction what are the indispensable aspects of your story? Your story must be grounded in some absolutes, at least when you begin. (You may find that these might need readjusting as you go along, but you must have some specifics to begin with.) These may include setting, themes, voice, language, time span, tone, etc. Once you decide on one of these, the others may take shape. For instance, if you

are writing about 19th century West Virginia, that should inform the language of your story.

4. Research. Double-check everything you can. Memories are one thing. Narrative is another. As the authorial voice, you must be a reliable storyteller so if you aren't sure of a given detail, check it out. One detail out of place can pull the reader out of the world you've worked so hard to create. Research can be fun. I introduced my husband to a whole new world when we grabbed cameras and went into remote areas of Puerto Rico to shoot old houses. People were incredibly generous when they found out what we were doing and often contributed to our growing stock of unsolicited stories.

5. Make it seamless. Toni Morrison writes about the need to make a story seamless. If the reader sees the seams, the world you are creating begins to fall apart. This is especially difficult when you are asked to make substantial cuts in your work. How do you cut 200 pages and not affect the story? I look at the finished work as a puzzle. It's difficult to take any one piece out without destroying the whole. But you may have to do just that. Now that's painful. It may be necessary but never fun.

6. Be prepared to let go of some details you may love in the service of the piece as a whole. That story of the cute baby may have to go. Uncle Joe's funeral may have to go. (Save these for another book.) I had to let go of whole chapters, characters and wonderful imagery. I had to learn to be ruthless for the sake of the book as a whole.

7. Be honest to your work. No story can exist without conflicts, just as no life can exist without conflicts or mistakes. No matter how perfect you think your family might be, there is no such thing as perfection, especially in modern fiction. Sometimes exploring the most painful aspects of your personal stories

may be vital to your fiction. No one wants to read about pure perfection. Readers can smell dishonest a mile away (forgive the cliché)

8. Be prepared to write many, many drafts.

9. Consider keeping your work to yourself. Sometimes getting too much feedback from loved ones can derail what you are trying to do. Share your work with professionals who have a more objective view of the narrative and an understanding of your process. There will be time enough for feedback after the publication.

34. Poetry Makes An Honest Woman of You

Rosemary Moeller

My husband takes pride in knowing that when I write about him I'm more likely to get published. Of course he doesn't read my poetry, just likes being the focus of another part of my life. He is my muse, like it or not, intrinsically woven into all my words and my reality.

Writers are cautioned to write about what they know best, yet my family confuses and confounds me regularly. I am often surprised by their strangeness and unfamiliarity. Writing about them is my way of holding on to the mystery of bonded relationships. Like it or not we're in this together. So I write about what I'm learning.

Images from moments of unexpected confusion are a fertile starting place. Confusion's rampant where there are sons and daughters, parents and spouses. This doesn't mean anything will suddenly become clear, just that there will be a pause in the attack of contrary emotions while sorting through the knots in memories like the necklace chains in a jewelry drawer. There are parents to take care of, listen to and ignore. There are grown children going through crises that are reruns of our own, but don't want to hear the platitudes of wisdom we learned. We have young ones struggling with truths that we forgot existed in our adolescences, yet now resurface like algae in August. These times of confusion, uncertainty about who is feeling the new emotion and who is remembering what should have been forgotten, are poetic moments waiting to be balanced on metaphors so all doesn't tumble into a hole of self-denial. I love these moments. I believe in chaos as unorganized beauty. This is the time to reflect on the blurred image before us, knowing the blur is from time passing so quickly.

A wealth of writing comes from frustration, repeated frustrations that can never be celebrated as final because no one knows the last time the door will be left open for the flies to come in. And there are frustrations that are not spoken, ever. The "I told you so's" that are all swallowed, washed down with a beer. The dates and times of lies are not challenged because it's better to appear dumb to grown children than admit you knew all about their escapades and intricate plans. But, remarkably, they don't see themselves in my narratives, don't recognize their idiosyncrasies in my characters. A simple, "It's fiction. Get over it," explains research into murder scenarios to everyone's satisfaction.

One of my favorite sources of inspiration for family writing involves acts of kindness that I never really did but wanted to. When written about as if it happened, it eventually changes from myth to memory. I create effortless goodness. One of the graces of writing is that one can "do over" what happened, because in the family, no two memories are the same anyway. The printed story becomes the real one. It's the nature of writing. We who write become the storytellers, those who remember otherwise become the spoiled sports.

My sappy writings are in praise of good deeds and better intentions. I like them. As writers, feeling good about ourselves doesn't pop up too often. It is a job of constant self-criticism and evaluation on a vicious grade curve. So those moments of pure appreciation for someone doing something special, that time of reflection when we can Photoshop the scenes in our minds and remove the imperfections of family members is a blessing. I like to feel good once in a while. Not too often, because it dulls the sarcasm fairy's nails. It adds to the myth that we are all one happy family, which is why holidays exist, and why we rush back to numbing quotidian schedules as soon as we can after holidays to sigh in relief and breathe the air of honesty again. But once in a while a few words of praise are nice. My children actually eat it up.

Speaking of holidays, there are gifts. Gifts from one's own children are especially interesting. There is often the desire to ask, "Is this how you see me, using this, wearing this, dusting this, hand-washing this?" As mothers we know we'll never ask until we're so demented by age it won't matter if we do. But for now, it's a topic to be explored in lyric or polemic verse. Writing is the most personal way to expose oneself there is. It takes an exhibitionist to dangle these dark secrets in front of unknown editors, hoping for some affirmation that we're not the only one with nipples that look like this. In our extremely materialistic society we have numerous opportunities to give thanks a black eye or two, and deservedly so.

There is the challenge of lists. Dave's Top Ten is a perennial favorite for a reason. Every now and again some people list their pallbearers, rewrite their obits, decide which child they would save if only one could be saved, and most don't eat the pieces of paper after they're ripped up but some do. But there are lists of priorities and that kyrielle of valuables that means nothing to our survivors. It's all worth the paper it's written on because it is a flash of the moment. Whenever we think about eternal things we wind up being caught in the now. And that is one of the best places to be for writing about family. Capturing those stupid, petty, small-minded moments makes for great irony.

Photo albums are the visual record of where light hits the surface, bounces or bends, and we see what we thought we remembered. Narratives and lyrics are the subsurface of meaningful people and events. Our poems are the real feelings from the multiple perspectives of every woman who is mother, aunt, wife, daughter and lots of other Eves, all folded neatly into one tissue box of life-experiences, waiting to be sneezed at, cried on or used to wipe away the messes of life.

35. Writing Poems About Grandparents

Karen Coody Cooper

Some of the tightest human bonds involve grandparents, the people who most adore and spoil us. Youthful emotional memories of grandparents are sometimes more accessible to a writer than esoteric explorations of other topics. And if you never experienced the nostalgic form of fond relationship with a grandparent, you might have some other sorts of feelings worth exploring in poetry or stories.

Writing about grandparents can serve as simple, yet productive, exercises. Think of an activity or event that strongly linked you to a grandparent. What is the central emotion or outcome you experienced during that event? What message or theme would you like to explore? See the setting, if possible. Think of ancillary actions or items and consider whether they can fold into the story, or frame it as beginning and ending points.

Begin writing. Find a rhythm that suits your message; it may be soothing, energetic, choppy, or a classic form. Use poetic embellishments such as alliteration or rhyming. To create a past setting, use words as they were spoken in that place and time. But don't overwork or overwrite. After I capture the thought and mood, I begin pruning. Remove sucker roots and lop off limbs sprouting in the wrong places, create a poem with tight sparseness, yet keep, when possible, the most beautiful lines you wrote (or save such lines for use in another poem). The poem should start with a thread, and the thread should run true to the end. If a stanza doesn't work with the rest, it should be deleted or reworked.

The time I spent with my grandparents on their small Oklahoma farm presents me with intense emotional memories.

Those memories often leap forth, full-fledged and brightly hued. Since I savor enjoyment from childhood pleasures, I am eager to capture such moments in written form. By writing about grandparents we are assured the enjoyment of them will be preserved.

The Carapace

I tasted the melon and the parched face
with the eyes of summers I can never see
came to me in clarity.
The porch supported the two of us again,
the lilac bloomed,
the portulaca waved from its black kettle.

All the scents and sights returned and I was
there again as if I had never left—
a taste, a smell, a word, a touch—
returns the comforting mantle
and I am carapaced in love long past—
forever enduring. (Fine Arts Press 1982)

I wrote this piece as a young bride, removed 1500 miles from my grandparents. The scent of a fragrant melon in my kitchen reminded me of the fresh melons my grandparents had grown, and of the porch where summer foods were enjoyed. Homesick, I relished the memory of sharing a melon with my grandmother. As memories flooded into my head, I enjoyed the tantalizing images. I also remembered the meadow behind my grandparents' home where hundreds of painted box turtles erupted each spring. With the thought of terrapins in my mind, the word carapace sprang to use, and the poem took shape.

However, not all memories are purely sweet. Some can be jarring, and haunt us with a sadness we'd rather forget. When writing about something bothersome, I hope to exercise control over it, taming it, and defuse it. By linking my beloved grandmother to a troubled scene, I am able to say life has both good and bad components.

Grandma's Quilt

The paisley piece
Warmed grandma's bent back
The summer day we bought the birdseed
For the infant sparrow hatched
by the TV's warm tubes.

That striped patch
Brightened a nursery
In a room with a mirror near the floor
Where baby brother and I huddled
While our parents' voices raged and tore.
They held our security in their anger.

The green plaid
Protected from pinches
On a St. Patrick's Day playground
A girl too shy to chase and pinch the ones
who had forgotten.

Grandma's quilt
With a bit of mama's Sunday dress—
Patchwork pieces of my life.
The sparrow died.

The poem took shape while examining a quilt my grandmother had made for me as a wedding gift. Fabric swatches from my mother's sewing projects especially prompted memories. Surprisingly, my mood made me recall sad moments. It seemed fitting to include a recollection of a hatchling sparrow's death in the poem.

As a new poet, I submitted these early pieces unwittingly to vanity anthologies, the makers of which gain income by selling thick volumes to several hundred submitting authors. The collections include good works mixed in with poor ones. At the time, I didn't have the funds to buy any of the copies. Nevertheless, inspired by being published, I kept writing.

By 1985, I found discerning local outlets for my work. If they didn't pay, at least they gave me free copies of the issues using my poems, and they were more selective of what they published. A memory of my grandfather bringing home an opossum, carrying it by its tail while it hung without movement, was often on my mind. The memory of the possum coming to life so excited me that I have taken to viewing opossums as a metaphor for life: when threatened, roll over, keep a low profile, take action later.

Grandpa

Grandpa, in baggy overalls
with pouches like the marsupial,
cackled and clucked us to him –
little chicks of grandchildren
streaming to the wings
of the wise old chanticleer.
He held a critter at arm's length
and pointed our eyes to it,
and laid it lifeless upon the
dry, dusty ground.

'You've killed it,' I pouted. 'Killed it.'
'Naw," he crowed, laughing
(and how could he, I thought).
Then he jabbed the unkempt
mass of scraggly fur.
Suddenly teeth snapped the air,
little legs did a whirlwind dance,
the cluster of cousins fell over one another
in backward jumps.
Then over their shoulders they saw
that all was peace again
as the possum curled into another embryo pose.

And I stood there loving the resurrected animal.
Loving it for its ploy.

Loving it for its patience.
Loving it for its audacity.
Loving it for its very being.
Loved it so much I became it.

It finally wandered off
after the cousins drifted away, still themselves.
But, I was transformed.
I went with it to the trees.
It went with me to school.

Poetry can be found in incomplete relationships as well.
Attending the funeral of an estranged grandparent provides an
opportunity to tap into feelings in search of lessons.

Grandfather R

We sat in the car
Watching the black garbed
Mill around.

It was
Hot –
Too hot to enter into
The uncooled sanctuary.
Father swallowed.
Wishing no one had called.
Mother, caught in this web
Like I,
Tried to understand.

When all had entered
We went
And sat against the back wall
But when it was over
She saw us there
And made her way to us

And said how glad she was
To see that we had come.
We cried (at least
Mother and I did)
And I thought –
This is the
Wife of my grandfather
A man I didn't know.
And who is he,
That young boy,
To me?
Son of my grandfather
But not of my grandmother.
Who is he
And who will love him now
Except this
Tired Woman?

In 2005, an editor contacted me hoping I could provide an essay or poem about women and food for an anthology. I wasn't sure I had anything to say since I've never enjoyed cooking, a faulty trait passed on from my mother. And, truthfully, my maternal grandmother prepared plain, simple food. I never thought about whether she enjoyed cooking, or not. Her generation didn't have the opportunity to seek what they enjoyed. Their days had been full of what had to be done. But soon I was remembering the beautiful preserves Grandma produced. If she didn't enjoy making them, she surely enjoyed having achieved the "putting up" of the farm's bounty. As a child I loved the sweet treasures she created. Grandma again gave me a poem, and the editor was pleased.

Sand Plum Jelly

The women call an alarm.
"Car's coming?"
Shirttails fly to our faces

Arming us against the rooster-tail of dust.
The sand plums thrive on the shoulders
        of backwoods dirt roads.

The squat, frail sand plum trees,
Confronted by willowy aunts and uncles,
Yield tart golden orbs plunked into tin pails.

The jars of sand plum jelly,
        lined on storage shelves,
        look like a beekeepers' product
            tinged with pale rouge and glints of sun.

The jelly sparkles like jewels.
Amber, topaz, sunset and salmon colors.
Grandma knew each batch by its hue
"This was when Euless and his kids helped."
"The rosy ones are when you were here."
"The pale is from the drought."
The jelly was both bounty and art.

It recorded history, you see,
Events beyond the kitchen's reach,
Stacked in the root cellar,
In the memories of fledged offspring,
The jelly was riches and thrift.
The jelly was farmhouse repast.
The jelly was my family working together.

The jelly was summer and childhood.
The jelly was Grandma
            and everything I treasured.
The jelly was beautiful.
Light gently played through each jar
And cast a pink-gold aura
            throughout the tiny house
Where my strongest memories of women
        and love began.

There are no sand plums where I live.
But memory endures.

If you become proficient in capturing the value of a grandparent, you might be asked to write about someone else's grandparent. The next poem was written about a man I had never met, but having heard him so reverently described by his grandson (a grandfather at the time), I knew I could focus on the strong link between the two.

As the Prow Cuts Through Water

He shaped the steamed wood
 Into pieces for a vessel
That would carry them back
 To familiar headwaters.
He shaped the young boy
 Into a vessel
Who would move forward through
 The arduous currents of time.
There is never silence in the woods,
 The grandfather said,
 For even silence is a sound.
You're never alone outside, he said,
 There are always ears listening
 And you may as well learn to talk to them.

He made the child bathe in winter streams
 Which taught the boy to curse
But such a grandfather as walks on the surface
 Of snow is a tangible savior
 (and fine craftsman of snowshoes).
While weather-hardened hands
 Shaved gunwales to hard satin
And split slats to their thinnest possibility,
 The young boy watched
And patterned himself in

The image of his grandfather.
As the prow cuts through water,
    Ripples become
    The journey's record of memory
And while following those ahead of you,
    You make your own ripples.
    And yours join theirs.

In a canoe you face forward
    Toward the things you follow.
When the boy became a grandparent
He still followed the Grandfather before him.

While we know there are evil grandparents, we also know how dear the grandparent/grandchild relationship can be. Relieved of the duty to provide daily discipline and care, grandparents can enjoy the antics of grandchildren without the tension parents are likely to experience. This is the sweetest relationship people can know. It is one enjoyed around the world and throughout time, and should ever be so. May you capture the special love, and the heightened awareness that comes with that love, as you write poems about your own grandparents.

References

Cooper, Karen Coody. "As the Prow Cuts Through Water." *Gatherings: Volume XII: Transformation: En'owkin Journal of First North American Peoples*. Ed. by Ostrowidzki, Eric and Florence Belmore. Penticton, BC: Theytus Books, 2001.

Cooper, Karen Coody. "The Carapace." *Poetry of Love, Past and Present: A Treasury of Classical and Contemporary Love Poems*. Ed. by Lincoln B. Young. Kingsport, Tennessee: Fine Arts Press, 1982.

Cooper, Karen Coody. "Grandfather R." *Fireweed: A Feminist Quarterly of Writing, Politics, Art & Culture*. Issue 2, Winter 1986. Toronto: Fireweed Inc.

Cooper, Karen Coody. "Grandma's Quilt." *College Poetry Review*: Vol. 42, No. 1. Agoura, Calif: National Poetry Press, 1979.

Cooper, Karen Coody. "Grandpa." *Rooted Like the Ash Trees: New England Indians and the Land*. Ed. by Richard G. Carlson. Naugatuck, Conn: Eagle Wing Press, 1987.

Cooper, Karen Coody. "Sand Plum Jelly." *Through the Kitchen Window*. Ed. by Arlene V. Avakian. Oxford: Berg, 2005.

Part VI

Finding Your Writing Style

36. Becoming a Parenting Advocate for Moms through Writing

Judy M. Miller

Personal experiences are often the seeds for writers' articles and essays. This is true for me. I discovered my voice and reclaimed some of myself in the process of becoming a writer. I learned that being a mom did not preclude me from being an intelligent advocate for my children and for other parents that followed in my wake. Quite the opposite. My experience as a mother provided me with insights, encouraged confidence, and taught me how to approach others. I found that I had something, actually a lot, to say and that I wanted to be heard, to educate more than one person at a time, and to engage others in thought and conversation. My challenge was how to say it so others would listen.

Upon entering the mother "club" I took on new identities. I became known as one or more of the following: the mother of each of my four children, as in "Lizzie's mom;" the mom with the multiracial family; the mom with the special needs child who patiently waited each and every time she melted down; the overly involved mom; and/or the mom who drove the custom-topped blue van (people could see me coming…).

Motherhood, transracial adoption, and special needs seized me within fluid arms, starting around my ankles and holding on tight until I was treading the emotions that rose up, surrounding me and threatening to pull me under. At first I willingly bobbed in the flood-waters of love, but later I found it hard to keep my head barely above the surface. "Me" was concealed within the identity of motherhood. "Me" felt stifled, silenced. I was at risk of drowning.

Parenting children who were adopted transracially (across race, for example I am a white mom to Asian and Hispanic children) became challenging, only because there seemed a never ending line of people who felt they needed to talk to me, similar to a reception line at a wedding. Parenting kids who didn't match was a non-issue for me. Many outside of my family, circle of friends, and adoptive parents were having a difficult time understanding how I could parent and love children that I didn't give birth to and in no way resembled me.

In a short matter of time, educating others at the spur of the moment or answering people who felt they were entitled to know about me and my family began to wear. I felt exposed and even worse; I was worried about how my emotions and responses were affecting my children. I did not want to share my kids' stories. Those were their stories. People continued to press.

Maintaining a calm temperament while dodging or addressing comments and answering questions from well- and not-so-well-meaning people, often in front of my children, became harder. I developed sensitive radar, adept at knowing when a person was going to lob one of their "zingers" at me:

"God bless you!" (Give me a break. I adopted because I wanted more children. I'm not a saint or someone special. That is the plain and simple of it. Sorry that I can't give you a better reason.)

"Are you their real mother?" (Do I look un-real?)

"Are they sisters?" (Do you seriously feel that it is all right for you to ask me that question? Well?)

"We thought about adoption but we could have *our own*." (I didn't know you could own a child. I mean, aren't they all gifts from something greater than ourselves?)

I was often met with questions and comments, like the ones above, with silence or asked, "Why do you want to know?" while I ran what I really wanted to say through my head (indicated in the above parentheses.) You see, my mother raised a "nice" girl...

I believe life's purpose is to grow. Growth develops through personal challenges, exploration, and experiences. Personal growth lays the foundation to provide service to others. But, shortly after becoming an adoptive mom, I chose to look down and inward, to not grow because I didn't know how. I didn't care what others thought. I hid, disappearing into my private world with my children.

Well, life is funny. Life threw me a curve ball and it came in the form of my daughter with special needs. I landed in a foreign country, without a user's manual. I didn't know the language or the customs. Everything was unfamiliar. The mothering plan that I used with my other kids didn't work. As I set out to learn what I could about my new destination, I had to disengage my mother autopilot, because it was ineffective in this new place. Intuition was my guide and it served me well.

I didn't know what was amiss. Words fail to describe what I felt. All I can say is that I knew something was terribly wrong and that I was lost. My daughter showed me how to parent her by demonstrating what worked to calm her and help her connect. I was a very good student, but she did not improve. I wrote down what I observed and, after being evaluated by specialist three times (and diagnosed as "normal"), it was my meticulous notes that unlocked what was going on with my daughter. My notes assisted the specialists in diagnosing and developing treatment to save her.

What can one say about that? Well, I found I had a bottomless well of what to say about parenting a child with special needs. I wrote to process my emotions and to make sense of what occurred. I wanted to share. I also wanted to extend my hand to other parents out there who felt as I had—frightened and sick with worry. I wanted to give them hope.

I stumbled upon an online class, targeted at writer mamas. The class, "Writing and Publishing the Short Stuff," taught by Christina Katz, promised to teach me how to write, assess my work and get my articles and essays to print. The class sounded perfect, so I registered. The class was just what I needed. Christina was the gentle taskmaster; a woman who was a mom and a gifted teacher. With her encouragement, I submitted the article I finished in class.

"The Dragons Rest" was published in two regional parenting magazines. The essay chronicled the journey of having my daughter diagnosed and watching her improve. Of course I was thrilled, but of more significance was how empowered I felt. Editors believed that what I had written was important enough to be published, to be shared with other parents. And they paid me for it.

As I grew in confidence, I wrote, submitted and became more published. I wrote about topics in which I had expertise—adoption, motherhood, general parenting, and raising teens—with a decidedly informative bent. I wanted others to know what it is like for parents of special needs kids and how adoptive parents and families feel. I also reached out to my own tribe, developing an online class for parents of tweens and teens who have been adopted, adding adoptive parent education, coaching, and speaking to my resume.

How do you arrive at that place where people value what you have to say? How do you develop a voice that others want to listen to? With encouragement and diligence you can become prolific in your work and use your writing voice to effectively advocate, to persuade others to take action because of what you have written. Consider these points to increase your chances of being heard.

- **Believe in yourself.** Work on building your confidence. Look at your everyday relationships and how people react to you. Pay special attention to others in your life, such as your spouse, family, friends, and colleagues. Their responses to you are indicators of how you affect them. Better yet, ask them what they think of you. Most likely you will be pleasantly surprised.

- **Give yourself permission to express yourself and to write.** Many writers worry about saying what they think or writing perfectly. Be genuine and your voice will evolve. So will your confidence. Your readers will be inspired and motivated by you when you write from your authentic center.

- **Discover why you like to write and what you like to write about.** What are you passionate about? What do you know or want to know more about? I write about adoption, parenting, and special needs. I am a passionate advocate for all three of these topics and that comes through in my writing.

- **Determine who your audience is.** Are they other moms? Moms and dads? Professionals? Your audience determines your tone and style. My audience is typically other parents, but sometimes it is adoption professionals, teachers or therapists. My vernacular changes when writing for each audience as does my formality.

- **Make sure your message is clear.** Decide what you want to say. What is the message that you wish to convey to others? What is your intent? Is your experience enough or do you need expert opinion, quotes and research to support what you advocate? Much depends on the intention of your writing, your audience's general level of knowledge of your topic, and the type of piece you are writing. Are you writing to inform? Persuade? Inspire?

- **How do you make what you write, what you have to say, memorable?** Figure out what format of writing comes easier to you, for example, the reported essay. You can write a story within your article. You can use humor or an analogy. You can present a problem, resources and solutions.

- **Write tightly.** Your reader is busy, so keep that in mind when you are writing.

- **State your point or argument and then set about supporting your position or premise with facts and expert quotes.** Are you able to challenge, support and defend a position or idea? If necessary, provide documentation, expert quotes, and results. Make recommendations and provide resources. I wrote an article about an oral sex discussion I had with my then fifteen year-old son. Although I offered my expert opinion as a mom, I included statistics and quotes from experts to give my article more credibility.

Writing has the power to heal, offer reflection, and provide introspection. Writing helped me grow and to control the floodwaters of love and identity crisis that were engulfing me. Writing has the ability to entertain, inspire others, and affect lives by introducing and defending different viewpoints. Writing has the power to motivate people into action and to temper opinion.

In the process of learning how to write so that people want to listen, I discovered my voice. By sharing my voice I inspire and encourage others to educate those they come in contact with, to embrace the children they parent and to fight for their children and themselves. My voice is the advocate for moms—of special needs children, children who have been adopted, tweens, teens, daughters, sons, and multiracial families. Moms like me. How will your writing be a means to advocate for what you believe in?

Resources for inspiration and guidance on how to write and where to submit:

- **Begin writing your own blog.** You can even keep it private if you wish. A blog is a great place to plant seeds, establish a writing rhythm and your voice.

- **Local writers' centers and organizations.** Most likely there is a writer's group near you. If not, check online for a network that can provide emotional and professional support and constructive critique.

- **Libraries are full of writing resources and support.** You also might be able to find a group of writers through your librarian or start something yourself.

- **University and colleges.** Again go online and peruse through the offerings that are locally available and fit into your schedule.

- **Consider taking an online course.** They exist. I took a number of very helpful classes through Christina Katz ~Empowering Writers christinakatz.com/

- **Consider writing for your local paper.** The pay won't be great, but you can get your feet wet.

- **Regional Parenting Publications of America** parentingpublications.org Offers resources and a list of magazines to submit to. Regional parenting publications are a great place to begin submitting.

37. Critique Groups for Women with Families

Colleen Kappeler

A good critique group can be crucial to getting a piece ready for publication or learning ways to improve your craft. As a woman with a family, there is no time to waste on mediocre feedback. It's crucial to find, or develop, a group that meets your needs as a writer with a family in the time you have available.

What to Look for in Joining a Group

Be sure there is a mix of experience in the group. If all members are beginners, this is great if you want to write for fun. But if you are looking for serious critique you want a group with at least one highly experienced writer so that you can be sure to get some feedback that is worth your time.

Find out what their guidelines are for critique. You want to be sure the group has some ideas on what they are looking for in a critique so you can avoid falling into the "that's so great" syndrome.

Are there other group members who write in the same genre as you? You want to have at least a couple others who share the same genre writing to help encourage constructive critique.

Who is the facilitator? Unless you want the responsibility, be sure there is a good facilitator who is in charge of setting meeting times and dates, checking out new group members, and keeping the discussion on track.

If you are joining an online critique group, find out something about the writers involved. See if you can get some recommendations from other writers as well.

Creating Your Own Critique Group

There are several ways to set up a critique group that can work with your schedule as a mother. To get started though, you need to decide on a couple things:

1. How many writers you want to include (12 or less works best); and
2. How you want to meet.

There are several options for meetings: online, a central meeting spot, at homes, or with a writers' co-op. Online critique groups can be great for those with very little time to spare or for groups that consist of members all over the country. The easiest way to run a group online is to set up a yahoo group account open only to members. You can send each other your work for evaluation, as well as share feedback as a group. The downside is that you often don't get the personal involvement that comes from meeting with others locally; the upside is that you avoid becoming too personal with each other and sugar-coating your critiques.

More personal groups can include meeting at a local coffee shop, each other's homes, a library, or setting up a writers' co-op. The first three are self-explanatory. The co-op involves developing a group of mothers who want to write and critique, then holding a monthly meeting at a member's home. You can alternate meetings with morning one month and evening the next. In between meetings you can share babysitting hours, thus giving members time to write when necessary. You can also get together with other moms who share the same goals and write together while the children play.

No matter what meeting format you choose, you will need to find members who share the same goals and willingness for honest critique as you. You will need to have guidelines for discussion, including questions to help guide the conversations. You will also want to develop some ground rules for how the meetings will be conducted and you should choose a facilitator who is in charge of announcing future meetings and keeping the conversation on track. Remember, this is a critique group and not a play date. You want to respect each others' time and not dwell on personal stories of your day or children, and not let the children interrupt more than is necessary. Having some ground rules at the beginning allows the facilitator and other members the freedom to bring up issues when or if they arise.

Finding Writers for Your Group

- Hang signs at local coffee houses and the library. As long as you're not asking for money, they are more than willing to support the growth of local writing groups.
- Put a listing on craigslist.com. People check here for local activities and groups and this can be a good start for finding writers.
- Contact your local paper--again, if you're not charging, neither will they.
- See if there is a state-run writing association that will list your writing group online.

Notes for Success!

- Have members bring copies of their work for discussion--this allows for easier critique and keeps everyone on the same page (literally!).
- Try to have at least a couple published writers in the group so that you have experience to call upon when necessary.

How to Avoid the "That's Good" Syndrome

Nothing wastes more time for a writer than hearing "That's good," every time they share their work. Having some guidelines for responses will help you avoid that situation.

General Critique Questions

- What was the purpose of the piece and was that met clearly?

- What specifically did you enjoy and why?
- What needs to be clearer, added, or taken out?
- Are you immediately drawn into this piece, is the lead strong?

Critiquing Fiction
- Is the point of view consistent?
- Does the author's voice overshadow the narrator?
- Is the dialogue natural and realistic?
- Is there an element of tension throughout the story making you keep reading?

Critiquing Nonfiction
Memoirs:
- Can you identify the theme and is it well maintained throughout the story?
- Do the dialogue and any exposition support the theme?
- Is the time and place easy to recognize?

Essays and articles
- Is there a strong opening hook to draw the reader in?
- Does the essay have a clear focus and theme and not read like a play-by-play of events?
- Are all emotions and thoughts presented in a believable and natural way?
- Does the ending satisfy you as a reader?

Critiquing Poetry
- Is the first line an attention grabber?
- Does the poem contain too many –ing verbs?
- Is there tension throughout the poem–can it be improved by playing with the line and stanza breaks?
- Does the last line carefully reflect the rest of the poem?

38. Editing an Anthology

Amber E. Kinser

I had a colleague once who told me, when I was editing my anthology, that he had both written a book on his own and edited a book with multiple contributors and that he preferred, hands down, to write his own book. Working with contributors, he said, was immensely frustrating and significantly more time consuming.

Having published in both formats myself, I find I like both very much, though for different reasons, and I found that working with contributors was interesting, intellectually stimulating, and a good way to build relationships in my area of interest. I was even a little sad when *Mothering in the Third Wave* went into publication because it meant I wouldn't have regular contact with the sixteen contributors with whom I worked on the project (I had only known three of them previously); they had come to be members of my professional circle. Editing an anthology is a challenging but rewarding way to get your ideas into circulation.

Crafting an anthology of fiction is different from crafting one that is non-fiction, and one that comprises previously published works is different from one comprising newly published works. While much of what I've written here can apply to many anthology projects, it is directed at bringing together essays that are non-fiction and not previously published. *Mothering in the Third Wave*, published by Demeter Press in 2008, was born out of my desire to bring together my interests in Third Wave feminist thinking and my experience—as both a writer and a mother—with feminist mothering. I wanted a book that accomplished the complicated tasks of making theory accessible to a broad array of readers, and of grounding feminist maternal writing in personal experience and narrative style. I wanted my title to be succinct and clear about the subject matter rather than playful or abstract, and I wanted to suggest my focus on Third Wave as an era of, rather than a defined politics of, feminist thought.

Getting a Clear Idea

The most challenging aspect of editing an anthology is producing a cohesive text that unfolds a coherent theme, and doing so by way of a diversity of multiple contributors, all of whom think and write differently, and all of whom are, by definition, focused more on their own piece than on the anthology as a whole. It is critical, then, that the editor take seriously the responsibility of having a clearly defined goal for the book and working from that to guide what the contributors write.

Developing Your Focus or Theme

The first step in editing your anthology is getting a clear idea of the book's focus. Your anthology's primary focus or theme should:
- Be clearly articulated.
- Be something about which you have a passion or affection.
- Offer something new to the market; this may mean a new idea or an old idea explored in new ways.
- Lend itself to being explored in a variety of ways, to allow for a diversity of essays.

Writing a Book Proposal and Developing a Marketing Plan

There is no shortage of advice online about how to write a book proposal. Spend some time working through a good bit of that advice, pulling from several sources to inform a proposal that will "sell" your book to publishers. It should be an uncomplicated document only a few pages in length. Note that many publishers do not accept uninvited proposals but may accept an initial "query" or an "inquiry" email (very brief) that asks whether they would consider reviewing your proposal.

In writing your proposal, one of the most important things you will have to identify is how your book relates to other books out there. If you argue that your topic has never been written about before, then not only will you come across as naïve, you also will give publishers no reason to take a risk on your book. They often want to know that books on your topic have sold before; they want to know that investing in your book is safe.

In order to argue that your book is a worthy investment for the publisher, you will need to do your research so that you can answer questions such as:

- What other anthologies are like yours and in what ways? What about these did you want to model and why?
- What other anthologies are different from yours and in what ways? What about these did you want to do differently and why?
- What topics or formats or styles have been overdone and how is yours different from those?
- What new twist does your anthology offer?

Getting Contributors

You will need to get authors to submit their work to you. Authors are more likely to trust you with their work if you communicate a coherent vision for your book and come across as having a game plan for its publication, even if you don't know yet who the publisher will be.

Craft your Call

Sometimes referred to as a "Call for Papers" (or CFP), a "Call for Submissions," or a "Call for Subs," this is the way you invite writers to share their work with you.

What to Include in Your 1-page Call

1. Tentative title of your anthology
2. Description of your vision and goals for the book
3. A list of possible subtopics. You might say: Topics include but are not limited to...
4. Request for chapter title(s), abstract(s), and brief synopsis (ses) of their essays. Include a word limit; I prefer about 150 words
5. Request for a Contributor Bio. Include a word limit, maybe 50-65 words. You may use the bios in your book proposal, and you will use them later for the "About the Contributors" page of your anthology
6. Deadline for submissions and what contact or affiliation information you want from them
7. Your own contact information, including an email address to which they should submit their work and your website address if you have one.

Distribute your Call Widely

Your anthology will benefit from being able to feature very different kinds of writers who span an array of life experiences. This will provide breadth to your book and will increase the likelihood of appealing to a wide readership. Email your call to people you know who may be interested and have them forward to others who may be interested (that's how I came across the call for this book; a friend forwarded it to me.) Distribute the call at conferences and other gatherings. Here are some other ways to get your CFP out:

- Join groups whose membership may have interest in your topic and post on the group's website, and/ or distribute through the group's listserv. Be sure to include the URL to your website if you have one.

- Create a website. If you've never created a webpage before, an exceptionally easy and free web builder, which I still use, is weebly.com. You really can know nothing about web design and still create a simple website. I built my site (amberkinser.com) and still maintain it through Weebly, but there are a host of other free and easy web builders. If you already have a website, add a page to it that hosts your call for subs and allows you more space for information than your listserv announcements, flyers, or emails might offer. One advantage of this approach is that contributors can see what other work you've done and can better sculpt an essay that is likely to appeal to you and the kinds of writing you value or the kinds of audiences you tend to target. The point is, potential contributors can have ongoing access to the call and can direct others to it. Then, once you have selected contributors, you can use the page for announcements or contributor updates.

- Send direct email to people you've heard or read about; ask them to consider contributing or to forward the email to others who may be interested. When I was editing *Mothering in the Third Wave*, I discovered an announcement about a conference in my region on the topic of motherhood, which I wasn't able to attend. I found the conference poster online, which listed many of the speakers, then tracked down their contact information and sent emails to each of them individually.

Choosing Essays, Contributors

You should make no commitment to a contributor until you're sure you have an essay that: meets your goals for the book, is well written, and fits with the style of the other essays. Don't let "feeling bad" for the contributors weigh on you too heavily; do what's right for the book and contributes best to a cohesive whole.

Let the Essays Move You

As an editor, you need to both stay true to your vision and let your vision evolve. Figuring out how to work this paradox will result in a stronger anthology. That is, you won't be able to offer an anthology that has a coherent tone or theme if you don't stay focused on your vision, yet it is good, creative process to let the project evolve relative to what the other authors contribute.

Write Your Feedback with Care and Respect

You can be very up front about what you need and still create a collaborative, professional feel to your correspondence. Using phrases like "I'd like you to consider changing X so that it accomplishes Y in a clearer way. For example, what if you…" is one way of doing this. Again, you have the responsibility of helping to sculpt different works into a coherent whole, of making 15 essays or more look like they were planned and written in conjunction with each other.

Organization

Once contributors have returned their essays to you, they have been edited to your satisfaction, and you have selected which ones will be part of your anthology, the next step is to identify the primary themes that are emerging from the essays so you will know how to separate your book into different sections. Choose some of the most dominant themes coming from the essays and use them to divide your book into three or four sections. You will have an opportunity to explain these themes and how they relate to the focus of the book when you write the introduction.

Front and Back Matter

By the time you've made it this far through the process, it may be hard to imagine that there still are portions that need to be written. There remain, though, some important pieces:

Introduction and Preface
My anthology (and most of the works released by my publisher) had only an Introduction, though others will have both. If yours features an Intro and no Preface, you will use it to tell the reader what brought about the book—what your relationship to the topic is and what ideas were burning for you, what you saw as missing in other literature, and what you hope your anthology will accomplish. You also will discuss the theory, methods, framework, or approach you and your contributors used. Most Intros discuss each section of the book and how it unfolds the book's overall vision. You might also talk about how each chapter unfolds its section's purpose. Be careful not to say too much about the essays so you don't "steal the thunder" that your contributors worked so hard to craft. Academic Intros will also include an accessible review of the literature that positions the book and shows what gaps it is meant to fill.

If your book has both a Preface and an Intro, you will essentially split up these foci, and may also elaborate them. The Preface would cover the author's relationship to or credibility with the topic, the genesis of the book, and what it was meant to accomplish. Some authors offer brief mention here of people or organizations that supported the project but are not discussed in the Acknowledgements, or were primary and so bear mentioning again. The Introduction in this case would focus more pointedly on the subject matter of the book and what the reader needs to know, or point of view s/he should adopt, to most effectively grasp the book's purpose. It forecasts what will unfold in the book both in terms of content and structure. The Introduction functions as part of the book's text; the Preface is separate from it.

Acknowledgments
Begin a draft of this very early on in your process and keep adding to it. Throw into it the name of everyone who helped

you in the slightest way. You can expand on what you will say about them later if you want, but at least include in the document their name and what they did for you. By the end of the process you are likely to have forgotten the people from the early stages. Include everybody, even if all you include, in the end, is their name. This is a serious responsibility of any writer.

Contributor's Notes/About the Contributors
Work from the author bios you compiled early on to tell your readers briefly who each of your contributors are. Allow contributors an opportunity, once the manuscript has taken shape, to see the whole Contributor's Notes document so they can edit theirs according to the now clearer shape of the book and according to what other contributors say about themselves.

Sculpting the Manuscript

Allow for diversity in style from your contributors. Resist the temptation to edit all the essays so that they read as if you had written them. This meddles in the spirit of an anthology. It should read with a coherent tone, but not as if it were a monograph authored by you.

Once you've sent the complete manuscript to your publisher, s/he will send it out to knowledgeable people in the field or subject area for their recommendations. Typically, I followed the reviewers' suggestions, even when I didn't quite agree, because by this point I knew I had lost all objectivity and knew I needed to take seriously how other people were reading the manuscript. Sometimes I did not follow a reviewer's recommendation and explained to my publisher why.

When I first started my anthology project, I got terrific advice from a professional colleague: Be a hands-on editor. I found this advice to be invaluable because it allowed me to take primary ownership of the project and was the means through which I was able to realize that paradoxical goal of staying true to my vision while letting it evolve.

39. The Ideal Reader as Family

Anne Valente

As creative writers, most of us envision an ideal reader. We use this imaginary model to hone and shape our work, and to visualize how our work will be received. Sometimes that ideal reader is entirely invented, as with John Updike, who has said that he imagines a teenage boy randomly pulling books from library shelves, seeking literary adventure (Moyer). But other times, the ideal reader is someone we know intimately. Stephen King considers his wife Tabitha to be his ideal reader, and says that though she is the perfect commentator for his work, her critiques often come with initial disagreements and hurt feelings (King). Presumably, this is common for writers who use a family member as their imagined reader.

Relatives can be tremendously valuable resources for our writing, particularly if they know us well and intuit what we are trying to say. They often know our emotions and intentions, and they can tell us whether our purpose is apparent in our words. Though such intimacy makes us choose family members as ideal readers in the first place, it is also precisely why the writer-relative relationship comes with distinct challenges. Our confidence in family members makes their feedback all the more valuable, but also all the more hurtful if it is not what we want to hear. Family members may find their feelings hurt as well, if they read themselves into the work. Ultimately, if we are to use a family member as our imagined reader, we must first determine our intentions in wanting their response, and our ability to withstand their honest opinion.

Our Wounded Ego

The scenario is a familiar one for most writers—we finally finish a section of our manuscript, and we send it immediately to our favorite reader. We have spent inordinate amounts of time perfecting single lines and images, and we've imagined that our sister—or mother, father or cousin—will recognize the profound nuances of our language. We dash off a quick email with the manuscript attached, and we wait for resounding praise to fill the inbox. Except that when the feedback finally arrives, it comes with unexpected questions. *I like what you have, but where is this going? Would your main character really say that? Why is your choice of metaphor so obvious?* The praise is there too, but it sinks to the bottom amid the choppy waves of criticism.

Such a situation is not rare. Though at first it may be difficult to accept that a family member could criticize our work, we must ask ourselves why we wanted their response in the first place. Do we really want honest feedback, for our own consideration when making revisions and determining where to go next? Or do we simply want a comforting pat on the back, someone to make it all better when we are unsure?

There is, of course, nothing wrong with wanting encouragement. Family members are often a safe haven, reading our material before we make it widely public, and before we release ourselves to an audience who does not intimately know us. It is okay to want a family member's gentle prodding, or a thumbs-up that we are on the right track. However, in making a family member our imagined reader, we must also accept that their feedback will include constructive criticism, and that in logical terms it would be unrealistic for them to praise everything in our work. In fact, it might be suspicious—and even unfulfilling—if they offered nothing but positive comments, all the time. We might begin to question their critical ability or their honesty, which may be even more undesirable than smarting from their initial observations.

Their Wounded Ego

Beyond our hurt feelings, of course, lies the possibility that those of our ideal reader will also be harmed. Most creative writers are well-acquainted with the sting of harsh commentary, but equally familiar is the frequency with which family members, partners and friends read themselves into what has been written. Though this can sometimes inspire laughter and affection, it more often than not summons bruised egos and wounded feelings.

This can arise in a couple of ways. It can occur in our details, which may have been drawn into the work subconsciously but without deliberate attachment to a particular person. For example, suppose we have created a character who cheats and steals, and we are fumbling for a specific article of clothing she might wear—suddenly, a red trench coat comes to mind. Fast-forward to our sister's feedback, who says she thought the character was believable, but did we really have to include the red coat? We *know* our sister owns one too. What exactly are we trying to say?

The other pitfall, not surprisingly, is that our ideal reader will assume our relationship with them has naturally been reflected in our work. If we write about a mother who has neglected her children, our own mother may deduce that we too have unresolved abandonment issues. If we write about a protagonist who ends up committing fratricide, our own brother may presume that we secretly despise him.

Such reactions are mostly beyond our control, other than simply reminding the ideal reader that our work is not about them, and that writers often incorporate a pastiche of real details that combine to create a single character. We can also remind our ideal reader that we chose them in the first place because we trust them, and that in return, they must trust us too.

References

King, Stephen. *On Writing: A Memoir of the Craft*. New York: Pocket Books, 2002.

Moyer, Steve. "Biography: John Updike." Humanities, May/June 2008. *National Endowment for the Humanities*, neh.gov/whoweare/updike/biography.html

40. Lists, E-mail, and Facebook: Crafting Fiction and Nonfiction from Everyday Writing

Yelizaveta P. Renfro

There's so much you want to say, but sitting down to write, you find yourself stalled because you don't know how to organize all of your experiences and ideas. How do you structure your piece? With limited time to write, how do you get it all down? In fact, you are most likely already doing quite a bit of writing on a daily basis that can help you get going on your fiction and nonfiction. Stop to think about the writing you do during the course of the typical day. Do you write shopping lists and "to do" lists? Do you dash off e-mails to family and friends? Do you post status updates on Facebook or use other social networking sites? Do you send text messages? If so, then you're already writing! These forms of "everyday" writing can help you to organize and structure your short stories and essays.

Lists

Many women with busy lives are compulsive list makers. Lists of things to fix, things to buy, people to call, and errands to run help many of us to organize our days. Why not use lists to help us organize our writing as well?

If writing nonfiction, generate a list about your subject. For example, if you want to write about your baby's first year, make a list of all the objects that you associate with that time: the baby monitor, the nursing bras, the swaddling blanket, the rubber-coated spoon, the soft leather shoes, etc.

Space out the list and write a paragraph or two on each object. As you write, focusing on specific objects, a detailed picture of that special time will emerge.

If you're working on a family history, make a list of family members, and then write about each one. Even a "to do" list can be a good starting place. If you're a working mother, make a detailed "to do" list of all the things you must accomplish in one day. Then go through and flesh out each item. Even a "how to" list can become an essay. You might tackle a step-by-step project like building a birdhouse, or you might use the "how to" format in a more unorthodox way. For example, imagine crafting an essay-list on "How to Be an Amazing Grandmother" or "How to Raise a Budding Paleontologist."

List making can be equally valuable in fiction. If you can't figure out where to begin your story or are stuck halfway through, try making a list of all the scenes that you think will be in the story. List them as they occur to you, in no particular order. Making lists can be freeing because you're less likely to hold yourself to high literary standards when you're simply listing things. After all, lists are something you just dash off in a minute.

Once you have your list of scenes, go through and start fleshing in the details. Write a bit of dialogue or description. As you work, you will see your story emerging. Later, you can go through and rearrange the pieces. The list is often just the scaffolding that holds the story up in the early stages, and all traces of the list disappear in the finished work. Sometimes, however, the list remains as a central structuring device, as is the case in my short story, "A Catalogue of Everything in the World."

E-Mail

For centuries, the epistolary novel—written as a series of letters—was a popular genre. In fact, one of the first novels, Samuel Richardson's *Pamela*, is a collection of letters. As computers have come to dominate much communication and traditional letter writing has become less popular, the new epistolary format in fiction may very well be e-mail. Consider writing a short story as a collection of e-mails between two or more characters.

Think about the ways in which people use e-mail. Depending on your characters, you might use abbreviations and omit capitalization and punctuation to lend authenticity to your work. In my short story, "Panhandlers," written as a series of e-mails, I chose to adhere to the rules of grammar and capitalization because my narrator is a stickler for correct language usage.

E-mail can be an aid in writing nonfiction as well. Many of us dash off regular e-mails to keep faraway family and friends updated about our lives. We write about the garden, the weather, the annoying neighbors, and our children's milestones. Sometimes, e-mail is the only place we get all this information down. If you're trying to reconstruct a time in your children's lives or write about a stressful or exciting event in your own life, try going back to your e-mail. Find all the messages you sent, and string them together in a document. Read through them, and you might find that you have the rough outline of an essay. The concrete details and immediacy of your thoughts and feelings come through in the e-mails; now is the time for filling in the gaps, making the transitions, and polishing your prose.

Texting and Social Networking

If you belong to Facebook or another social networking site, you might have noticed that certain friends update their status messages multiple times a day. As you read through them, often clear narratives emerge. They are, in effect, telling stories, one update at a time. Look through your own updates. What stories are you telling? How can a list of status updates serve as the outline for a work of nonfiction or fiction? If you or your friends prefer text messaging, you can use the text messages the same way. Make a list of the updates or messages, and then build a story around them. Fill in the gaps with narrative.

As social networking sites become more popular, writing that makes use of Facebook or MySpace or Twitter are gaining acceptance. For example, Lori Walker's "Allison Trainor is Talking to Strangers, 23 Minutes Ago," a short story featured at *Literary Mama*, makes extensive use of Facebook updates. The journal *Iron Horse Literary Review* also recently announced a Facebook Issue. Clearly, these types of "everyday" writing are, more and more, being accepted as valuable and enduring forms of fiction and nonfiction.

References

Renfro, Yelizaveta P. *A Catalogue of Everything in the World: Nebraska Stories*. New York: Black Lawrence, 2010.

Walker, Lori. "Allison Trainor is Talking to Strangers, 23 Minutes Ago." *Literary Mama*. 13 Feb. 2010. Web. 30 Apr. 2010.

41. The Roles of Women in Narrative

Mary Rice

Family narrative is about creating a coherent sense of community among the characters. A woman is often at the forefront of these stories. How women became the centerpiece of so many family narratives is not the subject of this chapter. Using that structure in order to build a paradigm of "us" in any story—fact or fiction is. In my work as a folklore archivist, I was able to sort through many personal narratives. Reading narratives about family revealed that many of the same things that make a family narrative worth archiving also make a family story—fictional or otherwise worth publishing. Considering narratives about women demonstrates the power that women wield for holding the family and its story together.

Women as keepers of experience
Many of my narratives that I looked at dealt with family stories of grandmothers. The narrators in these stories communicate family expectations for women and these descriptions often include some kind of description of toughness. It seems to make sense to assert that in the narrator's mind, a strong woman makes for a strong family. Occasionally there are even nicknames for these female family members that emphasize their toughness.

　　　The grandmother is an ideal candidate for such attention in narrative because she is removed from the immediacy of judgment that falls on mothers because mothers are still raising children. Grandmothers have earned respect. They lived exotic lives in different times. They have secure identities and can say what they really think. If they are no longer living, then the mere mentioning of their names is a hallowed experience. Grandmothers also represent collective wisdom because of their age and experiences. This also helps them serve as archetypes for various time periods. Narrators have confidence telling stories about grandmothers because their listeners tacitly agree on the sacredness of grandmothers.

Women as keepers of identity

Another circumstance that makes narratives about women unique is women's willingness to be laughed at, and therefore serve as important cultural forces. Women were more frequently the focal points of stories of chagrin in the narratives I looked at. The ability to laugh at the follies of women builds collective identity through shared humorous experiences. Some of the narratives that I read took pause to discuss why this might be. It may be that in some families, mothers do not do funny things intentionally, and so when humorous things happen to mothers, they are more worthy of a story because they are rare or because mother was not planning on their occurrence. There is also the possibility that women are enculturated to be self-deprecating and so they feel they deserve to have their faux pas canvassed. Other women may just be confident and while a particular event may seem embarrassing to some, to women, the event was not a big deal and therefore, they do not mind if the story is told.

The fact that women seem to be accepting of stories about their foibles is an interesting aspect of the collective description of womanhood because they are the keepers of stories in family. They get to be keepers for two reasons: because they tell many stories, and because many stories are told about them. In fact, many families have more stories about the women of the family than they do about the men. Therefore, when authors wish to depict women in family narratives, those stories need to be ones that represent women that commit a variety of actions, lest they become stale as characters. Stories with women as central characters need to stand as a ballast against all of the other interactions can be judged against.

Another interesting aspect of narratives about women is that women seem to have stories about them telling stories to a greater extent than men do. This double layering adds to the complexity of any plot by keeping the story in the point-of-view of a third party who is by no means omniscient, but at the same time has credibility. Letting women tell stories-within-stories can add to the intimacy of a story by allowing the reader to respond to both narrators instead of just one. It also helps the readers to be able to interpret the actions of the main plot through the lens of another narrator. There is often no assumption that this meta-narrator is objective. Rather, it is usually assumed that a woman telling the story about another woman telling a story is heavily invested in the woman whose original story she is canvassing. Within this context, judgments can be made by in and out of narrative space about all of the women involved resulting in a highly complex story. While most writers work to create linear stories, using a woman narrator to tell a story about another woman can add depth and interest.

Women as keepers of truth
Women are not the only ones who tell stories about women, of course. Men also tell stories about women. These narratives usually portend towards a question about what constitutes the truth in a given situation. This phenomenon seems to match the assertion of many sociolinguists including Deborah Tannen from Georgetown University that men primarily communicate as an amoral information-seeking enterprise. Women, by contrast, communicate to build relationships and their exchanges are based in a kind of dynamic morality. It is not that women do not care about information or men do not care about relationships, it is just that they tend to use what they learn from exchanges to achieve different goals.

In light of Tannen's theory about gendered communication, it is interesting that, instead of narratives that describe relationships, the stories that men tell about women are often about depicting events. To add layers to stories that are set up where men discuss women, authors can build a narrative where multiple men tell slightly different versions of an event. In this type of a story, all the storytellers can claim to be the keeper of the most accurate version. In the narratives I looked at where this phenomenon was occurring, the men were usually family members of some type, such as father and son or brothers. The version of at least one of the narrators can be very detailed. The additional narrator's version may be more vague, except for one or two critical details that the first narrator omits.

Building a family narrative with one plot where the finer points differ depending on the teller, could result from a combination of factors, but because this phenomenon exists, it brings with it the potential for really thick plotlines and perspective possible for authors. Also, if authors wish to make one character look more trustworthy to readers and another less, they should allow the preferred characters to tell stories with better detail and the ones they want to seem less trustworthy to tell stories that are less descriptive. This technique can also be used to throw readers off of the trail of a character's true malevolence when the plot calls for this.

In the end, the reader is left with an unclear vision of exactly which narrator is the more trustworthy person, or had the closer contact with the woman about whom he is narrating. At this point in the story, the author can then revert to literary theory in order to help resolve this conflict and reveal which of the authors should be believed. The author could impeach one or both of the narrators as the story progresses or write the ending in an ambiguous manner so that readers are left to decide what truths are revealed and hidden through the course of the story.

Another option for building family narratives with multiple narrators is to build parallel plotlines. These plotlines can appear to be unrelated initially or not, but as the story progresses, they can be brought together gradually in a climax that helps the reader reconsider the positions of all of the characters involved. It is also possible to embed a narrator within the story who is relating other narratives throughout the story instead of giving every narrative and every narrator equal weight. Again, this technique could prove to be an important one for strengthening symbolisms, showing the dynamics of relationships, proving or disproving the integrity of other characters, and allowing other literary elements such as symbolism to manifest themselves.

Women as keepers of humanity

One particularly interesting motif in many of the stories that I read was women's hair. Not only is hair the essence of femininity in many cultures, it is also, ethologically speaking, what makes a woman a mother. Some developmental psychologists have observed that mammals like to hold on to their mother's hair while they are eating and thus a mother's hair is an artifact that is common to many. Anyone with long hair who has ever fed a baby can also attest to the fact that it gets pulled. In her ruminations about growing up in Los Angeles, Sandra Cisneros, a Latina author, devoted an entire vignette in her book *The House on Mango Street*, to hair. She started her chapter by looking at her own hair and worked her way back through all of her family members to her mother's hair, which smelled like bread and made Sandra feel safe. Another great narrative about women's hair is O. Henry's classic short story, "The Gift of the Magi." In this tale, an indigent young married couple, very much in love, both sacrifice special possessions in order to give one another gifts for Christmas. Della, the wife in the story sells her hair. In Louisa May Alcott's classic *Little Women*, Jo, the most outspoken of the March sisters, sells her hair for the train ticket her mother needs to visit her wounded husband. Finally, the young adult novel *Adaline Falling Star* by Mary Pope Osborn fictionalizes the life of Kit Carson's Native American daughter who is left to live with a family that does not understand her culture. In a drastic act of self-expression, Adaline cuts her hair — an act that is described as a mourning ritual for Native Americans in the book.

Capitalizing on the humanistic qualities of women and the stories that get told about these qualities is another way to gain credibility as author and help readers connect to the characters in a text. While it may not be necessary to specifically mention hair in a particular work of fiction, it may be fruitful to spend time observing women in the context the writing project focuses on, taking note of the simple, subtle things that the women do, and then incorporating those subtle details into the project.

Looking at women from an anthropological standpoint carries the idea that women have an influential role in the collective identity full circle. In her science-fictional work, *The Host*, Stephenie Meyer builds a family out of necessity in the Arizona desert, most of which are unrelated, but who would like to avoid having their bodies overtaken by an invading army of extraterrestrials. Even more traumatic than losing your soul while an alien absconds with your body is the fate of Meyer's principal character that mistakenly ended up with two female souls, one alien and the other human. Once the group accepts Wanda the alien in Melanie's body, they appoint her a teacher. As resident educator, Wanda's job is tell stories about her former lives on other planets over the course of her extra long life span. Wanda's storytelling is ultimately what brings the strangers in the desert together and makes them a society. A woman and her stories brought all of the characters together and effectively becomes the spokesperson, not only for alien kind, but all of humanity.

Blurring the line between fiction and reality
The examples in this chapter were selected to demonstrate that stories about women in narrative perform the essentially same function that women in reality do. They are bonding agents, making sure that there is a story to tell at all. They are willing to have stories be told about them for the benefit of the whole family. They not only have stories told about them, but they have stories told about them as storytellers. Watching women reveals new and interesting ways to interpret not

only the experience of the women characters, but of the family or families whose experiences are being chronicled. The wise author depicts women in such a way that readers feel not only connected to the family in the story, but all of humankind.

References

Alcott, Louisa M, and Valerie Alderson. *Little Women*. Oxford: Oxford University Press, 2008.

Cisneros, Sandra. *The House on Mango Street*. New York: Vintage Books, 1991.

Henry, O. "The Gift of the Magi." *The Best Short Stories of O. Henry*. New York: Modern Library, 1994.

Meyer, Stephenie. *The Host: A Novel*. New York: Little, Brown and Co, 2008.

Osborne, Mary P. *Adaline Falling Star*. New York: Scholastic Press, 2000.

Tannen, Deborah. *You Just Don't Understand: Women and Men in Conversation*. New York: Morrow, 1990.

Part VII

Publishing, Marketing,
&
Promotion

42. Cybermoms: Opportunities for Women Writers on the Web

Anne Witkavitch

Looking for places to publish your work? Need clips to build your professional writing portfolio? There is a growing demand on the web for women who write, whether your focus is on family, work/life balance, or personal growth. Blogs, e-zines, and online literary magazines, as well as web versions of traditional print publications, offer numerous opportunities to showcase your work, and many are on the look out for new and emerging writers.

The key to writing success in the world of the web is to understand what online markets are best suited to your writing; take advantage of blogs and websites to showcase your talent and collect clips; and use technology to manage your productivity and track your progress.

Researching Markets on the Web

There are several advantages to writing for the web:

- Many online publications replenish content more frequently than print publications.
- There is a shorter lead-time for publishing on the web; you may have a clip for your portfolio within weeks instead of waiting months or years.
- The submission process is easier and faster. Most online publications prefer to receive queries by e-mail and often accept or reject submissions within a reasonable time frame.

- Online publications offer many ways to contribute content, from reader comments and blog posts to book reviews and contests.
- New online publications, including those targeting women, working mothers, and parents, are often looking for new writers with strong voices to help them launch.

Targeting Your Markets

One of the best ways to research online markets is to set aside time and "surf the web." First, start with the traditional print magazines you have targeted on your publishing wish list. Using a search engine like Google, type in the name of the magazine and find its website. Just as you would do when researching a traditional publication, take time to read and study the web content and determine how what you write might fit.

Next, find the submission guidelines. This may be tricky and take some detective work. Some publications, particularly those who openly accept submissions from freelance writers, often have a direct link to the "submission guidelines" or "contributor guidelines" on the home page, clearly visible on the top or side navigation bars.

If you have trouble finding submission information, check the "About Us" or "Frequently Asked Questions" links. These typically show up as smaller print at the bottom of the home page. If you still cannot figure out how to submit a query, simply e-mail customer service via the "Contact Us" link and ask to receive their submission guidelines for writers. You will usually receive a reply within days.

Continue your market research by typing into the search engine various descriptions of markets you want to write for. For example, you can type in phrases like "working women online publications," "parenting websites," and "literary online magazines for mothers." You will find more publications listed, some which are published strictly online, and which you may want to query. Follow the same process described previously to locate submission guidelines. Again, just like for print publications, do your homework and invest time to get familiar with the contents.

Organizing Your Information

As you do your research, use technology to boost your productivity by developing an electronic process for managing information and processing queries. For example, create a folder in Favorites and call it "Submission Guidelines." As you uncover links to the publications you want to target, copy and save the web address into the folder for easy reference. You can also create a folder in your personal e-mail files for "Submissions" and include subfolders for "Outgoing," "Accepted," and "Rejected." As you query and submit your work, save any correspondence or responses in the appropriate folders.

Other Online Resources

You will also find links to websites that aggregate information about writing markets and post them in directory format. However, always check with the publication's website first before sending your query to verify that the information is accurate. Sometimes contact information or guidelines are out-of-date.

The Business of Blogging

Blogs are terrific vehicles for women who write. Search for blogs that focus on women, mothers, and parenthood. Visit and bookmark the ones you find particularly interesting. Study what makes them work. Are they visually appealing? How frequently does the blogger post?

How Specific is the Content?

Once you get comfortable with other people's blogs, you can create your own. Blogs are easy to set up, most are free, and they are a great way to build discipline into your writing practice.

If you do set up a blog, there are several things to keep in mind:

- To be a successful blogger, you should plan to post an entry at least three to four times a week.
- Title your blog using descriptive phrases and key words that will raise your visibility in search engines and attract readers who are interested in what you are writing about.
- Link to other websites and blogs to build reader traffic, especially those that target the same readers you want to attract. Remember, the Internet is a giant web and making connections is critical in order to grow your readership and gain further visibility for your writing.
- Share your blog address with everyone you know. Put the link in your e-mail signature to ensure it appears every time you send an e-mail.

Be aware, however, many publications consider the writing you have posted to your blog as previously published material. If you are writing something you plan to query to either a print or online publication, it is best to find out first what policies, if any, exist for essays or articles originally posted to your blog.

Tracking Your Progress

Once you've researched markets and targeted where you want to publish, you need to start sending out queries. You can track submissions using the task tool in your e-mail program:

- For each query or submission open a new task.

- Decide on a standard submission line to describe the task; for example, "Submitted [name of essay/ article] to [name of publication.]
- Create a category called "Magazine Submissions" and mark each task appropriately. You can later sort your tasks by category and view all of your submissions together.
- Use the date you e-mailed the query as "Date Started." Use the expected response period noted in the contributor guidelines as the "Due Date." For example, if you send your query on April 1 and the response time is eight weeks, choose June 1 as the due date.

Ensuring Your Success

The web offers a wonderful oasis of opportunities for getting published. But it is important that you do not ignore print publications as vital markets for publishing your work. Submitting online can give you visibility and get you clips, but you still need to break into more traditional outlets. Also, it is important that you balance "surfing the web" with your writing practice, and manage blog postings as part of your daily writing discipline.

By managing your online writing as an integral part of your career, you will immerse yourself into a virtual community for writers that provides plenty of channels for publishing, networking, and continuous learning.

43. From Pitch to Publication: Learning How to Work With an Editor

Caroline M. Grant

All writers want to be published, and an essential step toward seeing your work in print is learning how to work well with an editor. While your focus on family writing – whether it's a personal essay or an advice piece – might tempt you to treat your editor as casually as family, you should always take your editorial relationship as seriously and as professionally as you do your writing. If you devote the same care and consideration to the process of submission and revision that you do to the writing process, you can look forward to developing a productive and lasting partnership with your editor.

The best start to a great working relationship with your editor is, of course, to submit your very strongest writing. So once you feel your piece is finished, take a break from it. You won't be able to follow the old advice to "kill your darlings" – editing out beloved but tired phrases – if they are still fresh in your mind. Take a couple days or a week to work on something else, and then print out your piece and give it one more careful read-through before submitting for publication. Printing and reading aloud, with a pen in hand, lets you see and hear things you might miss if you just read from the screen, so take time for this step.

In this final edit, try to imagine how an editor would mark up your text. Remember that what is new and creative to you might not be so innovative to an editor who reads family writing for a living. Over my years of reading submissions for *Literary Mama*, I've learned that there is no limit to the imaginative ways a writer can describe love, guilt, or fear (three of the predominant emotions in family writing) and if you come up with something unusual and effective, you'll get — and hold — an editor's attention. But if you write that you were born as a writer when you birthed your child, or if you make comparisons between producing a manuscript and delivering a baby, your editor's eyes will surely glaze over. So this is the time to ruthlessly excise adverbs, clichés, and forms of the verb "to be." Editing can provide a valuable break from writing; it gives you the opportunity to look at your writing with a different perspective. Further, editing is work that has a more definite end point than writing does, so it offers a useful respite to you as a writer. Take advantage of the change in your focus to see your writing anew.

For writers focused on family issues, this is the time to consider, too, the extent to which this piece of writing might expose those who appear in your story or essay. If you are writing about your children, parents, siblings, or other close family members, always be sensitive to perspective. What reads like a funny story to you might not feel so funny to its newly-public subject. Use the "playground test:" as you consider an anecdote to share about your family, consider how you would feel if it were read out loud on the playground. If there's any discomfort in that, maybe you shouldn't share the story.

Also, think critically about your objective with your writing: is what you're revealing crucial to the story, or is its impact more personal? You don't want to write in anger or for retribution; save that tone for the op-ed page. As you edit, make sure the story is always driving your decisions about how much and what to reveal. You don't want to censor yourself while you're writing; indeed, you should allow yourself the freedom to write the strongest, most revealing version of your story, knowing that later, away from the computer, you can consider what belongs in the piece and what might better suit your journal. The thinking that you do about this will slow you down and improve your writing.

After this final editorial review, you're ready to submit your writing for publication. You may have written the piece with a particular journal or magazine in mind, or perhaps this was a piece that demanded to be written, and you haven't yet thought about a home for it. Either way, take time now to consider your full range of options. Is the piece a literary essay, an advice article, a funny sketch? Think of the different kinds of publications in which it might fit, and don't forget that newspapers and general-subject magazines generally maintain a regular space for family writing. Once you've developed a list of potential outlets for your piece, consider whether it would be similar to other writing the journal publishes or more of a stretch, so that you can craft your cover letter accordingly. Make sure your cover letter complies with the publication's submissions guidelines, and keep it professional; just because this may be a quite personal piece about your family, there's no reason to diverge from the standard cover letter. Finally, read every detail of the submissions guidelines carefully; if they request that you submit using FedEx and pink paper clips, then by all means, use FedEx and pink paperclips.

Some journals request that you pitch your ideas first, and of course once you've established yourself professionally, you will always want to pitch first and insure a home for your piece before you take the time to develop it fully. Make your pitch specific and concise, just a paragraph, but allow for the possibility that the finished piece may vary somewhat, especially in its conclusion, from your pitch.

If you're in the fortunate position of having a piece of writing solicited by an editor, don't then presume that any of these guidelines go out the window. You've been invited to the party, but that doesn't give you leave to flout the house rules. Follow the submissions guidelines, write an appropriate cover letter, and send in your work.

After an editor responds positively to your writing and asks to work with you on it, the fun really begins. But before embarking on revisions with your editor, take a moment to think about your relationship to this particular piece of writing. Is this something you've worked on for years and submitted for numerous rejections? Did you just finish it and get lucky with your first submission? Regardless of the time you've spent with the piece and its past history, your editor knows nothing of that – and doesn't need to. The editor likes this piece now and wants to publish it. See it through her eyes. Working with this editor allows you to start fresh with this piece of writing.

The relationship with your editor might not feel very balanced at first: you want your work to be published, and the editor is the gatekeeper. If you don't have a lot of experience working with an editor, you might find yourself feeling very protective of your work. Writers occasionally have trouble with the editorial process because they are put off by an editor's suggestions, especially if they seem brusque. Take a deep breath if you are hurt by an editor's comments, and never respond while upset. If you are feeling defensive, consult with a supportive friend who can remind you what a great writer you are, and who can also help you consider the editor's comments with an open mind. Remember that an editor is a collaborator, and that constructive critique is engagement with your work. It indicates a serious investment in your writing. Always keep in mind that you and your editor both have the same goal: publishing your writing.

As you work with your editor, keep in mind these three basic points:

1. *Follow your editor's lead.*
Each editor will have a slightly different working styles. Get to know how this editor works and respond appropriately. For instance, if your editor emails attached documents and uses Word's Track Changes feature, learn it and use it when you respond to editorial suggestions. If she pastes your document into an email and puts her comments in brackets, then you can do the same. If you are uncertain of how she wants to see your revisions, simply ask.

2. *Respond promptly.*
Be responsive. Always acknowledge receipt of edits,

and if the editor hasn't set a deadline for response, let the editor know when you will return a revision. Whether the editor sets the timeframe or you do, don't miss that deadline. Prove she can rely on you.

3. Be cordial.

This should go without saying, but always keep in mind that this exchange began because the editor likes your work and wants to publish it. Look for the positive in all your editor's suggestions. Be thoughtful, considerate and courteous in your communication with her. Most editorial discussions take place via email these days, and tone can sometimes be hard to read, so politely request clarification if you're uncertain about something.

Whether you are a new writer (feeling supplicant to the editor) or a more experienced writer feeling confident that your piece doesn't need many edits, keep the editor's perspective in mind. She is trying to shape your piece to fit in to a particular issue, edition, or anthology. She has a word count to meet and, likely, an editor to whom she needs to answer. You aren't able to see the full context into which your work will go, so trust that your editor is doing her best to balance your piece with her vision of the project as a whole.

So in your questions about editorial suggestions, maintain a polite and neutral tone; "I want to understand…" or "I'm curious…" are more inviting openings than "I don't agree with…" If you feel your piece is being cut or altered aggressively, try pushing back gently with a line like "This edit seems to flatten the tone" or "I was trying to express…"

Also, take full responsibility for the work your editor asks of you. There is a fine line between asking questions to clarify an editorial suggestion and trying to get your editor to put words on your page. Make sure not to pester your editor with questions in an attempt to get her to do your work.

If you're not thrilled with the editorial suggestions you receive, it may help to think of this simply as one version of the piece. Writers often publish different iterations of an essay in a number of different venues. Read your contract or contributor's agreement carefully, and if you retain the rights to the piece, consider submitting the original for publication elsewhere.

If the editor asks for changes with which, after careful consideration, you really disagree, talk to her candidly. You certainly don't want to publish a piece that you're not proud of, and ultimately, no matter how much the piece changes in accordance with your editor's suggestions, it will forever be your name in the byline, not your editor's. So make sure you are satisfied with the revision. If not, you can withdraw the piece and resubmit it somewhere else. But don't do this hastily; make sure you've thought through your reservations about the suggested revisions and discussed them with your editor.

Ultimately, consider what is more important to you: getting the piece published and seeing your name in print, or preserving your sense of the integrity of your writing? You might have to sacrifice getting published if you're determined not to make changes to your piece, and then you've lost the chance to share your ideas with the broader world. Remember, writing is communication. If your writing isn't published, you're not communicating with anyone.

A good editor is essential to any professional literary career, so don't embark on this correspondence as if it will be the only time you work with this editor – take the long view. Work to establish a friendly relationship with your editor, and she may invite you to pitch ideas via a quick email rather than a formal query. Consider connecting with her on Facebook, Twitter, LinkedIn or other social media services so that you can see what else she is involved with and vice versa; you may discover shared personal interests that lead to more professional assignments.

If you make an investment in this person, she might invite you to write for her again, but think bigger. Establish a real connection, and you could find that your editor truly shapes your career.

44. Identifying Potential Markets for Family Writing

Rebecca Tolley-Stokes

Getting your work published brings to mind the chicken and egg conundrum. Should you write your piece first and then seek a market for it? Or is it best to identify markets and write specifically for their audience? The answer is: A little of both. This article offers strategies for writers for identifying potential markets for their work. It covers finding journals and magazines by searching the web, browsing newsstands, and using library resources like *Cabell's*, *Ulrich's*, and *Writer's Market*, and provides an annotated list of both print and on-line journals and magazines in this category.

The first place to begin is with you. What magazines do you read? Which ones do you subscribe to? It's likely that you're drawn to content that shares a similar sensibility to your writing. A quick look around your home or workplace may reveal markets to submit your work. It's easier to start with what you know. If you've read a magazine for several years, then you know what type of stories they like, and definitely mention your long relationship with the publication to its editor in your query. At first glance, there may not be an obvious connection between family and the magazines fanned across your coffee table. Everyone writes about family whether they acknowledge it or not, because everything relates to family, or can relate to family in some fashion. Whether you pitch your idea around family activities, traditions, or experiences, you can identify a market for your article.

Include stops at your public library and local bookstores in your market-seeking mission. Both offer a rich variety of resources. Expand your search for markets by looking through your library's current periodical subscriptions. You can browse the print issues and easily locate online journals via your library's website and/or online catalog. Other library resources can help you identify markets for your family writing. Remember: your local and state taxes pay for public and academic libraries. You are entitled to use them.

Cabell's Publishing is an online directory of academic journals, more typically available at a university library. Each journal has an entry, which includes information such as subject area, type of readership, editorial policy, manuscript guidelines, review process and timeline, review type and number of reviewers, and acceptance rate. While not all family writing would be appropriate or acceptable in these journals — which are scholarly in nature — exploring the value and applicability of family management skills to the workplace in an article submitted to one of the management journals covered by *Cabell's* is a wise strategy. Likewise, incorporate your family wisdom in articles tailored to journals compiled in *Cabell's* education and psychology directories.

In print it's known as *Ulrich's Periodical Directory*, but online *Ulrichsweb.com* helps writers identify potential markets for their work. The print version offers detailed, comprehensive, and authoritative information on serials published throughout the world. Ulrichsweb.com is especially helpful given its search capabilities and contains more than 300,000 periodicals of all kinds. A keyword search of family returned 3,718 individual periodical titles. If you do an advanced search and limit the results to actively published titles as well as typing "family" in the subject field, your search results are refined to 18 titles. *Grand Magazine* and *Today's Dad* appeared in that list and would be appropriate markets to pursue.

Ask a librarian to help you refine your search of *Ulrichsweb.com*. Her help will save you time and energy that you should devote to your writing. Another strategy to use in searching *Ulrichsweb.com* is by subject. When you look up a title like *Family Circle* and view its entry note the subjects or, how *Ulrichsweb.com* has categorized or tagged the title. Clicking on "home economics" or "women's interests" will reveal magazines that cover similar topics that you could pitch your family-related article to.

When you change search tactics and try "family" via Title (keyword), more than 1,000 titles appear: *Adoptive Families, AKC Family Dog, Arkansas Family Historian, Bilingual Family Newsletter, Black Parenting Today, Catholic Family Perspectives, Children and Families, Exceptional Parent, Family Business, Family Camping, Health, Home Educator's Family Times, Kiwi, Parents, Successful Farming, Thriving Family, Travel + Leisure Family,* and *Your Stepfamily.*

And an advanced search limiting the results to English-language periodicals published in the U.S. with the subject "children and youth—about" elicits: *American Baby, American Mother, Baby Couture, Big Apple Parent, Exceptional Parent, Gay Parent, Growing Child, Mothering, Single Mother, Teen Food & Fitness, Toddler, Twins,* and *Wonder Time.*

The largest hardbound book of U.S. and Canadian periodicals is *Standard Periodical Directory.* It compiles and organizes over 65,000 magazines by category. It's valuable for presenting key staff names and contact information. Similarly, the *Gale Directory of Publications and Broadcast Media*, considered a venerable print reference, entries provide full contact information, including address, phone and fax numbers, e-mail addresses and Web site URLs, listings of key personnel, including feature editors and owner information. As of 2012 this resource was available in print and eBook.

Published annually, *Writer's Market* is invaluable, but be cautioned: some editorial staff at magazines revealed that the contact names published in the book are facsimiles and queries addressed to those names are automatically rejected. Research the magazine and to whom to pitch. Phone the office to ask for the names of editors. *LinkedIn* or *Ulrichsweb.com* can uncover that information as well. The Deluxe Edition published in 2010 included a one-year subscription to the publication's website, *WritersMarket.com* which gives owners access to an additional 2,500 entries not in the print edition, thus making over 6,000 markets available to writers. In conclusion, consider this list of magazines and online media to inspire your family-infused writing:

- Billed as "for a new generation of parents," **Babble. com** publishes writing that "bypasses the clichés" of parenting. Articles tout traditional parenting advice alongside the latest childhood development research. Their blogs, columns, and features cover products, fashion, entertainment, health, and travel.
- **Bitch Media**, formerly *Bitch: Feminist Response to Pop Culture* publishes features, interviews, and reviews with a popular culture context. Articles informed by feminist perspectives draw heavily from "personal insight and wit" and include topics such as unschooling.
- **Brain, Child** goes beyond parenting tips and advice from experts to get at the heart of the motherhood experience and provide a venue for "thinking mothers" with articles exploring breastfeeding, sex education, spanking, and evolution and many others.
- **Bridges: A Jewish Feminist Journal** features essays, fiction, poetry, art and reviews on the cutting edge of feminist Judaism. The editors publish essays, fiction, poetry, art, translations, and reviews that celebrate and illustrate the complexities of Jewish women's identity and social justice activism.
- **Bust** proudly tells the truth about the female experience including dealing with our families with an eye toward challenging cultural stereotypes. Pitch your family-related stories to their Real Life section, which explores "all the ways we do that every day voodoo that we do so well."
- The online venue *errant parent* publishes humorous "essays, fiction, poetry, parodies, rants, confessions, and more" featuring a gritty or clever voice.

They don't go for "cutesy or anecdotal" but pay $25-$50 per submission upon publication.

- *Family* is a monthly magazine that covers all aspects of parenting and family life, but specifically needs book excerpts, new product reviews, personal essays, and advice on raising teens.

- *Family Circle* is published every three weeks and features stories about women's lives and interests with an emphasis upon family, specifically families with children ages 8-16. The magazine seeks anecdotal stories, service journalism, essays, and opinion pieces.

- *The Family Digest* is a quarterly magazine written for a Catholic audience. Its editors consider nonfiction on the topics of family life, parish life, prayer life, spiritual life, and Catholic traditions.

- Focused on family play and activities, *FamilyFun* contains article about "all the great things families can do together." Their nonfiction needs include: book excerpts, essays, general interest, how-to, crafts, cooking, educational activities, humor, personal experience, and travel.

- Articles published in **Good Housekeeping** may focus on childcare and range between these types of writing: human interest stories, articles on social issues, money management, health, relationships, and travel.

- Politically minded **HipMama.com** is an online magazine that represents the stories of progressive families. They seek "fresh, authentic writing from the trenches of motherhood."

- *Ladies' Home Journal* serves a female audience ages 30-45. They need highly focused features on aspects of family.

- *Living* is a quarterly tabloid that seeks general interest, how-to, humor, inspirational, and personal experience stories about family life at all ages and stages. "Non-white writers" are encouraged to submit to the tabloid.

- The online journal **Literary Mama** bills itself as "reading for the maternally inclined" and features book reviews, columns, creative nonfiction, poetry, and profiles of mother writers. Devoted exclusively to writing covering the experience of motherhood, they seek "beautiful poetry, fiction and creative nonfiction that may be too long, too complex, too ambiguous, too deep, too raw, too irreverent, too ironic, and too body conscious for other publications."

- Another online journal of literature and art by women is **Melusine**, or **Woman in the 21st Century** (melusine21cent.com). They seek reflective essays, autobiographical sketches, and reviews of art, film, literature, and music reflecting the female experience.

- *Mothering* welcome unsolicited articles with a strong point of view that originate from the heart and focus on the "inspirational and spiritual side of nurturing." Midwifery, home births, breastfeeding, and homeschooling and unschooling topics as well as recipes, parenting tips, and poetry are welcome. *Mothering* pays pay between $200 and $500 for a 1,500 to 2,500 words magazine article.

- *Parents* is a nationally circulated monthly magazine that specifically seeks 1,000-word submissions in their "As They Grow" column which tackles issues on different stages of development.

- *Parenting* is a print magazine published 10 times each year and features stories for mothers of children from birth to age 12. The editors desire book excerpts, personal experience, and child development/behavior/health.

- *Plum* magazine is an annual publication that covers health and lifestyle for women over the age of

35. It is distributed via obstetrics offices and available at some newsstands.

- *Redbook* accepts nonfiction articles on parenting that apply to the magazine's audience—women between the ages of 25 and 45.
- Published by the University of Chicago Press, *Signs: Journal of Women in Culture and Society*, accepts major articles, comparative perspectives symposia, retrospectives, new directions essays, and book reviews that provoke readers and scholars of women's studies.
- A monthly magazine, *Skirt!* is all about women, including their family life. They seek essays, humor, and personal experience with a "spirited, independent, outspoken, serious, playful, irreverent" attitude.
- *Today's Christian Woman* is a bimonthly serving a broad audience of women of all ages who are homemakers and career women. The magazine seeks submissions that help women deal with contemporary issues in light of Biblical perspectives. How-to, narrative, and spiritual articles should contain a "distinct evangelical Christian perspective."
- *Twins Magazine* serves an audience of parents who have twins, triplets, and other sequences of multiple births. Published eight times a year, the magazine features positive and personal articles providing informational and educational stories about parenting multiples.
- *Women Writers: A Zine* is another online journal (womenwriters.net) that does not pay but that gives new writers a break in getting their work published. The zine is published two or three times each year and accepts fiction, poetry, and book reviews from professional scholars and academics featuring a third-wave feminist perspective.

- *Working Mother* seeks nonfiction articles in humor, service, child development, and material pertinent to the working mother's desire to balance demands of work and family.

These titles represent a few markets that women writing about family topics might consider when querying editors. Do keep in mind that any magazine may be interested in your family-related topics, so don't limit your queries to magazines for women, parents, or grandparents. Family anecdotes intersect with pets, hobbies, education, travel, food, and almost any topic that broad audiences want to read about.

45. The Importance of Face Time: Making the Most of Writing Conferences

Kate Hopper

The Internet has certainly made leading a writer's life easier (and in many ways less lonely). You can e-mail stories to your editor, participate in online writing classes, and develop an international network of writer-friends, all from the comfort of your own home. But as helpful as the Internet is in our daily lives, we can't forget how valuable it is to meet other members of the writing and publishing industries in person.

Writing conferences offer the perfect opportunity to meet face-to-face with other writers, editors, and agents. And the connections you make at a conference can develop into friendships, lead to work opportunities, and even help you sell your book.

Choosing a Conference

Your conference goals should dictate the kind of conference you attend. Don't pick a random writing conference in Florida just because you need a break from a long, Midwestern winter. (You might as well plan a beach vacation instead.) And don't agree to attend a conference with a friend before researching whether the conference will also meet your writing or publishing needs.

Asking the following questions will help you decide which conference will be the best fit for you. Are you primarily interested in:

- Focusing on craft issues and improving your writing?
- Specializing in one genre, such as nature writing, personal essays, romance writing, etc.?
- Expanding your network of writer friends?

- Pitching articles to magazine editors?
- Pitching your book to editors and agents?

Once you've decided on your goals (which can be a combination of the above), do your research. Ask your writer friends which conferences have been most helpful to them. Check out websites like *ShawGuides* and *Poets & Writers*; these sites each publish a comprehensive list of writing conferences and residencies. Make a list of potential conferences and then figure out the when, where, what, and who. (This information is usually available online and easily accessible.)

- When and where is the conference taking place? Does the location and timing work with your schedule?
- What is the content of the conference? Will the schedule provide you with opportunities to meet your conference goals?
- Who will be presenting at and participating in the conference? Will meeting and/or working with these people help you meet your conference goals?

As you consider which conference is best for you, keep in mind that the conference's size may impact your experience. Though a larger, national conference may draw more editors and agents, small regional conferences are sometimes less overwhelming and competitive in terms of getting face time with an agent or editor. Similarly, a larger conference may draw well-known writers to give craft talks, but you may be sitting in a room with 400 other writers. After the talk, you may have to jockey for position in order to greet the writer. Keeping your goals in mind will help you choose the conference size that will be a fit for you.

Preparing for the Conference

Once you've chosen your conference, you can start preparing. Again, how you prepare for your conference will depend on your conference goals. If your goal is to pitch articles to magazine editors, have a couple of article ideas ready for each magazine you're interested in. If your goal is to find an agent, make sure you know what kind of books/authors each the participating agents represents.

One of my goals when I attended the AWP Conference a few years ago was to talk with editors of small publishing houses and university presses to see if any of them might be interested in my memoir. I poured over the list of publishers who would be in attendance, visiting their websites and reviewing the kinds of books they published. When I found presses that seemed like a fit, I compiled as much information about their books and editors as I could. When I boarded the plane for the conference, it was with three typed pages of publishers in my hand. I was ready to pitch my book.

If you *are* pitching a book, make sure you can do the following quickly and clearly:

- Describe your book in one-two sentences (What is it really about? What is the universal theme in your story that will appeal to readers?)
- Describe the market in two sentences (Who will be your book's audience?)
- Describe in a few sentences how your platform makes you the ideal person to write and sell this book. (Editors and agents want to know that you will be able to sell and market your own book.)

If you are attending a craft-focused conference or retreat, familiarize yourself with the writing of the presenters. Make a list of craft questions you'd like addressed. Are you struggling with scene or dialogue in your writing? Make sure you attend sessions that will be most helpful to you.

Success at a Conference

The most important thing to remember while you're at a conference is to be professional and courteous. Don't rush to an editor after a panel presentation and hand her your 400-page manuscript. (Actually, don't hand anyone your manuscript. It will probably end up in the recycling.) Have a short pitch ready based on your pre-conference preparation. Or introduce yourself and say how much you enjoyed the presentation. You can follow-up with this person in an e-mail and mention that you met him/her.

Sometimes, it's the informal conversations at a conference that can be most valuable. Maybe you end up sitting next to an editor or another writer at the hotel bar, and this leads to a magazine article or a writing collaboration down the line. Be open to new relationships and experiences and be a good listener. Asking other writers about their work is a great way to break the ice.

Being "on" at a conference can be exhausting, so take breaks when you feel you need one. Take a short walk outside or retreat to your hotel room for twenty minutes a few times a day. And pace yourself. Networking nonstop at a conference can be draining for even the most enthusiastic extrovert.

Post-Conference: Following Up

Don't forget to follow up with your new connections after the conference. Send an e-mail to a new writer friend saying how nice it was to meet him/her. Follow up on article ideas with the editors you met. Send off your book proposal to interested agents.

If you've met agents or editors in person, they will generally give your submission more attention than they do the multitude of blind submissions they receive daily. Mention meeting him/her at the conference and, again, remember to be professional and courteous in all your communications.

Have Fun

With research and preparation, a writing conference can lead to new work, new friendships and even a book sale, but don't forget to have fun! Writing is isolating work, and a conference can provide an opportunity for you to feel you are part of a community. Allow time to meet up with friends or go for coffee or a drink with new acquaintances. If you have small children at home, a conference can not only boost your career, it can provide a much-needed break and help reenergize you. Relax and enjoy it!

46. Locating Markets for Writing about Family

Colleen Kappeler

Mothers are busy people. We spend the majority of the day with our families, so it's natural that this work provides fodder for writing. And it's natural that mothers want to read about family life. Our stories help others learn new techniques, give hope to those who feel hopeless, and make them laugh when they feel like the only ones out there having a hard day. The stories come naturally, but finding sources for publishing them can be daunting.

Study the market!

Take note of what is out there. Remember, there are many markets women with families can look into, not just parenting. Don't discount decorating, cooking, local, and educational magazines to name a few.

- *The Grocery Store Checkout Line.* Keep your eyes open at the grocery store and bookstore for new magazines. When you are waiting in those endless checkout lines, look to see if any new magazine titles catch your eye and flip through them for ideas. Look at the free publications in consignment shops and on your way out of the stores.
- *The Bookstore.* Take your kids to the bookstore and before you settle them at the train table, pick up a handful of magazines to browse through. Here you will have entertainment for the kids, a coffee for you, and a huge selection of magazines–many of which you may never have seen before!
- *The Library.* Libraries usually have children's areas with computers to play on, books to read, and some-

times even toys to keep them busy. Before you head in there, quickly browse through the stacks of magazines or the piles of new non-fiction books. Grab any that catch your interest and settle in with a pencil and paper while the kids play and read. You can also use the time to go online through the library computers and do research for online markets.

- *Free Publications.* Never discount the free publications. Anytime you are on your way out of a coffee shop, bookstore, eatery or grocery store, check out the racks by the door. They often include local free publications and magazines for parents such as *Metroparent*. These publications focus on local activities and ideas for families. They are often in need of freelance writers.

- *Local Newspapers.* Call the editor at your local paper. There are often sections of the paper that are open for freelance writing—like recurring columns that they have open for different writers each week. If you have inside information on local activities for families with children, ask if you can cover it for them. You may be surprised at their willingness to give you the work—even if they don't pay, it's good experience!

- *The Pediatrician's Office.* You're stuck in the waiting room anyway, may as well check out the magazines they have lying around. Your kids should have something to do with the books and toys, so you may actually catch a free moment to browse.

- *Don't Forget to Go Online!* Much of the writing market is heading toward online publication. There are tons of e-zines looking for stories on parenting. Do a general search and see what story assignments are out there for online publications. There are also several online magazines that are looking for columnists. Many of these publications do not pay at all or very little at the most, but the credits and experience are often worth the work.

Learn What Readers Want to Read

Next you want to think about what unique twist or story you have to share. Is there something you have experienced that could help others? Did your child struggle or succeed in an unusual way? Many parents face the same issues and, although we've been talking about it for years, we still want to read about what other's experiences are. Some of these common subjects can be: choosing schools, setting up bedtime boundaries, instituting allowances. Find a way to write about it that isn't out there right now and you've got a marketable piece.

- *Talk to the Teachers.* Teachers are with the children every day of the school year, usually for more hours than most parents. Find out what their biggest issues are, what is bothering the children they know the most, and what is going on in the school systems. These are all good ways to learn information for developing an appealing article for any market.
- *Talk to Librarians.* Find out what the librarians tend to read or recommend most to children of various ages—especially the age group you may want to write a children's story for. Also, ask them what information parents are most likely to come in asking about. Librarians are a wonderful resource of information to get you started. And they can help you find good research materials too!
- *Ask your Pediatrician.* Pediatricians get a lot of feedback and questions from families. Find out what the most common concerns are, what parents most often misdiagnose, and what pediatrician's biggest concerns are. These are hot topics that are sure to find a place in the writing market.
- *Don't Forget Your Friends!* Talk to your friends and find out what they are reading, what they are interested in reading about, what they wish someone would write about. These are your readers so

find out what is important to them. And just listen. Sometimes you will hear the same story over and over–you may hear from many how disorganized they feel—and you will find a good topic for writing.

You may be sharing a common job, parenting, but you have many individual stories to share with the community. Don't be afraid to give it a try!

Markets to Research
- *Working Mother*
- *Adoption Today*
- *Conception Magazine*
- Cookie
- *MOMSense* (a publication of Mothers of Preschoolers)
- *Metroparent* (a local newspaper type publication available in most cities)
- Anthologies (think *Chicken Soup, Cup of Comfort*)
- Online publications such as *Mommies Magazine*

Stories to Consider
- Holidays
- School Issues
- In-laws
- Medical Conditions
- Adoption
- Conceiving
- Decorating
- Cooking
- Going Green

47. Self Publishing a Book

Gayle Zinda

I've got the gift of gab, it's true; but when people used to tell me over and over I should write a book, I'd laugh it off.

Through my work with cancer survivors and those with other medical challenges, I met my future husband, and things in my life began to change. I began to develop a speaking career motivating others, but in the back of my mind kept coming the idea of writing a book, a way for me to tell my stories on a larger scale.

Step 1: Have a Story to Tell

Having a great story, a story that's aching to be told, is the first step in writing.

My story wasn't complicated. It was nonfiction, true stories of my experiences as I struggled to raise my two sons alone, care for women struggling with the effects of breast and other cancers, run a growing business with no, and I mean NO business experience or money, and finally find some joy and peace for myself. I wanted to share this story because I felt that others could be helped by hearing it. It wasn't just about me, it was about the amazing courage and support of the people I'd worked with all those years, but I didn't have a clue as to where to begin the book writing process.

I borrowed my husband's Dictaphone®, lit a candle, asked for guidance and began to talk. Eleven hours and a very sore throat later my chapters were born. I then took them to my husband's secretary to transcribe them. I thank God Michael was so supportive and that Elli was able to take my words and put them on paper.

But, once I saw the words on paper, I realized that this was going to be more complicated than I thought. Telling a story, talking out loud about your experiences, is a very fluid thing. Reading those same words on the page, they didn't sound quite right. I wanted my voice to come through but I knew I had to get some help making my book a page-turner.

Step 2: You Will Need Help Along the Way

After seeing the first 3 chapters, I decided I needed an editor. I found my first editor and was relieved, but, after great pains and a lot of money, I realized that he was not a match for me. He was in his 70's and a former banker and I was in my 40's and a previous nurse. Now for another situation this might have been great, but for my brand of story telling, we were not a good match.

Having a professional edit your work can be an expensive process. Editors can improve readability, correct punctuation and grammar and help create a manuscript. But all of these things take time, and editors usually charge either by the hour or by the page. As I got into the editing process, I found myself increasingly unhappy with the results. I felt that something was wrong. I didn't think that the beginning chapter was going to make people want to keep reading. So I sent those chapters to five people, who I felt would give me good advice. The first four said the chapters were great. The fifth, my illustrator John, told me the truth. I learned later that the problem was that the edited story no longer had my voice.

So, even though I'd already spent money on my first editor, I decided to take my book back and begin again. And that's when I finally found my editor in my illustrator. John had never edited a book, but he had listened to my stories for years; we were a perfect match. John and I were partners rather than a client/vendor relationship.

If you do get help with the editing or revision process, remember to keep control of the result. It's your book, and the story must be your story, or it just won't be as compelling.

Choose people to help who can give you honest feedback. I've had people from Africa to Ireland tell me they couldn't put the book down, so I know that my choice to change editors was the right one.

Help can also come in the form of support from your family. My husband put up with my ridiculously long hours because he believed in my story and that it needed to be told. My son Nick, who lives several states away, called me weekly to ask how it was going, and would send me items he had found on the Internet to help with research or the writing process. My son Adam believed in me so much, he moved from Kentucky to Wisconsin and became my Marketing Director.

Near the end of the writing and editing process, just as the book was getting ready to go to the printer, I was diagnosed with lung cancer. Suddenly, my motivation was gone, and I had no interest in finishing my book anymore. But motivation to finish came from my grandson Colin, who said to me one day, "Grammy, when are you going to finish *Pink Lemonade?* I want to take it to school with me." And that was all I needed to get it completed. I found people to help and together we worked the process of getting the book completed and to the printer.

Step 3: Research Your Options

As John was shaping up my book, I was focusing on the next step, getting it to the public. While writing, I subscribed to writing magazines, took writing classes, and immersed myself in the process of writing a book. Now, as I moved on to the publishing stage, I decided to research that aspect of this business as well.

I belong to the National Speakers Association, and had heard a lot about Dan Poynter and his book, *The Self Publishing Manual*, so I bought it. I read it cover to cover numerous times. I slept with that book on my nightstand. I marked it up so much that there wasn't a clear sentence left after I was done. That was such a valuable tool for me. I learned how to put together my book, what paper and color to use, the size that mattered on a bookshelf, cost effectiveness, how to obtain an ISBN number, you name it, it was in there. I was so excited about all I had learned, well worth my $20 investment.

While I was going through the decision-making process about whether to search for a publisher or pursue self-publishing, I went to the National Speakers Convention in Atlanta. As I frequently do, I struck up a conversation with a woman attending the conference who, after hearing my story, directed me to a workshop about book publishing. To my shock and delight, the speaker in the workshop was Dan Poynter. Of course, I had my book with me, battered and marked up as it was, and I asked him to sign it. I wanted him to know how important his book had been for me.

I knew from reading Dan's book that unless I was well known, the likelihood of a publisher picking me up was small. So, after much thought, prayer and consideration, my husband and I decided to try it on our own. We were fortunate to be able to take this chance.

Self-publishing options are growing for writers, allowing them to put their books out there for the public. Because John, my editor, had worked as an illustrator in the textbook industry for many years, he was aware of several possible printing houses that would meet our needs. I found many opportunities through the Book Expo of America Convention, and the Publishers Marketing Association, as well as *Literary Marketplace* and *The Self Publishing Manual.*

When talking to printers, it's important to do your research. They expect you to be able to talk intelligently about your needs before you call them for information. You will need to know things such as the number of pages you have, the size of the type, number of words on the page, paper type, binding type, etc. Again, I learned a great deal from *The Self Publishing Manual* and through working with John, my editor.

I submitted *Pink Lemonade* to several printers, and got quotes based on the information I provided. Sometimes the printer will be able to offer a price break for a larger order, however, more books is not always better. It's important to know your market so that you don't order too many books.

Step 4: Commit to Marketing Yourself.

I knew that since my husband and I had published my book, there would be no marketing support or book tours unless we did them. I also knew that books don't get sold unless they are marketed. For me, the answer to marketing my book was easy. I am a motivational speaker. I travel the country speaking to groups about hope for cancer survivors, through *Pink Lemonade*. But just because it was easy to come up with a method to market my book, doesn't mean it was easy to do. Here are some suggestions.

Speak out about your topic. Approach libraries, women's groups, churches, or any group of people that might be interested in the topic of your book, and offer to speak. I started out small, talking to church groups and women's groups, often for free, only asking that I be able to sell my book at the end of the talk. As I stood in front of these groups, talking about how they could find inspiration, I wanted them to carry that message home. Seventy-five percent of my book sales come from back of the room sales.

Create a buzz. My son, Adam, was hired on to direct marketing and sales. Who better to promote me than my first-born? I knew that travel to book signings and speaking engagements would be necessary but also painful. You see I have had two back surgeries and a hip replacement and sitting is the worst. To alleviate some of the pain of travel, we bought a 31 foot RV. Adam, being a great marketer, suggested that we "go big or go home." We couldn't go home at this point, so we went big and wrapped the RV in advertising, creating a mobile billboard, the "Motorvator." We have traveled 40,000 miles inspiring people to embrace their life no matter where it is and to read *Pink Lemonade*.

You can also create promotional pieces, donate copies of your book to libraries, special events or giveaways, or create a press release to let people know when your book becomes available in their area. Having a website where people can read more about you and buy your book is also invaluable. Create an e-newsletter, with topics from your book, to help drive interest back to your website.

Submit your book for awards. To find the awards we wanted to submit to, Adam Googled "book awards." Here is another area where knowledge of your market is essential. You need to know what genre your book belongs in, and if you fit the award criteria. If you send your book in, and it doesn't fit the criteria, you've just wasted your time and theirs, and possibly some money as well. There are awards that accept submissions for free, while others may charge a fee to be considered. We submitted *Pink Lemonade* to several awards processes and, as a result, *Pink Lemonade* won three national awards, including a gold USA Books Best Book Award and two silver IPPYs, Independent Publisher awards, and was a finalist in the Nautilus awards.

Ask for endorsements. Many people buy books based on the comments on the cover. Also, don't be afraid to ask for a review from an admired writer or person in your field. Often, if you give them a book and ask for comments, a potential reviewer will be happy to oblige, especially if the book relates to their life or passion as well. You only lose if you don't try. Once you get your reviews, you can put them on your website and your cover, when you reprint.

48. Self-Publishing from Manuscript to Finished Book: Eight Steps in Eight Months

Anne Ipsen

Self-publishing is a time-consuming and possibly expensive undertaking, whether your family writing project is a memoir, fiction, or non-fiction. Who will be your readers? Is the public interested in your topic or will the book be circulated only to family and friends? What follows is a month-by-month countdown of the tasks that will produce a professional book for public sale. It is based on my experience in self-publishing five books, two of which were memoirs, the others historical fiction. I formulated the outline during the preparation of my fourth book and used it prospectively for my fifth. I wish I had had this guide for my first three.

Why eight months? Much of the time elapses waiting for others to carry out their tasks, to answer your emails, and to write reviews. Reaching the public requires publicity and getting reviews take time. Remember that those you work with have their own schedules and your project may not be their top priority. You may elect to hire a publicist to carry out an intense publicity campaign, but consider carefully whether additional sales will materialize in sufficient quantity to offset the cost.

On the other hand, if your book is only for limited circulation within the family or organization, many of the tasks can be simplified or even skipped, particularly those dealing with publicity during the final months before publication. Thus the actual work-time for the production of your book can be condensed, but if your time or budget is limited, eight months may still be needed.

The task ahead may seem daunting, but breaking it into steps makes it manageable. Parts may require you to learn new skills and some tasks may be less enjoyable than others. Rather than focusing on huge sales (unlikely for self-published books), remind yourself that the goal is to reach readers; selling books is merely the means to that end. Anyone can be a writer, but publishing makes you an author. That gives you the credentials to talk about your work to an interested audience and will bring as much joy as the writing that began it all.

Before starting the production of your book, you need an electronic document of your manuscript that is as polished as you can make it with the help of friends, writers' groups, or even a professional editor. The manuscript should be saved as a .doc (or .docx) file in Microsoft Word, preferably in standard submission format. If these terms are not familiar to you, consult the help screen on Word, a knowledgeable writer friend, or your public library. This preliminary step is no different from preparing a manuscript for submission to an agent or publisher, but by self-publishing you continue to be in charge of your project instead of waiting (possibly in vain) for replies from agents or publishers. You will do what you can yourself, but will hire skilled contractors for those tasks that you either cannot do, cannot do well, or for which you do not have the time.

MINUS 8 MBP: (8 months before publication) **Prepare Manuscript.**

- Network: ask friends and fellow writers, consult writing magazines, and join online writers' chatgroups for advice on self-publishing.
- Identify the **POD** (print on demand) company that will print the book. There are a multitude of such companies, the best known are: Lightning Source (a division of Ingram), LuLu, Create Space (a division of amazon.com), Xlibris, and Author House. I have

used the first two; friends have used others, including small local companies. Explore their websites and compare their services and price structures carefully. Having your book printed on demand (i.e. ordering in small print lots) is recommended so you don't have to warehouse a large number of books nor pay for them until they are needed.

- Decide whether you will use the **imprint** of the POD company or publish under your own **press name**.
- Identify those persons who will **design** (format) the text, design the **cover**, and **proofread** (line edit) the book. Do *not* do any of these yourself unless you have professional and technical expertise. Most POD companies provide 'packages' of these services, but working with independent professionals will give you more personal input although it will probably be slightly more expensive.
- Run the manuscript through **spell check** one final time before sending to the proofreader for line editing. This is not the time for major rewrites, but for identification of typos, bad grammar, repetitions, and awkward sentences, i.e. line-by-line rather than comprehensive editing.

MINUS 7 MBP: Finalize Manuscript and Plan Pre-publication Marketing

- Request permission, as needed, for reproducing any copyrighted material such as pictures, photographs, maps, and quotations. Proper citations will need to be placed by the material reproduced and/ or on the copyright page.
- Purchase an ISBN number(s) either from your book designer, the POD Company, or directly from Bowkers.com. Obtain corresponding LOC (Library of Congress) numbers. Remember that you need separate numbers for each planned version of your book: hardcover, paperback, and e-book format.

- Write Front and Back Matter, i.e. the copyright page, dedication, acknowledgement, and author biographical sketch.
- Correct the proofed manuscript, including front and back matter and send to the formatter or book designer as Word .doc or .docx electronic file(s).
- Endorsements. Make list of potential authors or relevant professionals to write endorsements for the back cover and other PR materials.
- If you want and can afford, hire a publicist to carry out or advise on marketing your book. Such a professional can carry out many of the following steps.
- Who is most likely to be interested in your book? That is your market. Draft a Marketing Plan listing specific groups and organizations and their contact information. Since big bookstores will seldom sponsor events for self-published authors, identify independent booksellers in small communities. If your memoir deals with an ethnic group, social problem, health issue, or similar, focus promotion on those organizations.
- Make a preliminary budget for production and initial marketing costs and add estimated cost to each step of your marketing plan. Consider the cost effectiveness of each item.

MINUS 6 MBP: Manuscript to POD Print Company

- Work with the designer to draft the cover of the book, including spine and back 'blurb'. Approve or modify the final design.
- Approve or modify book design. Pay attention to how the book will look by examining font choice and size, space between lines, size of margins, chapter beginning, headers and footers. Carefully proof the front and back matter.
- Make a list of potential reviewers, including *Pub-*

lishers Weekly, Booklist, Library Journal, Midwest Review, Readers' Views, alumnae magazines, local newspapers, and relevant special-interest newspapers/newsletters. Read their guidelines and check conditions for reviewing a self-published and POD book. Make a schedule of when each needs preliminary or final copies of the book—some require up to four months lead time before publication.

- Create a one-page 'sell-sheet' with a picture of the cover, basic publication information, brief description and biographical sketch of the author. Print only a few copies so it can be modified for different purposes. Add any endorsements and brief quotes of reviews as they become available. An alternative version that is half of an 8.5 x 11 sheet with the biographical sketch on the back, works well for some purposes.
- Query potential endorsers for their willingness to provide a brief review and endorsement. Enclose a sell-sheet or similar summary in the letter or email.
- Upload or have the formatter upload the .pdf files for the book text and cover to your POD print company. Order one galley copy.
- ARC Distribution List. Add to the reviewers list all those who will receive free pre-publication ARCs (Advance Readers Copies), including early reviewers, endorsers, persons identified in the acknowledgement as having contributed significantly to the writing of the book (usually 25-50 copies).
- Using the final book page count to compute the actual print cost per book for different price points. Add this print-cost-per-book to your preliminary budget plan, including printing and mailing of ARC (advance readers copies). Calculate the break-even point for direct sales and use this to set/adjust the cover price so you will break even after direct sales of about 200-250 books.

MINUS 5 MBP: Distribute ARCs and Develop Publicity Materials

- Review the galley and make final corrections to text and cover design, if needed. Order ARCs (Advance Readers Copies).
- Order (100-200) postcards, bookmarks, and/or business cards with cover picture and basic publication information.
- Send ARCs books to those on the distribution list according to the schedule. Include sell-sheet and/or postcard as suitable.
- Create a press kit, consisting of a sell-sheet, postcard, bookmark, and/or business card.
- Pick and query venue(s) for launch party(s).

MINUS 4 MBP: Pre-Publication Publicity

- Purchase your own URL (.com), if you don't already have one (about $10/year). Suggestion: use your full author name rather than the book title, in case you write more books and so people searching for your name will find your URL. Create or re-design your website to anticipate publication. There are many sites that will host a website for free or at low cost. They also have templates to help you with the process. Add a 'PayPal' shopping basket for customers to securely pay for direct sales by credit card. Their website will walk you through the process. You may need technical help, but be aware that hiring a professional website designer will be expensive.
- Schedule launch party(s).
- Develop articles or talks on relevant topic(s) and market. Negotiate whether you will waive speaker's fee in return for direct sales of books.
- Contact booksellers, museums, and libraries for possible readings or talks. Offer to mail or deliver

an ARC—some places will return these. Discuss whether the venue will order books directly from you or order from their usual distributor. Popular places may schedule book events a year at a time, so don't be surprised if the next open date is months away.
- Give ARC's to anyone who has helped you (including those you hired) and those relatives/friends that expect free copies.

MINUS 3 MBP: Continue and Wait

- Continue to follow-up on any lose ends, as needed.
- Set up or add the book title and cover image to an author's page on Facebook and begin to promote the book release here.
- Open accounts on Goodreads.com and Librarything.com.
- As any endorsements or reviews become available, add these to the back cover, sell-sheet, and other PR materials.
- Make a list of essential corrections to text. Keep these to a minimum as major changes are expensive.
- Arrange to display and sell your book at book fairs and conferences.
- If there is to be a hardcover version of the book, design the back and flaps of the dust jacket using material from the Back Matter and back cover of the paper version. Similarly format the e-book file(s).
- Have the book formatter correct text and back blurb. Prepare final files for all versions of the book. Upload to the POD company.

MINUS 2 MBP: Final Preparations

- Order launch books (100 copies is a practical number).
- Launch the sale of the book on your website with

pre-publication special deals or prices.

- Mail/email launch announcements and invitations. You can print these on the back of your postcards and mail in matching envelopes.
- Arrange with POD company to distribute the book to Amazon, Barnes & Noble, Ingram, Baker & Taylor, etc.
- On the page with your book on Amazon.com, click "I have copies for sale" to arrange for direct sales (more profit than with Amazon sales).
- Change your accounts to 'author page' on Amazon. com, Goodreads.com, and Librarything.com. Promote the book with sample chapters and/or a personal statement about you.
- Practice reading aloud from your book. Speak sl-ooow-ly, loudly, and distinctly. Learn to project to the back row of your audience.

LAUNCH MONTH: Launch!

- Continue to arrange and promote your work at book events. Offer to meet with local book clubs and prepare a list of discussion questions to mail to participants.
- Fulfill direct orders from your website and other sources promptly. Keep track of your customers and their addresses for future promotions.
- Enjoy meeting your readers!

49. What To Do When the Byline Buzz Wears Off

Madeleine Kuderick

As I stood before a packed audience at the International Reading Association conference in New Orleans, I suddenly felt this speaking engagement was the biggest mistake of my life. I was a writer, after all. Not a performer. And judging by the knots in my stomach, I should have stayed home, safe and sound in my writer's cave. But, it was too late. Brod Bagert, the charismatic poet and master of ceremonies had already made my introduction. So, I gripped the podium and began to speak.

Authors who write about family experiences don't always get the opportunity to see how their stories impact readers. They might receive positive feedback from family members or catch a congratulatory comment from a neighbor or two. But beyond that, the writer can only guess if her story made a mark on someone's heart—unless she chooses to step outside of the writer's cave as I had done in New Orleans.

There, I recited a poem about my son's struggle with dyslexia. My voice cracked as I delivered the line "all I want for Christmas is to learn how to read". My hands began to tremble and the blood drained from my face. I was convinced this had to be the most unprofessional performance the audience had ever seen. But then, the strangest thing happened. Purses opened. Kleenex flew out. The woman in the front row dabbed away a tear. By the end of the poem, the audience was on their feet, clapping and crying all at the same time. My hands tingled and my heart skipped a beat. I didn't know you could *feel* a standing ovation.

Later, several teachers approached me. They spoke of the struggling students in their own classrooms and told me that hearing this poem had changed them as educators. Starting Monday, they were going to try extra hard with Tyler and Michael and Sue. Maybe those children felt just like my son, they said. That's when I realized my story had a purpose bigger than our family's experience. That it was going to change lives far beyond our own.

As a newly published author, this was an extremely important epiphany for me. To my surprise, the thrill of seeing my byline in print only lasted a short while. The buzz of being published soon faded and the book containing my poem settled quietly on the back of a shelf. I might have forgotten about it. But that audience in New Orleans wouldn't let me. Their feedback kept me energized and focused on writing new material. That's what connecting with your audience can do for you as a writer. It's the ultimate validation. It will inspire you long after the excitement of seeing your work in print has worn off.

Connect With Your Reader Through Small Speaking Venues:

There are many ways to engage with your audience. You don't have to subject yourself to large conference venues and knee-knocking public appearances if that seems too formidable. Perhaps you can target smaller audiences. Consider your topic. Are there groups or organizations who would relate to your story? Teachers at your local elementary school? Residents at the nearby nursing home? Scout troops? Youth soccer teams? Church groups? Be creative and identify places where your story will make an emotional impact. Then, it's time to take the leap of faith. Believe in your story and yourself. Contact the group leader and present your speaking idea. Be flexible about scheduling. Adapt your presentation so that it is age appropriate and relatable to that specific audience. Sometimes speaking to smaller, more intimate groups can be the most rewarding of all.

Reaching a Wider Audience with Conference Presentations

If you choose to pursue larger conference venues, select events that have a specific connection to your topic. I shared my poem about dyslexia at the International Reading Association because I knew many educators and literacy specialists would be in the audience. I thought they'd identify with the poem. Since then, I've shared the same material at a conference hosted by the Council for Learning Disabilities and I've submitted a proposal to speak at the International Dyslexia Association's annual event.

You can find connections for your topic too. Consider the type of events and organizations that would attract your audience. If you're not sure where to begin, you might want to explore a reference like the Directory of U.S. Associations which lists more than 60,000 professional, business, and trade associations as well as 501(c)(3) non profit organizations, charity and community institutions. Once you have identified your target venue, research it thoroughly. Conference proposals are usually due months before the actual event. So be proactive and aware of approaching deadlines. Be sure to follow the conference proposal process precisely, just as you would strictly adhere to writer's guidelines before submitting any manuscript. Remember, speaking engagements at national events can be very competitive. So don't get discouraged if some of your early proposals are rejected. Patience and persistence will prevail.

When your proposal is accepted, there are a couple techniques that will make speaking in front of a large audience feel more comfortable. I wish I'd known them in New Orleans and I use them to speak more naturally today. If possible, try to talk with audience members before you're ever introduced. A friend of mine who is a professional speaker says he talks to people on the airport van as it shuttles them to the hotel. He speaks to them on the elevators, in the breakfast line, and in the hallways. He always shows a personal interest, asking why they've come to the meeting, or how they're enjoying the conference so far. Through this process, he transforms the audience from an anonymous blur into what they really are. People. Just like himself. Then, when it's time to speak, he only thinks about four or five people he's met. He pictures the ones who will truly benefit from his talk, people he made a connection with.

You can use this same technique. Not only will it ease your speaking jitters, but your audience will perceive you as someone who is caring and approachable. They will be more likely to seek you out after your talk and share their feedback. Remember, it is their input that you are really after, their emotional response that will fuel your writing in the months ahead.

Leveraging Book Signings for Reader Engagement

Book signings can also provide a unique opportunity to engage with your reader. Whether you schedule an event at Barnes & Noble, an independent bookstore, or your local coffee house, there are a couple key steps that will maximize your reader interaction. The first step is promoting your event. Unlike conferences, where your target audience is sure to be present, you will have to work harder to attract your readership to a book signing. There are several ways to get the word out. Community newspapers will often run a short promotional piece. You can promote your book signing through social media like Facebook, Twitter, your blog or webpage. Sometimes the store will promote the event for you. For example, Barnes & Noble publishes upcoming engagements in the "Stores & Events" section of their website.

Once you've attracted some readership through promotion, you need to focus on the second key step—how to lure the random store visitor to your table as well. In order to do that, your book signing space must look attractive and feel approachable. Consider adding a few eye catching table-top decorations, an assortment of playful pens, and a dish of chocolates. Remember to smile as people walk by. Say hello.

Invite them to chat. Keep your goal in mind. It's not just about signing books. It's about engaging your reader.

If you're fortunate enough to have some theatrical friends, ask them to participate in the signing. A goofy gimmick can be amazingly effective. At a December Barnes & Noble book signing for *Christmas Miracles*, a member of my critique group arrived fully costumed as a Christmas elf. She proceeded to mingle with patrons, share quips from my story and point people to my festive table. In just a few hours, the store sold out of inventory—more than fifty books!

But, the most measurable achievement was not ringing up at the cash register. Instead, it was registering in my heart. That afternoon, I had the opportunity to talk to countless holiday shoppers. Most of them were not even acquainted with my book. But within minutes of chatting, each person seemed to discover some synergy with my story. They began to share anecdotes from their own lives, to talk about miracles and God, about losing faith or finding it, about what Christmas meant to them and their families. In that moment, I realized how much people long for a universal experience and how hard they will squint to see an inch of common ground.

As women who write about family, it's important that we craft our stories to feel relatable and timeless, to be universal. But, I didn't discover that tip in a writing how-to book or hear it in a literature class. I learned that lesson one Saturday afternoon from the random readers who approached my book-signing table. What revelations might be awaiting you, the next time you step out of the writer's cave?

Interacting with Your Reader Through Social Media:

In addition to speaking opportunities and book signings, there are other ways you can connect directly with your audience. Many authors choose to blog. Some encourage audience feedback through their websites. Today, even a Facebook page can generate lively exchanges with your readers. But, you don't need a mega presence on the social media scene to be inspired by your readers. When it comes to inspiration, the volume of traffic doesn't really matter. Sometimes a single message can ignite your writing muse for months to come. Take this email I received from a reader half way around the globe:

"While reading your story in *Chicken Soup*, my heart was deeply moved. I wrapped my arms around my 2-year old daughter and kissed her on the head. This story had a very positive impact on my life." — Hamza

When I wrote that story for *Chicken Soup* about a wish my son made while blowing on a dandelion, I never imagined someone in Saudi Arabia hugging their child or feeling renewed hope because of my words. Yet, that's exactly what happened. Because of Hamza's feedback, I was inspired to write about other family experiences. His comments energized my writing. We are so fortunate to write in an era where our readers are just a keystroke away, where an email or blog post or Facebook comment can rejuvenate our craft.

So, when the byline alone doesn't sparkle for you anymore, it's time to connect with your reader. Even if that feels like the biggest mistake of your life. It's not. Your reader can validate the importance of your writing and trigger the ah-ha moments that will spur future stories. They will energize and invigorate your words. With so many creative options for connecting, you simply need to choose the one that's in your comfort zone. Make yourself accessible through a website or social networking, blogs or speaking engagements. Schedule a book signing. Put on an elf hat. It doesn't matter which method you choose, as long as you step out of that writer's cave and listen to how you've touched the reader's heart. You will be inspired...beyond words.

50. A Writer's Thoughts on Book Marketing

Ann McCauley

I've learned the hard way that after the writing and the publishing, *it's the marketing that counts*. But *always* be prepared and present your work as perfectly as possible. Why perfection? With 800 books published every day, the competition is fierce. This includes major publishing houses, university presses as well as numerous small independent presses. It comprises service manuals and family genealogies for family reunions. It also includes a glut of self-published books; most will sell 75 copies or less.

Even writers lucky enough to have large publishers behind them are still putting lots of their own cash into marketing their books. Most publishers put the majority of their limited marketing budget behind their guaranteed best selling authors. It costs much more than most writers can afford to have an eye-catching display inside every major book store in the country. The publishing world is in a state of transformation. Writers are creative enough to write books, and we must use our creativity to think outside the box and find special niches to let readers know about our books.

Tried and True Low Budget Strategies
- Don't be afraid to give a few books away. On average, for every book *strategically* given away, I sell ten. So don't stand on a street corner and hand out books to every third person who walks by!

- Have a professional press pack printed which includes a cover letter, a press release, professional book reviews, a brief author bio, short synopsis of the book, a book mark with a photo of your book on one side and short blurb or review on other side. It should also include your website address. Yes! Every writer needs a website.

- Listen to local un-syndicated radio stations, become familiar with their programming. Then contact a person at each station that feels like your book could fit an angle with their show. *If* they agree to an on air interview with you, give them five or six copies to give away to callers in the days preceding your interview and save one or two for the day of the interview. Each time they give one of your books away; you get a few seconds of free advertising. Participation is rarely a problem, radio stations love to give prizes, and more people will listen because everyone loves to win a prize.

- For a wider audience, consider checking out Voice of America Radio, Talk Radio Network, and other Internet interview formats. There are many different radio hosts who are looking to fill airtime with interesting guests. It's easy; most do their live interviews by phone so there is little travel necessary to tell the world about your book. A word to the wise...if you have a dog and he's anything like mine, it would be a prudent decision not to have it in the same room with you when you do the interview!

- Most small radio station interviewers do not have time to read many books. Be kind; give interviewers a short synopsis of your book and a list of interview questions to use at their convenience. Most will appreciate your thoughtfulness. And it makes the interview easier for you.

- Focus on the season your book might fit their programming needs most readily. For example with my first novel, *Mother Love*, I focused on publicity blitzes around Mother's Day. I wrote an essay about motherhood that garnered the attention of local newspapers as well as regional magazines and our regional public broadcasting stations. I was invited to appear on the local PBS television and radio shows to talk about my novel. There is no need to take your own questions with you to PBS. They read the book and are prepared for in depth interviews. For first time authors, it's almost an author beware situation!

- With my second novel, *Runaway Grandma*, I had an essay contest for elementary age children, "Why MY Grandma Would Never Run Away". I gave the six children's winning entries $50.00 savings bonds, an autographed copy of *Runaway Grandma* and computer-generated Commendation Certificates. Honorable mentions received free copies of the novel to give to their grandmothers as well as Commendation Certificates. All other entries received a Certificate of Participation. The hardest part was judging which essays were the best! I visited many classrooms and truly enjoyed the children's interest and questions and another way to keep my book in the newspaper.

- Make the Internet booksellers your friends. All books should be available on Amazon and Barnes & Noble. If we want readers to buy our books, then they must be able to order them from mainstream book selling sites. Make sure your book reviews are posted as well as your public appearances. Keep people thinking and talking about your book.

- Be sure your publisher makes your book available for electronic book devices. Most readers still prefer a paper book but there is an ever-growing trend toward e-books and our books should be available in all formats.

Is It Worth It?

Most writers cringe at the thought of talking in front of people, talking on the radio or heaven forbid, television! We writers are by nature shy and solitary creatures. We prefer life on the sidelines, watching others and then twisting those observations into stories. But that doesn't sell books. That's why we must be willing to push ourselves to do what it takes to get our books in the hands of more readers.

I also speak at many service organizations and have actually learned to enjoy it. I'm an avid reader and I always hand out lists of my favorite books and authors when I finish speaking to groups. Sometimes people who are a bit skeptical about me and my books will recognize an author's name on my list and buy autographed copies of my novel simply because we like the same writer.

Word of mouth sells books; but if readers don't read our books, they'll never be able to tell their friends about them. If we write and publish, we must find ways to get our books into reader's hands and these are a few methods that have proven to be effective for me.

I also donated more than two hundred copies of my first two novels to libraries with a S.A.S.E. to return a receipt for the donation, which I use for my taxes. In these days of slashed library funding, these donations are even more appreciated. (Library addresses are readily available on the Internet.) This has generated several library reading groups to choose my books for their book clubs.

I know of book clubs in Pennsylvania, New York, Arizona, North Carolina, Florida, Texas, and California that have chosen to read *Runaway Grandma*. It made The List of Top 100 Book Club Choices in 2008 by BookList.com. True, that's not *The New York Times* Bestseller List, but it was something and it happened on its own momentum.

A writer's survival is closely related to his ability to develop thick skin; there will always be some readers who do not like our work. The old cliché, *you can please some of the people some of the time but you cannot please all of the people all of the time, exists because it is true.* Fortunately, I've received dozens of kind words about my books, yet one unkind comment or review by a stranger online has the force of gale winds to a writer's confidence. We must have faith in our calling and push on.

A few weeks ago, I received an email request from a distant library requesting fresh copies of both my novels because their copies were falling apart. *Mother Love* had been checked out and read forty four times and *Runaway Grandma* thirty! They had no budget to replace them. I immediately mailed them two fresh copies.

Writing, finding an agent, publishing and marketing is a long tedious process and requires a deep commitment. If anyone wants to write to get rich, I might suggest they buy a lotto ticket instead!

Part VIII

Building Your Confidence

51. Finding My Voice

Ingeborg Gubler Casey

I struggled in college writing classes. My stories earned mediocre grades, so I concluded that I had no talent as a writer. When the idea of writing a book took hold of me, it seemed impossible. But it refused to let go. I had a story to tell and, stubbornly, doggedly, it pushed its way out of me.

It was through my work as a psychotherapist that I discovered I had a story worth sharing. In listening to my clients' stories, I was surprised to hear familiar themes. I had thought my own coming of age—with my schizophrenic mother—would fall into a category by itself, with little relevance to others. Yet, whether our mothers were psychotic, alcoholic, depressed or normal, my clients and I all struggled with the same dilemma. We needed to find a way to become ourselves yet maintain a connection with our mothers. We grappled with similar questions: How can I be true to myself without disappointing mother? When is it okay to be selfish? How can I be loyal without letting her control my life?

Because of the extremity of my mother's illness, my very survival depended on my resolution of these issues. In the struggle, I learned much. Drawing on my own experiences to help my clients, I began to appreciate the value of my story. I felt a deep impulse to share, but the task of writing felt almost impossible. I pushed aside the idea as an impractical fantasy.

Then the recurring dreams started. I would wake with anxiety, a sense of urgency—something I needed to do—time was running out. It was the exam dream, always the same one: *I suddenly realize I'm back in college and registered for two classes. I always meant to study, even though I never went to class;*

but now it was final exam time. Why hadn't I just dropped the class-
es? Now it was too late and I would fail.

Why, when I had been finished with school for more than fifteen years would I have this dream? The classes, always biol-
ogy and history, led me to the answer. The dream was insist-
ing I was running out of time to write my *"life history."*

My anxiety only increased. How was I going to accomplish this impossible task? I was plagued with inner conversations: *"You've got to write it."*

"I can't." I protested. "I'm not good at writing."

"But you're the only one who can tell this story."

"I don't have time. Besides, no one would want to read it."

At a therapy workshop, I confided my problem to one
of my teachers, Sonia Nevis. Without hesitating, she said. "I
want to read it. You write the first chapter and send it to me."
She had quickly sized up my first problem: I was still living in
my childhood world where no one listened to my stories. My
job was to listen to Mama, not burden her with my feelings.
I had no voice because I had never expressed myself. In one
fell swoop, Sonia challenged my unconscious belief. I went to
work and when the thought *"No one is going to read this"* discouraged me, I would retort, "Sonia will." Then I went back
to work. I sent her my first few pages, but after that my own
interest sustained me.

After I began my project, I felt a great sense of peace.
No matter the outcome, I was honoring my deepest impulse.
I set aside three hours a week for the task and told myself it
didn't matter how long it took. The important thing was that
I had started. I began with my memories. They were crystal
clear; that is the nature of traumatic memory. I could re-enter
scenes from my childhood and replay conversations in my
mind. But in addition to memory, I needed to express my own
thoughts and feelings. In the process, I was surprised at what
I uncovered. Even though I thought I had already worked
through everything in psychotherapy, I was deepening my
understanding and making new meanings. Writing stimu-
lated something deep inside: my own voice, awakening and
rejoicing at last.

I began to see a similarity between writing and therapy: both involve a struggle to identify, clarify and express feelings. Both require an attitude of openness, an honoring of inner experience. Finding a voice, whether in therapy or through writing, is a powerful act of self-definition. And both lead to the satisfaction that comes from communicating what is most deeply felt.

After completing my first draft, I found a gifted writing teacher through the extension of our local university. She taught me how to write a scene, how to write transitions, how to eliminate unnecessary detail, how to eliminate unnecessary details that detracted from the story, and how to develop the two voices, adult and child, in my story. When we were finished, I knew I had a good book. Nevertheless I didn't succeed in finding a publisher. The only way to share my story with the world was to self-publish and so that is what I did.

I believe in the power of sharing. It is healing for both the teller and the listener, writer and reader. It breaks the power of shame and brings us out of isolation into deeper connection with one another. In sharing my story, I defied my mother's rules about silence and secrecy. Sharing my story has been gratifying and deeply satisfying.

52. On Believing What You Have to Say Is Worth Writing

Sheila Bender

Whether we live on farms or in city apartments, grow up in logging camps or in suburban homes, move all over the world or remain in just one town, take on unusual jobs or work at home, we can become shy about what we write. We convert that shyness into thinking that whatever it is we would write is not important or interesting enough for others to read. We begin to believe that our reflections on experience and our taste in subjects are not worthy of words on a page. We suffer from doubt that we can write what we have to say well enough to honor our subject. And we might suffer from fear that we don't have the right to speak up about things others in our family may see differently or do not want to make public. We worry that we will offend people by saying what it is we have to say or that we will not get things right enough to satisfy everyone.

When I feel this way, I like remembering what the Nicolas Cage character, who was immortal and, therefore, without the five senses of us humans, said in the film *City of Angels* when he was courting the mortal character played by Meg Ryan. As she cut a pear, he asked, "What's that like? What's it taste like? Describe it like Hemingway." She answered, "Well, it tastes like a pear. You don't know what a pear tastes like?" His reply is good instruction for all writers, "I don't know what a pear tastes like to you." Our writing's reason d'etre is to describe what an event, person, dilemma, or memory tastes like to us; what we hear, touch, smell, see and taste helps us make our writing come alive. When we involve the five senses with specific details and images and allow ourselves to use metaphor and associative thinking to explore the subtext of our subjects, we begin to evoke universal human experience. When we do that, not only do we learn more about what has shaped us, what we can offer the world, and what we will do as consequence of examining our experience, we also create writing that has meaning to others. Through our writing, others relive feelings and perceptions they have had and often times overlooked or not taken the time to reflect on. They grow as we grow. This includes our family members. You can use these understandings to override any fear that your writing will not be welcomed and will be judged unimportant, whether by you or your intended audience:

- First, realize that only you have lived your experience and it is yours just as the dreams you have while you sleep are yours. No one would expect you to not describe a dream you had merely because it was yours or because you might not be remembering it correctly or in its entirety. Feel about your writing as you start that you are as empowered to write your experience as to have dreams from it.

- Second, accept that what you write as a first draft might not be as rich as the ideas and feelings seem when you think about writing them. Writing allows you to see and perceive more than you could otherwise, but your ability to say what is at the bottom of your heart and mind takes time. Learning the techniques of the writing craft helps, and luckily, every writer has access to such learning through writing classes, writing books written by writers, magazine articles by writers on writing and attendance at writing groups for peer response to work-in-progress.

- Third, remember that writing is something you will get better and better at through experience and willingness to enter and enjoy the revision process.

I have never met writers who have had the good fortune of producing perfectly shaped writing each time they set words on the page. It is actually a surprise when a piece arrives almost whole. Most often, writers write and look for what is shaping up in their words; then they apply the craft of writing to find the rest of what their piece wants to be or the rest of how to evoke their subject. Understanding this will make you comfortable with the process of putting your words on the page as best you can and then learning where to go with them.

- Fourth, your writing is smarter than you are. When writers proclaim this they mean that their words lead them to deeper connections than they would have made if they hadn't started to write their experience. Wisdom is a consequence of writing about something, rather than a reason for writing. To write, you must have a desire to write. Gaining knowledge and insight is a result of the explorations you'll make through writing.

- Fifth, to live fully, you must be heard. Sometimes you write to read your truths to people who come to hear you read. Sometimes you write to send your truths out for publication. If you are not writing what you want to write because you fear someone else's reaction, you are muffling not only your voice but also your presence in the world. You are not here to be invisible; you are here to be part of the whole. The more you immerse yourself in the writing life, whether online or in person in groups, classes and conferences, the more you will honor writing and believe passionately that you deserve to write.

Rainer Maria Rilke's poem "Archaic Torso of Apollo" offers us motivation to overcome fear of being visible. The last two lines of the poem go like this: "burst like a star: for here there is no place that does not see you. You must change your life." There is a place in which you are already seen; you must write to see that for yourself.

References

Rilke, Rainer M., and Stephen Mitchell. *The Selected Poetry of Rainer Maria Rilke*. Edited and Translated by Stephen Mitchell; with an Introduction by Robert Hass. New York: Vintage Books, 1989.

53. Preparing Yourself as a Writer: How to Risk Baring Your Soul While Writing Your Truth

Kezia Willingham

The biggest hurdle I faced when becoming a writer was to silence my own inner critic. I was adept at finding reasons why I couldn't write: I'd never taken a creative writing class in school, I had trouble learning the names of the parts of speech as child, the idea of even trying to write fiction made me feel guilty for telling lies. I'd been a voracious reader all of my life, but it took years before I allowed myself to write for publication. I knew I was lacking in the practical training aspects of writing, but facing the doubt I felt about exposing myself to the world at large was the biggest hurdle. Will anyone care what I have to say? Will people think I am stupid? Will I get in trouble?

As I contemplated the idea of writing, I kept reading. Memoirs have been my preferred genre for the last few years. I've read amazing books by writers who shared detailed, highly personal information in their books. None of them had died after their books were published. They'd lived and done it. I also read books by writers who seemed to even less formal training than I did. I thought that I could probably write as well as some of them. If they could write and get paid to do it, then perhaps I could.

I continued to have this internal dialogue with myself. I want to write, but I fear the outcome. I feared being told I was a terrible writer, I feared getting sued for sharing my frank thoughts and opinions about others, I feared hurting feelings of people I loved.

I began to read books about writing. The common theme in all of them was the message that perseverance trumps talent. In order to become a published writer, one must keep trying. I can do that, I figured. I'd transformed from being a high school dropout to earning two college degrees as a single parent. I survived bouts with welfare, public housing, dysfunctional relationships, and years of social isolation. If nothing else, I knew I was persistent when it came to achieving my goals.

Once I came to the conclusion that I would address my fears, I began to write. Early in the morning, when the rest of my family was asleep, I sat down at my laptop and began crafting essays. After proof reading and editing, I began to send them off for publication. I heard nothing. I continued to write and submit and hear nothing in response. Finally one day I got a rejection letter in the mail. At least there was evidence I'd actually sent something in.

At that time I was working a day job that was less than rewarding. I was facing some extreme challenges in my personal life. Writing was the thing I chose to focus on to keep me going. It gave me an outlet to express myself. If I was writing, then I was learning. My goal was not perfection; it was improvement. I figured that during the time I made to write, I was getting better. Perhaps the first hundred of my essays would be ignored or dismissed, but maybe the one hundred and twenty-fifth would be published. And that would be a success.

There were some weekends that I was too tired to write; I chose to sleep in instead. Or I felt I really needed to go to the gym. When I avoided writing, I knew that I was not continuing to learn and grow in this area. My secret goal was to become good enough to one day get a book deal. While I knew that was far fetched, it certainly would not happen unless I continued to write. Baby steps had always been my ticket to success. Continuing to write and read books about writing were my baby steps. I must keep going, I told myself.

Sometimes as I wrote, I would question what I'd written, thinking it sounded stupid. I had to learn to ignore the self-doubt in order to keep going. I decided that I would write my best on any given day, continue until I felt an essay was complete, and then send it off. The publisher could decide if they wanted to use it or not. I had to give myself permission to expose my vulnerability, to allow myself imperfection in the public eye.

One day I wrote and submitted an essay about writing. I expected no response, as that was the most common reaction I experienced. Surprisingly, the editor was interested! She told me I would have to do some major revisions, but she would like to publish my essay! Holy smokes, someone was interested in what I had to say! I eagerly plunged into the revisions, which I had to do a number of times, before getting to the final, publishable product. However, that encouragement gave me a high akin to the graduate school acceptance letters I'd received years before. It was amazing!

As I waited for the essay to post online, my old fears came back. What will people think? Why am I compelled to do this? What if I get in trouble? I contemplated rescinding my work before ultimately deciding to face my anxiety. I decided not to tell anyone in my family. I didn't want my fear of what they would think or say to inhibit me. Most people I knew did not read literary websites or journals, so what was the chance they would come across anything I wrote?

The essay was published a few weeks later. It did not change my life in any way other than the sense of accomplishment that I felt when achieving a goal I'd been working diligently to achieve. It gave me the ability to list a publication credit in my bio statement. From working with the editor, I absorbed the knowledge she shared about my writing and applied it to future pieces. Four months after setting my goal to become a published writer, I did! I was grateful for that valuable first publication experience.

Since that time I have had a number of other essays accepted for publication. I continue to read books about writing and publishing. I continue to write. I know that I will continue to learn and grow if I actively pursue my craft. Writing has helped me to confront my fears, to validate and express my feelings, to process my experiences. It keeps me grounded and focused. It is a method of communicating that doesn't require another person's immediate presence. My writing can help other people who have felt the same insecurities that I have faced. If nothing else, in addition to meeting my personal goals, I hope to encourage other women to write, those who feel they are not smart enough, educated enough, or creative enough to do so. You can write. You have a story to tell.

54. Professional Nurturer: How to Write about Family (and Still Be Seen as Professional)

Lee Skallerup Bessette

You have prided yourself on your professional achievements throughout your career; you have the credentials and the experience to prove it. Perhaps you sound like this woman: "She has high-caliber talent, she's quick and sharp, and she moves fast and is focused. Her door is open; she's calm, cool, and at ease with her team. They look to her for support and guidance, which she readily gives. She's bright, experienced, and respected. She exudes confidence and juggles her workload well. She seems to have it all under control" (Cormier). You are obviously and rightfully proud of your accomplishments, especially because you have managed to achieve a work-life balance that now you want to write about and share.

But now think of the experiences you will be writing about: the very emotional highs and lows of caring for children, parents, or a spouse or partner; the uncertainty you have faced and felt in yourself; and all of the time you have failed or when your decisions turned out to be very, very wrong. The image of ourselves that we portray in our professional lives is very different from the one we will be portraying when writing about family. As put by Cindey Paty Brewer, an academic wanting to write about work-family issues while not compromising her goal of receiving tenure, "How do you talk about a very personal, very emotional struggle to juggle work and motherhood when you were hired for your cool intellect, your seeming ability to step back from emotionally charged issues and view them with analytical objectivity?" This will be your challenge as a professional woman writing about family.

Professional women have long faced barriers to equal pay, promotion, and equal representation and status, particularly mothers, who often find themselves on the Mommy-Track. It is not just inflexible policies developed by a different generation of professionals (white males), it is also the perception of your colleagues and superiors; women are expected, to a certain extent, to be "men in skirts." Any deviation of that expectation is often punished — take this advice offered by "Ms. Mentor" to a young female professor on the tenure-track who (unapologetically) brought her baby with her to work: "a woman seen with a baby us believed to be "unserious." Viewing herself as a mom first, she's thought likely to drop her career at any moment. This unfair characterization is almost universal, and neither you nor Ms. Mentor can do much to change it"(Toth). Note how Ms. Mentor highlights how this perception is "universal"; extending outside of academia into most professional fields.

But writing about family, you say, isn't the same thing as bringing your baby into work with you or requesting flex-time to care for an ailing family member. No, but in the age of the Internet and blogging, the Mommy Blogger label is a hard one to shed; any indication that work is not your number one priority (no matter how unreasonable that expectation may be) can be used as an excuse to overlook you for a promotion, raise, or new job. Your *Ethos*, if we are to go as far back to Aristotle, is easy to know through a quick Google search; your Resume says one thing, but your digital footprint may say another.

I am not suggesting that you not write about family when you are a professional woman; in fact, these are reasons why it is important for professional women to use their voices to ensure that positive changes are made to their professions and also to foster a sense of community and understanding. Professional women are as deserving to have a voice when it comes to issues about family. In a *Harvard Business Review* Case Study about flexible schedules, a woman supervisor, Jessica, reflects back on the hiring of Megan, a mother who doesn't work Fridays or travel extensively for her job: "Jessica had second thoughts before hiring Megan-she had made so many demands in the interview...Megan's demands had left Jessica feeling uneasy. Part of the reason, Jessica realized later after much introspection, was because she had it much tougher when she was starting her career in the early 1970s" (Hayashi). Decisions about work-life policies (and their implementation) are made by human beings who are emotional, despite our best attempts otherwise. With more information and more voices that are heard on the issue of families within the professional sphere, better policies can be developed and applied. Or at least, that is the hope.

What, then, is a professional woman to do? What follows is some advice on how to mitigate the potential pitfalls of writing about family while being a professional woman. They will not be relevant to every woman; each of us is in our own unique situation and stage in our career and lives; the young, newly married professional weighing whether or not to have kids is in a much different situation than an older member of the "sandwich generation," perhaps caring for both adult children and elderly parents or siblings.

1) First and foremost, you need to ask yourself: why do I want to write about family?

Are you trying to work through issues that you cannot discuss with friends (because they are also colleagues), you don't have any friends who could relate, or you perhaps don't feel comfortable sharing that much detail about your private life? Certainly, keeping a journal is an excellent way to help deal with the pressures and stresses of balancing both a professional and personal identity. And if it is private, then you don't need to worry about any professional ramifications. You may decide later that your situation deserves to be shared with others to be used as a template or inspiration, but by then, you will have benefited from hindsight and be able to go back and edit your work according to that new purpose (more on that a little further down).

Are you writing to share news, events, or discoveries with your family and friends who may be scattered all over the country or the world? Then you may want to consider a private blog, accessible to only family and friends to whom you've given access. This allows you to decide who sees your writing about family, as well as what you write. Will it be a newsletter or digital scrapbook type work or a more in-depth semi-public account of your family? Again, because you control who sees your writing, you allow yourself the ability to decide when and what will be exposed to the public at large.

Are you writing to create a community? Sometimes, we think we're struggling alone in our unique situation and we certainly feel alone and isolated. Starting a public blog is one way to speak to others who may be in the same or similar situations to yours. You can search the Internet for similar blogs or discussion groups, join, and share your own blog within that community. The blog is more-or-less public, but you are free to blog anonymously or under a pseudonym, protecting your (and your family's) privacy. Or you could choose to blog as yourself, or some combination. Just because you start blogging under a different name doesn't mean that you can't reveal who you really are at a later date, nor does it completely guard against someone "outing" your identity. But it does provide some space to receive support and feedback on your writing to a sympathetic audience.

2) Stick to your purpose.

But maybe you are driven to write because the story you have to tell is important, relevant, or particularly inspiring. It is important to have a very clear purpose for your narrative; a reader (and, more importantly, an editor or publisher) needs to have something to take from an essay or book. What message or lesson to learn from what you write? You need to write this down and keep it next to you when you write; it will help ensure that any details about your life that you share serve the purpose of the message you are trying to communicate.

3) *As much as possible, write in a professional tone.*

As a professional, writing about the most personal and emotional topic will be expected to be handled in a professional way. You cannot just let go of all of what you have learned and mastered as a professional if you want to create a piece of writing that will get published and that people will read and find useful or valuable. And again, this will reflect back on you as a professional; if you still want to be seen as a professional and not a mommy, caretaker, or family historian, then what you write needs to reflect that.

4) Actively work to control and maintain your professional identity.

Again, depending on where you are in your career, this will vary. But if you are early in your career, then you need to make sure that the first thing an employer (or potential employer) sees is that you are a professional. This may even be relevant mid-career, because you never know when you will be up for a promotion or on the job hunt. Just simply having an online resume or more extensive CV or work history will make sure that when someone Googles you, what they find first is your professional image, not your personal one. Make sure that you have joined the professional social networking sites, such as LinkedIn, and you are active in other, more traditional professional organizations. If, between work, maintaining your professional image, and your personal writing, you have time, create and maintain a professional blog where you write about current issues in your profession. Any writing you do, be it professional or personal, will help you improve your writing more generally, so it serves a double purpose in this regard.

5) Find outlets for shorter pieces of your personal writing.

If your eventual goal is to be published, then the best way to start is to get your writing out there. Most magazines or websites targeted to specific professions (either commercial or run by a professional organization) have a section where they publish essays about work/life balance, family stories, or other personal anecdotes. Because it is in a publication that many people in your field read, you are at greater risk for judgment. But it is also a way of testing the waters to see how more extensive personal writing may be received later; a major backlash could mean that your dreams of publishing a book may need to get put on hold.

Another option would be to publish on websites or in publications that specialize in what you are writing about: parenting magazines and blogs, publications about special needs children, even smaller local newspapers are often will-ing to publish an essay that they think their readers would be interested in reading. While your audience may be larger, it may also be no less forgiving than colleagues, but in a dif-ferent way. Everyone has very strong opinions about women and their role within the family, and they are not afraid to share them. But you may also find a new support for your larger writing project.

In either case, there are two very important benefits from submitting small pieces of writing to various publica-tions: feedback and exposure. Even before you receive feed-back from the readers, you will receive feedback and advice from the editor. If your essay isn't accepted, they will prob-ably point to changes you can make to improve your chances or suggest more appropriate venues. Essays are rarely accept-ed without edits, and changes can be valuable to refining your writing style. Finally, when you go looking for a publisher, you can point them to your work and the reception it received, proving your abilities as a writer and that there is a clear and present audience for what you are submitting to them.

Despite the dire warning in the beginning of this essay, don't be afraid to write; just be aware and be proactive in maintaining a balance between worlds and words.

References

Brewer, Cindy Patey, "Madonna with Child: Untenured, but not Undone," in *Parenting and Professing: Balancing Family Work with an Academic Career*, ed. Rachel Hile Bassett (Nashville: Vanderbilt University Press, 2005), 62.

Cormier, Denise, "Why Top Professional Women Still Feel Like Outsiders," *Employment*.

Hayashi, Alden M, "Mommy-Track Backlash," *Harvard Business Review* 79 (2001): 35.

Toth, Emily, *Ms. Mentor's Impeccable Advice for Women in Academia.* (Philadelphia: University of Pennsylvania Press, 1997): 119-120.

55. Unlocking the Ties that Bind: Releasing the Writer Within

Laila S. Dahan

Writing about our own families is a rewarding experience. However, despite the great rewards, actually getting an entire book or article finished and published can be viewed as an overwhelming task. But it doesn't have to be. Our families are the closest people to us and writing about what we know is always easier than researching and writing about something we are not familiar with. Therefore, as someone who wrote and self-published a biography about my mother's adventurous life as an American in Libya, I have some tips and pointers on how to proceed.

Scheduling Time to Write

Since most women juggle a myriad of duties on a daily basis, our lives are quite different from most men who write. I am not being sexist, but as a general rule, we as women, handle most of the household chores and childcare duties. This was certainly my situation and I know many of you are in similar ones. With all the responsibilities we handle in a day it is imperative that we plan and maintain a schedule for writing that works for us. Because writing demands that we spend time on it daily. Scheduling writing time is important and if you hope to complete your book or article, you must give your writing ample time and contemplation. Here are some hints for managing your writing time:
- Schedule the time, put it on the calendar
- Write early in the morning or late in the evening
- Write when the children are napping or at school

- Write while you are waiting to pick up the children
- Have some special 'writing' time on the weekend
- Carry a notebook and pen at all times, inspiration can come at any time
- Do not let your writing interfere too much with your family's schedule
- Do not let the family end up resenting your 'writing' time

Writing about Family: Special and Emotional

When you write about family, you are writing about what you know best. These are personal stories and narratives about your life as intertwined with your family, or perhaps you on the periphery of the story looking inward. However you choose to go about the story, it is actually one of the simpler, and dare I say easier, types of writing because it is closest to you. These are tales from the heart, they might need some coaxing to bring them forth, but somewhere deep inside each of us are stories waiting to emerge and be told.

Therefore, I urge anyone who is thinking about writing about their families to take the plunge. It not only puts your stories out there for others, but is also cathartic for you as the writer. You may find that issues you had been unable to resolve, face, or even recall clearly suddenly become fixable, less frightening, or more lucid. This happens when we allow ourselves the freedom to write, especially about those people or issues we largely identify with, love, or dislike the most. You will be amazed at what can come forth from your pen or computer when you write about those as close as your parents, siblings, children, or other relatives. Permission to free yourself to put into words the joy, anger, suffering, or concerns you may have held about an event or a person, is enlightening and can lift your spirits as you cannot imagine. On the other hand, some emotions come forth that are more painful to deal with.

Many times during the writing of my mother's life story, I sat sobbing over the keyboard. I often was overwhelmed by the sadness I felt at having lost her so long ago and regret for all she had missed. But what also came forth was a stronger desire to be more like her. The memories that this type of writing will bring out can be extremely strong, and you must be prepared to face them. You cannot go into writing about family without uncovering some painful memories that must be addressed or perhaps an overwhelming sense of loss at the parents or relatives who have gone on. The following are some of the emotions every writer has to grapple with when the topic is family:

- Elation at old memories
- Happiness at discovering new facts about your family
- Encouragement at how much you know and can share
- Sadness at some of the memories you unearth
- Grief over the lives that may have been lost, but which you are bringing back in some way through your writing
- Uncertainty about the appropriateness of sharing family 'secrets' or private issues
- Concern over how your book will be received by an outside audience

Recruit the Help of Family Members

Any writing we do requires that we have some way of generating ideas. If we don't brainstorm or free-write or use some other method in order to produce ideas, we very often sit in front of a blank screen or piece of paper. Therefore the best way to generate ideas for writing about family is to enlist the aid of your family. If you have missing information or patchy areas of content, your best bet for filling in the gaps is contacting another family member. They may be able to help you address those gray areas. My brother and sister were full of useful information when I was writing, as were my Libyan and American relatives.

In order to get your family involved in helping you retrieve memories, if this is how you wish to proceed, you need to think about all those questions that need answers. Be ready to acknowledge that everyone in your family may have different memories of a particular situation, but another perspective and very often further details can help as you write up a specific incident or experience.

The great thing about writing on the topic of family is that you spend less time researching scholarly journals and more time writing and reacquainting yourself with family members. When you write about family the memories are mainly yours, peppered with some you obtain, borrow, or use from willing and interested relatives. Therefore, as you start writing about family, or if you have found yourself a little stumped, enlist the family by doing the following:

- Send out lists of questions about specific events, relatives, dates, etc.
- Ask family for stories about a particular relative or a specific event
- Ask if anyone has old letters (my cousin who lives in the US sent me stacks of letters my mother had written her over the years)
- Request photographs you could borrow, publishers will return originals
- Ask for any memories they can share

Imagine the End Product

Although no one can tell you how long your writing project might take, it is always good for the writer to imagine the finished product. This type of visualization goes a long way in helping you continue to write. Think about your article as it might appear in a particular journal or magazine; imagine the cover of your completed book and your family's excitement when they read it. These are the items that can keep you going during the writing process. Writing is a solitary pursuit and can leave you feeling lonely at times or frustrated with your lack of progress. But looking forward to the end product can honestly help carry you along.

You know you are writing something worth reading, something special enough about your family that you want read by a larger audience. You already have the spirit and desire to do this; and if you are already writing at this point you have taken that important first step. So now, anytime you lose the flow or feel blocked, think about what it will be like when the final creation is in your hands. Imagine your pride and that of your family. These sorts of tricks really can encourage you, and were instrumental in helping me finish my book.

When your piece is complete you will have a sense of accomplishment that gives you great happiness with yourself and your writing abilities. Keep in mind, as a wife, mother, teacher, or woman employed outside the home, your ability to write as much and as often as you want to is curtailed by virtue of your busy life. However, when you can hold up that article, or chapter, or book and see what emerged from your dedication to writing, though never at the expense of your many responsibilities, you will have pride in both yourself and your accomplishment. Therefore, no matter what might be holding you back from writing that family story, I urge you to start. What you produce will be for you, your family, and future generations. Here are some ways to imagine and visualize the finished product:

- Imagine the published bound book
- Visualize the beautiful cover, inspired by your ideas
- See your name in print on the cover
- Feel yourself holding the journal you are published in
- Envision how proud your family will be

Leaving Behind a Historical Record

When you hand down a written account of your family, you are leaving some history behind for future family members. What you write and publish becomes something that upcoming generations of your family can read and enjoy while understanding more about where they came from. Additionally, you leave a record for a wider audience to become acquainted with your family.

It is important for our children to be left with a written account of something related to them. My own children never met my parents, so by writing about their lives I have passed on a historical chronicle for my sons. I have left a piece of their grandparents in a form that will remain with them forever, not just memories, but written memories. Your own writing about family passes on the following:

- Memories for your children, grandchildren, and future generations
- Lessons from the past
- A sense of belonging or identity with the past
- The importance of the story to outsiders

Publishing your Work

Perhaps the biggest obstacle for writers today is the publishing process. Sometimes it feels like publishers set us up to fail. They don't seem to seek out new writers or those with fresh ideas who wish to share. Instead, they publish writing by big-names in the writing industry, or famous people, whose writing is circumspect, but will sell. Publishers are less interested in what writers have to say and more concerned about how much money they will make. Publishers also want writers to hire an agent, another unneeded expense. Frankly, many agents cannot do much more than you in shopping your manuscript around.

Luckily the option of self-publishing exists. Granted, this doesn't work for scholarly research, but when we really want to see our book in print, especially when it is as personal as a family biography, it is an option. As a writer who chose the self-publishing route after ten months of trying to find a publisher, I can say that it was worth it. It does cost the author money, but depending on the publisher you choose, you may have a lot of input on how the book turns out, looks, and sells.

Therefore, it is my belief that if you have something to say about family and you want it read by more than your personal circle of friends and family, then self-publishing can be the answer.

Conclusion

As women and as writers, we have things we wish to accomplish and many goals we hope to achieve. We can realize many of our dreams. If you want to write about family it will require time management skills, a strong desire to see your dream come to fruition, and a fervent belief in yourself and in your work. You *can* do it. It is possible. As a wife, mother, and full-time university instructor I went through the exact process outlined here and it worked. I am not saying it was always easy, but as a writer who often writes beyond the scope of family, I can say that writing about such a personal issue was eminently more satisfying and less painful than my other ventures in writing.

To every woman who wishes to write about family or beyond, I encourage you to start. Putting those first words down is the biggest motivator and once you start you have the potential to produce and leave behind a little piece of history.

Editors & Foreword Writer

Co-Editor Carol Smallwood's work has appeared in *English Journal, Michigan Feminist Studies, The Yale Journal for Humanities in Medicine, The Writer's Chronicle, The Detroit News*. She's included in *Best New Writing in Prose 2010; Who's Who in America, Contemporary Authors*. She edited *Writing and Publishing: The Librarian's Handbook*, American Library Association, 2010; was short-listed in 2009 for the Eric Hoffer Award for Best New Writing; she's a National Federation of State Poetry Societies Award Winner. *Compartments: Poems on Nature, Femininity and Other Realms* (Anaphora Literary Press, 2011) was nominated for the Pushcart Prize. *Lily's Odyssey* and *Contemporary American Women: Our Defining Passages*, are recent books.

Co-Editor Suzann Holland, 2010 Winner of *Public Libraries* Feature Award, has secured the permission of the Laura Ingalls Wilder estate to produce *A Little House Literary Companion*. She received a BA in History Education from the University of Northern Iowa and her MLIS and MA in History from University of Wisconsin-Milwaukee in 2000. She has served as an adjunct English Composition instructor, a public library consultant, and a public library director. Her works have appeared in *Public Libraries*, *VOYA*, and anthologies from Greenwood Press, Neal-Schuman, and ALA Editions.

Supriya Bhatnagar, Director of Publications at the Association of Writers & Writing Programs (AWP), editor of *The Writer's Chronicle* wrote the anthology's foreword. She has a Bachelor of Commerce degree from the University of Rajasthan, Jaipur, India, a BA in Nonfiction Writing & Editing, and an MFA in Creative Nonfiction from George Mason University. Her short stories and essays have appeared in *Femina* (femina.in), *Perigee*, and forthcoming in *Artful Dodge* and *NEO*, and in an anthology. Her memoir, *and then there were three...* was published by Serving House Books in 2010.

Contributors

Multi-award winning writer, **Diana Amadeo**, has written three books: *There's a Little Bit of Me in Jamey* (Albert Whitman & Company, 1989), *Holy Friends* (Pauline Books and Media, 2005), and *My Baby Sister is a Preemie* (Zondervan, 2005). Her essays have appeared in seven *Chicken Soup for the Soul* books and over 550 other publications. Yet, she persistently tweaks and rewrites her thousands of rejections with eternal hope that they may yet see the light of day.

Sheila Bender's memoir, *A New Theology: Turning to Poetry in a Time of Grief*, appeared in 2009 from Imago Press. Other books include *Creative Writing Demystified* (McGraw-Hill, 2010), and *Writing and Publishing Personal Essays*, Second Edition (Silver Threads, 2010). She's written for *The Writer's Chronicle, Writer's Digest*, and *The Writer*; she publishes weekly articles at Writing It Real.com.

Lee Skallerup Bessette teaches writing at Morehead State University in Kentucky. Dr. Bessette has a PhD in Comparative Literature from the University of Alberta, Canada. She has published numerous academic essays, but also has had her writing about parenting and work/life balance appear in *The New York Times* Motherload blog and on Insidehighered.com. She edited *Anne Hebert: Essays on Her Works* (Guernica Editions, 2010). Her blog is at collegereadywriting.blogspot.com.

After thirteen years in the secondary English classroom, **Jenn Brisendine** now pursues fiction and non-fiction projects and freelances educational materials. Her literary non-fiction essay "Twists in the Plot" appears in *The Maternal Is Political* (Seal Press, 2008), and her work has also appeared in *Mom Writer's Literary Magazine* and *Literary Mama*. She has an MA in fiction writing and lives in southwestern Pennsylvania with her husband and two sons.

Daphne Butas is a feature writer for AOL, and a specialist in educational content for various publishing houses. She holds a BA in American History and English from the University of Maryland, and her work has appeared in: *Motherverse, Momazine, The Virginia Construction Journal, Fighting With Jeb Stuart: Major James Breathed and the Confederate Horse Artillery*, and *The Navy Mutual Aid Association Newsletter*. Daphne lives with her family and writes outside of Washington, D.C.

Ingeborg Gubler Casey received her PhD in clinical psychology from the University of Wisconsin-Madison in 1967. She's taught psychology, including courses on the psychology of women, at the college level, practiced psychotherapy for forty years and given many workshops on understanding dreams. Her memoir about her relationship with her schizophrenic mother, *The Heart Moves in a Circular Direction: A Story of Healing* (iUniverse, 2007) includes dreams and inner dialogs.

After fourteen years at the Smithsonian's National Museum of the American Indian (NMAI), **Karen Coody Cooper** now works at the Cherokee Heritage Center, Tahlequah, Oklahoma. Initially studying journalism, she completed a BA in anthropology/sociology at Western Connecticut State University and a Master of Liberal Studies at the University of Oklahoma. She authored *Spirited Encounters: American Indians Protest Museum Policies and Practices* (AltaMira Press, 2007) and co-edited *Living Homes for Cultural Expression* (NMAI, 2005).

Laila Dahan teaches academic writing at the American University of Sharjah in the United Arab Emirates. She is the author of *Keep Your Feet Hidden: A Southern Belle on the Shores of Tripoli* (Melrose Books, 2009) and co-editor of the recently released *Global English and Arabic: Issues of Language, Culture, and Identity* (Peter Lang, 2011). Laila holds MAs in Political Science and TESOL and is currently writing her doctoral dissertation on language education and Arab identity.

Lela Davidson has built a writing career on everyday humor and candid observations. Lela is an essayist (*Blacklisted from the PTA*, Jupiter Press, imprint of Wyatt-MacKenzie, 2011), a journalist (the *TODAY Show Moms* blog), and a columnist for Brooke Burke's *Modern Mom*. Lela's humorous, inspirational essays have appeared in family and parenting magazines throughout North America, and in *Chicken Soup for the Soul: New Moms*.

Martha Engber received a 5-star rating from the Midwest Book Review for *The Wind Thief*, (Alondra Press, 2009). She appears in *Contemporary American Women: Our Defining Passages* (All Things That Matter Press, 2009). Martha wrote, *Growing Great Characters From the Ground Up* (Central Avenue Press, 2007). She's had a full-length play produced in Hollywood and fiction in *Watchword, Iconoclast, Anthology, Bookpress, Berkeley Fiction Review* and others. She maintains marthaengber.blogspot.com, a Q & A blog for writers.

Christin Geall teaches nonfiction at the University of Victoria. Her columns, reviews and essays have appeared on *Literary Mama*, in *Galleries West, Red Berry Review, Slow, Motherwords, Monday and Walk Myself Home* (Caitlin Press, 2010). Her work is forthcoming in *Becoming: Women's Stories* (Nebraska), and *21st Century Motherhood* (Demeter). A graduate of the Stonecoast MFA, Christin's thesis garnered representation from an American agency, and she has been struggling with retrospection ever since. www.christingeall.com/

Cathy Gildiner has written two memoirs entitled *Too Close to the Falls* (ECW Press, 1999) and *After the Falls* (Viking,

2010). The first was nominated for the Trillium Award and won the Different Drummer's Award. *Seduction* (Knopf, 2005) is a novel about Darwin and Freud and was listed in *Der Spiegel* in Germany as a top mystery. All three books have been on the best sellers' lists and have been internationally nominated for various prizes. Cathy presently lives in Toronto.

Caroline M. Grant is the editor-in-chief of Literary Mama, where she writes a regular column, *Mama at the Movies*. She is the co-editor of *The Cassoulet Saved Our Marriage: True Tales of Food, Family, and How We Learn to Eat* (Shambhala Press, 2013) and of *Mama, PhD: Women Write About Motherhood and Academic Life* (Rutgers University Press, 2008). Her essays have been published in a number of journals and anthologies. She lives in San Francisco with her husband and two sons.

Carol Hawkins holds a Ph.D. from the University of New Hampshire. She has taught writing and directed writing programs for over twenty years, in public and private colleges and universities, both nationally and abroad. Her writing appears in the *National Women's Studies Journal* and *Praxis: A Writing Center* Journal. Currently she is working on a memoir that explores the intersections of gender, economic class, and literacy.

Aubrey Hirsch's stories, essays and poems have appeared in numerous literary journals including *Hobart, Third Coast, The Los Angeles Review* and *The Minnetonka Review,* and in the anthology *Pittsburgh Noir* (Akashic Books, 2011). Her work has been nominated for the Pushcart Prize and the Micro Award and honored on the short list of *Glimmer Train*'s Fiction Open. She currently serves as the Daehler Fellow in Creative Writing at Colorado College in Colorado Springs.

Kate Hopper teaches writing at The Loft Literary Center. She has an MFA in creative writing and has been the recipient of a Fulbright Scholarship and a Minnesota State Arts Board

Grant. Her writing has appeared in *Brevity*, *Literary Mama*, and *The New York Times* online. *Use Your Words: A Writing Guide for Mothers*, is forthcoming from Viva Editions in 2012, and she's finishing a memoir, *Small Continents*. She's an editor at *Literary Mama*.

Anne Ipsen has self-published two memoirs: *A Child's Tapestry of War* (Beaver's Pond Press, 1998) about her WWII Danish childhood and *Teenage Immigrant* as a youth in Boston. The historical novels, K*aren from the Mill* (Beaver's Pond Press, 2005) and *Running Before the Prairie Wind* (ibus Press, 2009), follow Karen from adolescence on a Danish island to married immigrant life in Minnesota. *At the Concord of the Rivers* (ibus Press, 2011) is set in Puritan New England. An experienced teacher, Dr. Ipsen conducts workshops on being an independent writer.

Colleen Kappeler is a writing teacher, editor, and writer. Colleen has edited books for several published writers and taught hundreds of writers in the past 10 years. Her essays have appeared in national publications like *MOMSense*, *Adoption Today*, *The Christian Science Journal*, and the *Chicken Soup* series. She is a contributing editor for e-zines *Mommies Magazine* and *Expose Kenosha*. Colleen lives in Wisconsin with her husband and two children. She is currently pursuing an MA in Writing and Literature.

Amber E. Kinser is Professor and Chair of the Department of Communication at East Tennessee State University. She earned her PhD from Purdue University. She is author of *Motherhood and Feminism* (Seal, 2010) and editor of *Mothering in the Third Wave* (Demeter, 2008). Her work appears in *Encyclopedia of Mothering* and collections such as *Feminist Mothering* (SUNY, 2008), and *Mother Knows Best* (Demeter, 2009). To read her blog "Dr. Mama" and more about her work, visit amberkinser.com.

Madeleine Kuderick is passionate about writing stories that touch the heart. Her work appears in *Chicken Soup, Cup of Comfort, Hallmark Gift Books*, and other anthologies. She has a special interest in engaging reluctant readers and the teachers who touch their lives. Madeleine holds a Master's degree from Saint Leo University. She is a member of the Society of Children's Book Writers and Illustrators (SCBWI) and a graduate of the Institute of Children's Literature. More information is available on her website at: madeleinekuderick.com.

Diane LeBlanc is the author of two poetry chapbooks: *Dancer with Good Sow* (Finishing Line Press, 2008) and *Hope in Zone Four* (Talent House Press, 1998). Diane received the Bechtel Prize from Teachers & Writers Collaborative for her essay "Weaving Voices: Writing as a Working Class Daughter, Professor, and Poet." Her work appears in *Bellingham Review, Natural Bridge, Rhino, So to Speak, Water~Stone*, and other journals. Diane directs the writing program and teaches at St. Olaf College.

Jen Lee is a Brooklyn-based writer and a collector of stories, many of which unfold in her vibrant neighborhood or in the lives of her closest friends. A performer in New York City's storytelling scene, she has been featured on The Moth Mainstage. Jen is the creator of *Solstice: Stories of Light in the Dark* (audio), *Fortunes*, and *Take Me With You: A Journal for the Journey*. She leads workshops and retreats on storytelling, writing and the creative life. You can find her online at jenlee.net.

Corbin Lewars (http://corbinlewars.com) is the author of *Creating a Life: The Memoir of a Writer and Mom in the Making*, which was nominated for the 2011 Pacific Northwest Booksellers Award and Washington State book award. Her essays have been featured in over twenty-five publications including *Mothering, Hip Mama, The Seattle PI* and several anthologies. She has been a writing coach and instructor for fifteen years and assists clients on-line and in person. She lives in Seattle, WA with her two children.

Geri Lipschultz has appeared in *The New York Times*, *Kalliope*, *Black Warrior Review*, *Cezanne's Carrot*, *Kartika Review*, *Umbrella Journal*, and *College English*. She is among the thirty writers extensively interviewed for the recent book by Skyhorse Publications, edited by Eric Olsen and Glenn Schaeffer, *We Wanted to be Writers*, whose blog she occasionally writes for: wewantedtobewriters.com. Her one-woman show was produced in New York City by Woodie King, Jr. She received the Creative Artists in Public Service Fellowship, New York State Council on the Arts. She has an MFA from University of Iowa and is a doctoral candidate in English Literature at Ohio University.

After teaching English for many years, **Dahlma Llanos-Figueroa** obtained her MLS from Queens College of the City University of New York and served as a young adult librarian for the New York City Department of Education until her retirement in 2004. Dahlma was selected as one of two runner-ups for the 2009 PEN America Bingham Fellowship for Writers for her first novel, *Daughters of the Stone* (St. Martin's Press, 2009). You can contact Dahlma through her web site at llanosfigueroa.com.

Arlene L. Mandell, a retired English professor from New Jersey, now lives in Santa Rosa, California. A former writer for *Good Housekeeping*, her poems, essays and short stories have appeared in more than 300 publications, including "The Metropolitan Diary" section of *The New York Times*, *Women's Voices*, *Tiny Lights*, and 16 anthologies. Her most recent publication is *Scenes from My Life on Hemlock Street: A Brooklyn Memoir*, which can be read online at echapbook.com/memoir/mandell.

Ann McCauley worked as a freelancer for local newspapers and periodicals while working as an RN. She has authored two novels, *Mother Love* (PublishAmerica, 2003) and *Runaway Grandma* (Madison Avenue Publishers, 2007). *Mother Love* received the Reviewer's Choice Award in 2005. *Runaway Grandma* was nominated for Book of the Year in Women's Issues in

2008. Her third novel, *It Happened on Willow Lane*, is forthcoming. Ann enjoys gardening and traveling with her husband.

Judy M. Miller is an adoption educator and also teaches online through JudyMMiller.com. She presented at Story Circle Network's *Stories from the Heart V* conference in Austin, Texas (2010). She is a columnist for the online adoption site, *Grown in My Heart*. Her writing has been published in parenting and adoption magazines as well as *A Cup of Comfort for Adoptive Families* (Adams Media, 2009), *Pieces of Me* (EMK Press, 2009) and *Chicken Soup for the Soul: Thanks Mom* (Chicken Soup for the Soul, 2010).

Rosemary Dunn Moeller has been published in *Vermillion Literary Project, Mobius: The Poetry Magazine, Darkling, English Journal, The Upstart Crow, Encore, Quilt Stories, Life on the Farm and Ranch, Contemporary American Women* and has writing coming out in *Avocet, The Reach of Song, The Art of Music* and *Feile-Festa*. She and her husband farm in South Dakota. She's taught ESL in Bamako, Mali in the Peace Corps and in Miyasaki, Japan as a Fulbright Scholar.

Yelizaveta P. Renfro's short story collection, *A Catalogue of Everything in the World* (Black Lawrence Press, 2010), won the St. Lawrence Book Award. Her fiction and nonfiction have appeared in *Glimmer Train Stories, North American Review, Colorado Review, Alaska Quarterly Review, Witness, Blue Mesa Review, Untamed Ink, So to Speak*, and elsewhere. She holds an MFA from George Mason University and a PhD in English from the University of Nebraska-Lincoln.

Mary Rice is a former journalist and folklore archivist. She is a current faculty member at Brigham Young University. Her recent publications include articles in *English Journal, Educational Leadership, Brock Education*, and *Teaching and Teacher Education*. Her research focuses are literate identity and advocacy. She also teaches language arts and English as a second language classes to junior high students. She was honored as the 2008 Utah Bilingual Educator of the Year.

Lisa Romeo's work has appeared in *The New York Times*, *O: The Oprah Magazine*, literary journals, online venues and essay collections, including *Why We Ride: Women Writers on the Horses in Their Lives* (Seal Press, 2010). A former public relations specialist and equestrian journalist, Lisa holds an MFA from the University of Southern Maine. She teaches memoir and creative nonfiction in the Rutgers University Writing Program Extension and privately online, works as a freelance editor, and is writing a memoir of linked essays. Lisa lives in New Jersey with her husband and two sons.

Anna Saini has lived many lives as a political scientist, radical activist and multi-media artist. She completed a BA in Political Science from the University of Toronto and a MA in Public Policy from McMaster University. She works as a community organizer on issues of equality in higher education, prison abolition, gender-based violence and labor rights. Her writing appears in *Bitch Magazine*, *Diverse Voices Quarterly*, *Two-Bit Magazine*, *VOCES* and in the anthology *Colored Girls* (CreateSpace, 2010).

Cassie Premo Steele, PhD, is a Pushcart Prize nominated poet, writer, and creativity coach who lives along a creek in South Carolina. She is the author of eight books, including most recently *This is How Honey Runs*, an audio book of her poetry with original music from Unbound Content. Her writing and coaching focus on the themes of mothering, creativity, and living in relationship with the natural world. Her website is cassiepremosteele.com.

Rebecca Tolley-Stokes is writer, blogger, and librarian who writes about family and parenting both personally and professionally. Her encyclopedia entry "Blogs and the Blogosphere" is forthcoming in *The Multimedia Encyclopedia of Women in Today's World*. Her book reviews appeared in *Library Journal, Choice, Gastronomica*, and *Feminist Collections*. She's contributed encyclopedia articles to *The Encyclopedia of Motherhood, Women in the American Civil War: An Encyclopedia, The Business of Food: Encyclopedia of the Food and Drink Industry* among others.

Anne Valente's fiction has appeared in *Unsaid, Annalemma, Keyhole* and Dzanc Books' *Best of the Web 2010* anthology, among others. Her non-fiction has appeared in *The Washington Post*. She earned her MFA in creative writing from Bowling Green State University and her MS in journalism from the University of Illinois at Urbana-Champaign. She is the assistant editor of the literary journal *Storyglossia* and lives in Ohio.

Kezia Willingham, MSW, works for Seattle Public Schools. She graduated cum laude from Oregon State University with a Bachelors degree in Human Development and Family Sciences and from University of Washington with a Masters Degree in Social Work. Ms. Willingham has been published in *Literary Mama, Hip Mama,* and *Reality Mom*. Once a high school dropout and single mother on welfare, Ms. Willingham is now married and lives with her multiracial family in Seattle, Washington.

Anne Witkavitch has an MFA in Creative & Professional Writing from Western Connecticut State University. She is the editor of the anthology, *Press Pause Moments: Essays about Life Transitions by Women Writers*, recipient of a 2011 Clarion Award. She was managing editor of the 2010 *Thin Threads* anthology. Her work has appeared in *Miranda Literary Magazine, TravelingMom.com,* and *MariaShriver.com*. Anne lives in Connecticut with her husband, two children, a dog and a cat. Visit her blog at theeclecticwriter.typepad.com.

Gayle Zinda, a former nurse and business owner, travels the country speaking and writing on the issues of cancer awareness. Her first book, *Pink Lemonade,* in 2007, received a gold USA Book News Best Books Award and two silver Independent Publishers Awards. She received the Madison Business Woman of the Year in 2007. Gayle is a member of the National Speakers Association and the Women's National Book Association.

INDEX

Women writing on family :
tips on writing, teaching
and publishing